D1637654

WHO GOES THERE?

Authentication Through the Lens of Privacy

Committee on Authentication Technologies and Their Privacy Implications

Computer Science and Telecommunications Board

Division on Engineering and Physical Sciences

NATIONAL RESEARCH COUNCIL
OF THE NATIONAL ACADEMIES

Stephen T. Kent and Lynette I. Millett, *Editors*

THE NATIONAL ACADEMIES PRESS
Washington, D.C.
www.nap.edu

THE NATIONAL ACADEMIES PRESS   500 Fifth Street, N.W.   Washington, DC 20001

NOTICE: The project that is the subject of this report was approved by the Governing Board of the National Research Council, whose members are drawn from the councils of the National Academy of Sciences, the National Academy of Engineering, and the Institute of Medicine. The members of the committee responsible for the report were chosen for their special competences and with regard for appropriate balance.

This study was supported by Office of Naval Research Grant Number N00014-00-1-0855, National Science Foundation Grant Number ANI-0090219, General Services Administration Purchase Order Number GS00C00AM00228, Social Security Administration Purchase Order Number 0440-01-50677, and Federal Chief Information Officers Council Award Number GS00C00AM00228. The Vadasz Family Foundation gave supplemental funding. Any opinions, findings, conclusions, or recommendations expressed in this publication are those of the author(s) and do not necessarily reflect the views of the organizations or agencies that provided support for the project.

International Standard Book Number 0-309-08896-8 (Book)
International Standard Book Number 0-309-52654-X (PDF)

Cover designed by Jennifer M. Bishop.

Additional copies of this report are available from the National Academies Press, 500 Fifth Street, N.W., Lockbox 285, Washington, DC 20055; (800) 624-6242 or (202) 334-3313 (in the Washington metropolitan area); Internet, http://www.nap.edu.

Printed in the United States of America

THE NATIONAL ACADEMIES
Advisers to the Nation on Science, Engineering, and Medicine

The **National Academy of Sciences** is a private, nonprofit, self-perpetuating society of distinguished scholars engaged in scientific and engineering research, dedicated to the furtherance of science and technology and to their use for the general welfare. Upon the authority of the charter granted to it by the Congress in 1863, the Academy has a mandate that requires it to advise the federal government on scientific and technical matters. Dr. Bruce M. Alberts is president of the National Academy of Sciences.

The **National Academy of Engineering** was established in 1964, under the charter of the National Academy of Sciences, as a parallel organization of outstanding engineers. It is autonomous in its administration and in the selection of its members, sharing with the National Academy of Sciences the responsibility for advising the federal government. The National Academy of Engineering also sponsors engineering programs aimed at meeting national needs, encourages education and research, and recognizes the superior achievements of engineers. Dr. Wm. A. Wulf is president of the National Academy of Engineering.

The **Institute of Medicine** was established in 1970 by the National Academy of Sciences to secure the services of eminent members of appropriate professions in the examination of policy matters pertaining to the health of the public. The Institute acts under the responsibility given to the National Academy of Sciences by its congressional charter to be an adviser to the federal government and, upon its own initiative, to identify issues of medical care, research, and education. Dr. Harvey V. Fineberg is president of the Institute of Medicine.

The **National Research Council** was organized by the National Academy of Sciences in 1916 to associate the broad community of science and technology with the Academy's purposes of furthering knowledge and advising the federal government. Functioning in accordance with general policies determined by the Academy, the Council has become the principal operating agency of both the National Academy of Sciences and the National Academy of Engineering in providing services to the government, the public, and the scientific and engineering communities. The Council is administered jointly by both Academies and the Institute of Medicine. Dr. Bruce M. Alberts and Dr. Wm. A. Wulf are chair and vice chair, respectively, of the National Research Council.

www.national-academies.org

BRANDYE WILLIAMS, Staff Assistant
STEVEN WOO, Dissemination Officer

For more information on CSTB, see its Web site at <http://www.cstb.org>, write to CSTB, National Research Council, 500 Fifth Street, N.W., Washington, DC 20418; call at (202) 334-2605; or e-mail the CSTB at cstb@nas.edu.

Preface

The broadening use of the Internet implies that, more and more, people are communicating and sharing information with strangers. The result is growth in different kinds of demand to authenticate system users, and the different motivations for requiring authentication imply different trade-offs in evaluating technical and nontechnical options. Motivations range from those related to system security (for example, the ability to access critical systems or medical records) to those related to business development (for example, the ability to use "free" Web-based resources or to have access to elements of electronic commerce). The key questions surrounding these issues relate to what data about a person are shared, how they are shared (including whether overtly and cooperatively as well as by what technique), why they are shared (fitting the purpose to the nature and amount of data), and how the data are protected.

Concerns that arise about adverse impacts on personal privacy from particular approaches to authentication may reflect judgments about the rationale (e.g., how much information about a person is really needed to authorize access to a particular system) as well as concern about the soundness of the technical and procedural steps taken to protect the personal information gathered in the process of authentication. Those concerns are heightened by the growing ease of aggregation of information collected from multiple sources (so-called data matching), the observed tendency to collect information without an individual's knowledge, and the ease of publicizing or distributing personal information, like any other information, via the Internet.

THE COMMITTEE AND ITS CHARGE

In September 1999, the U.S. government's chief counselor for privacy, Peter Swire, met with the Computer Science and Telecommunications Board (CSTB) in Washington, D.C., and described his need for studies of biometrics and authentication. Enthusiastic support by CSTB members, given the importance of the topic and the ability to build on past CSTB work, led to further discussion about initiating a project. Richard Guida, former chair of the Federal Public Key Infrastructure (FPKI) Steering Committee and now with Johnson and Johnson, provided insight into federal agency thinking about authentication and encouraged FPKI members to be interested in and involved with the project. The scope of the project was broadened to encompass a range of authentication technologies and their privacy implications. Funding for the project was obtained from the National Science Foundation, the Office of Naval Research, the General Services Administration, the Federal Chief Information Officers Council, and the Social Security Administration.

The task of the committee assembled by CSTB—the Committee on Authentication Technologies and Their Privacy Implications—was to examine the interaction of authentication and privacy. The committee sought to identify the range of circumstances and the variety of environments in which greater or lesser degrees of identification are needed in order to carry out governmental or commercial functions. It also addressed ways in which law and policy can come to grips with the flaws that are likely in the technology or its implementation. It considered how the federal government can deploy improved authentication technologies consistent with the desire to protect privacy. It also examined the broad implications of alternative approaches to selecting and implementing authentication technologies by the federal government and others interested in their use.

Consisting of 16 members from industry and academia (see Appendix A), the committee was designed to have a range of technical expertise relating to different kinds of authentication technologies and information-system security technologies generally, to applications, and to the privacy impacts of information technology and related policy. The members possess a range of computer science expertise (e.g., information system security, cryptography, networking and distributed systems, human-computer interaction) and associated nontechnical expertise (e.g., privacy policy and law) as well as user perspectives (including organizations seeking to employ authentication and end users with various concerns in such sectors as banking/finance and health). One original committee member, David Solo of Citigroup, was unable to continue his participation in the project because of unforeseen time constraints.

PROCESS

Empanelled during the winter of 2000, the committee met seven times between March 2001 and August 2002 to plan its course of action, receive testimony from relevant experts, deliberate on its findings, and draft its final report. It continued its work between meetings and into the fall and end of 2002 by electronic communications. During the course of its study, the committee took briefings from information and authentication technology researchers and developers in industry and universities and from leaders in government agencies involved in the development and deployment of authentication technologies. It also heard from privacy and consumer protection experts and representatives from various sectors of industry that use authentication technologies for business processes and e-commerce. The committee also went to VeriSign in California for a site visit. (See Appendix B for a complete list of briefers to the committee.)

More than half of the committee's meetings were held and most of this report was written after the events of September 11, 2001. At its October 2001 meeting, the committee decided, with CSTB's encouragement, to develop a short report addressing the concept of nationwide identity systems—a topic that has received much media and policy attention since the terrorist attacks. Given that many of the committee's discussions and briefings were closely related to issues of identity and identification, the committee was well positioned to comment in a timely fashion on the topic. Supplemental funding for that activity was provided by the Vadasz Family Foundation. That report was released in April 2002 and is available from the National Academies Press.[1]

ACKNOWLEDGMENTS

As with any project of this magnitude, thanks are due to the many individuals who contributed to the work of the committee. The committee thanks those who came to various meetings to provide briefings and Warwick Ford for arranging the site visit at VeriSign in January. Thanks are also due to those who sponsored the study: the National Science Foun-

---

[1]Computer Science and Telecommunications Board, National Research Council. *IDs— Not That Easy: Questions About Nationwide Identity Systems.* Washington, D.C., National Academy Press, 2002.

dation (George Strawn and Aubrey Bush), the Office of Naval Research (Andre van Tilborg), the General Services Administration (Mary Mitchell), the Federal Chief Information Officers Council (Keith Thurston and Roger Baker), and the Social Security Administration (Sara Hamer and Tony Trenkle). We are grateful to Peter Swire for commissioning the project, to Richard Guida and Denise Silverberg for helping to muster support through the FPKI Steering Committee, and to Kathi Webb of Rand for providing early access to its biometrics study project.

Finally, the committee thanks David D. Clark, chair of the CSTB, and Marjory S. Blumenthal, CSTB's director when this study was being carried out, for valuable insights. The committee also thanks the following members of the CSTB staff for their contributions. Janet Briscoe provided crucial administrative support, especially with the October 2001 workshop. Suzanne Ossa was the initial senior project assistant for this project. Jennifer Bishop took over as senior project assistant and provided significant help with report preparation and editing; she also designed the covers of both this report and the earlier committee report and developed many of the diagrams. David Padgham provided background research and descriptions of various pieces of legislation. Wendy Edwards, an intern with CSTB in the summer of 2002, also provided some background research. Steven J. Marcus made an editorial pass through an earlier draft of the report, and Dorothy Sawicki and Liz Fikre made significant editorial contributions in preparation for publishing. Special thanks are due to Lynette I. Millett, the study director for this project. She worked very closely with the chair and other committee members, transforming their inputs into a coherent report that attempts to explain a complex topic in an understandable fashion.

Stephen T. Kent, *Chair*
Committee on Authentication
Technologies and Their Privacy
Implications

Acknowledgment of Reviewers

This report has been reviewed in draft form by individuals chosen for their diverse perspectives and technical expertise, in accordance with procedures approved by the National Research Council's Report Review Committee. The purpose of this independent review is to provide candid and critical comments that will assist the institution in making its published report as sound as possible and to ensure that the report meets institutional standards for objectivity, evidence, and responsiveness to the study charge. The review comments and draft manuscript remain confidential to protect the integrity of the deliberative process. We wish to thank the following individuals for their review of this report:

Ross Anderson, University of Cambridge,
Scott Charney, Microsoft,
Carl Ellison, Intel Corporation,
Joel S. Engel, JSE Consulting,
Michael Froomkin, University of Miami School of Law,
John D. Halamka, Harvard Medical School,
Jerry Kang, University of California, Los Angeles,
Sally Katzen, Independent Consultant,
Deborah J. Mayhew, Deborah J. Mayhew and Associates,
Jeffrey Naughton, University of Wisconsin-Madison,
Marek Rejman-Greene, BTexaCT Technologies, and
Barbara Simons, IBM.

Although the reviewers listed above have provided many constructive comments and suggestions, they were not asked to endorse the conclusions or recommendations, nor did they see the final draft of the report before its release. The review of this report was overseen by Mildred S. Dresselhaus and Randall Davis, both at the Massachusetts Institute of Technology. Appointed by the National Research Council, they were responsible for making certain that an independent examination of this report was carried out in accordance with institutional procedures and that all review comments were carefully considered. Responsibility for the final content of this report rests entirely with the authoring committee and the institution.

Contents

Executive Summary

As communications and computation technologies become increasingly pervasive in our lives, individuals are asked to authenticate them-selves—to verify their identities—in a variety of ways. Activities ranging from electronic commerce to physical access to buildings to e-government have driven the development of increasingly sophisticated authentication systems. Yet despite the wide variety of authentication technologies and the great range of activities for which some kind of authentication is required, virtually all involve the use of personal information, raising privacy concerns. The development, implementation, and broad deployment of authentication systems require that issues surrounding identity and privacy be thought through carefully. This report explores the interplay between authentication and privacy. It provides a framework for thinking through policy choices and decisions related to authentication systems.

Authentication's *implications* for privacy do not necessarily equate to *violations* of privacy, but understanding the distinctions requires being aware of how privacy can be affected by the process of authentication. Such awareness is usually absent, however, because authentication tends to be thought about more narrowly, in connection with security. In deciding how to design, develop, and deploy authentication systems, it is necessary to weigh privacy, security, cost, user convenience, and other interests. A key point is that all of these factors are subject to choice: Whether any given system violates privacy depends on how it is designed and implemented. Changes in technology and practice make this the time for broader, more rigorous analyses of options in authentication.

The complexity of the interplay between authentication and privacy becomes clear when one tries to define authentication, which can take multiple forms:

- *Individual authentication* is the process of establishing an understood level of confidence that an identifier refers to a specific individual.
- *Identity authentication* is the process of establishing an understood level of confidence that an identifier refers to an identity. The authenticated identity may or may not be linkable to an individual.
- *Attribute authentication* is the process of establishing an understood level of confidence that an attribute applies to a specific individual.

A common understanding and consistent use of these and other terms defined in the report are a prerequisite for informed discussion. The three variants above illustrate that authentication is not a simple concept: As the committee's first report on nationwide identity systems[1] argued, grappling with these issues and their implications is just not that easy (Box ES.1).

This summary of the report includes the findings and recommendations of the authoring Committee on Authentication Technologies and Their Privacy Implications. Each of these findings and recommendations, which are more fully developed and supported in the body of the report, is followed by the number of the finding or recommendation in parentheses. This number corresponds to the chapter where the finding or recommendation is found and its order of appearance in that chapter.

SECURITY, AUTHENTICATION, AND PRIVACY

Authentication is not an end in itself. In general, people are authenticated so that their requests to do something can be authorized and/or so that information useful in holding them accountable can be captured. Authentication systems are deployed when control of access and/or protection of resources, both key functions of security, are necessary.

The three generic means of authentication that tend to be used in practice can be described loosely as "something you know," "something you have," or "something you are." The systems discussed in this report—based on technologies such as passwords, public key infrastructures (PKI), smart cards, and biometrics, among others (see Boxes ES.2, ES.3, and ES.4)—generally implement one or a combination of these approaches.

---

[1] Computer Science and Telecommunications Board, National Research Council. *IDs—Not That Easy: Questions About Nationwide Identity Systems.* Washington, D.C., National Academy Press, 2002.

BOX ES.1
Nationwide Identity Systems

In the first report of the Committee on Authentication Technologies and Their Privacy Implications, *IDs—Not That Easy: Questions About Nationwide Identity Systems*, it was noted that many large-scale identity systems are in effect nationwide identity systems. In particular, driver's licenses and even Social Security cards qualify as such. Such large-scale systems pose significant privacy and security challenges, which were elaborated on in that report. A follow-on discussion is located in Chapter 6 that includes the findings and recommendations below.

Finding: State-issued driver's licenses are a de facto nationwide identity system. They are widely accepted for transactions that require a form of government-issued photo ID. (6.5)

Finding: Nationwide identity systems by definition create a widespread and widely used form of identification, which could easily result in inappropriate linkages among nominally independent databases. While it may be possible to create a nationwide identity system that would address some privacy and security concerns, the challenges of doing so are daunting. (6.6)

Recommendation: If biometrics are used to uniquely identify license holders and to prevent duplicate issuance, care must be taken to prevent exploitation of the resulting centralized database and any samples gathered. (6.3)

Recommendation: New proposals for improved driver's license systems should be subject to the analysis presented in this report by the National Research Council's Committee on Authentication Technologies and Their Privacy Implications and in the earlier (2002) report by the same committee: *IDs—Not That Easy: Questions About Nationwide Identity Systems*. (6.4)

Finding: Core authentication technologies are generally more neutral with respect to privacy than is usually believed. How these technologies are designed, developed, and deployed in systems is what most critically determines their privacy implications. (5.6)

But what kind of security is necessary, and is authentication required? When authentication is needed, which types might serve best? For example, when accountability is required, individual authentication may be

---

BOX ES.2
Passwords

Passwords pose serious security challenges. They are a commonly used form of authentication and are the quintessential example of "something you know." They require no specialized hardware or training and can be distributed, maintained, and updated by telephone, fax, or e-mail. But they do have serious disadvantages, among them susceptibility to guessing and to theft. In addition, passwords generally do not change without human intervention, leaving them open to compromise. Passwords are also easily shared, either intentionally or inadvertently (when written down near a computer, for example), and a complex, expensive infrastructure is necessary to enable resetting lost (forgotten) passwords. Because people have trouble remembering a large number of names and passwords, there is a trend either toward name and password reuse across systems, which undermines privacy (and security), or toward the creation of centralized systems to keep track of these names and passwords, which has the same negative centralization effect with respect to privacy and linkage.

Finding: Static passwords are the most commonly used form of user authentication, but they are also the source of many system security weaknesses, especially because they are often used inappropriately. (5.1)

Recommendation: Users should be educated with respect to the weaknesses of static passwords. System designers must consider trade-offs between usability and security when deploying authentication systems that rely on static passwords to ensure that the protections provided are commensurate with the risk and harm from a potential compromise of such an authentication solution. Great care should be taken in the design of systems that rely on static passwords. (5.1)

---

necessary; otherwise, attribute authentication (or no authentication) may suffice.

Finding: Authorization does not always require individual authentication or identification, but most existing authorization systems perform one of these functions anyway. Similarly, a requirement for authentication does not always imply that accountability is needed, but many authentication systems generate and store information as though it were. (2.1)

The use of authentication when it is not needed to achieve an appropriate level of security could threaten privacy. Overall, privacy protec-

---

BOX ES.3
Public Key Systems

Public key systems (sometimes implemented as public key infrastructures, or PKIs) employ a sophisticated approach to authentication that relies heavily on cryptography. Public key cryptography is often touted as a virtual panacea for e-commerce and e-government authentication and confidentiality challenges; however, implementation and deployment details are key to this technology's effectiveness, security, usability, and privacy protection. A critical component of some public key systems is a certificate authority (CA) that will certify that a particular key belongs to a particular individual. One way to implement this functionality is to use a public CA (or trusted third party) to certify keys for multiple users and organizations. This practice, however, places much control in a centralized location, raising privacy and security concerns.

The complexity of public key systems has made their ease of use and deployment a challenge. Getting the underlying cryptography right is only half the battle. Users must be educated with respect to how the systems should be used for maximum effectiveness. Certificates must be distributed securely and revoked when necessary. These systems require considerable storage, bandwidth, and computational ability. Their privacy implications depend on how they are implemented and used. The scope of the PKI (as with any authentication system) will be one determinant of how grave the attendant privacy risks are. At one end of the spectrum is a PKI designed to operate in a limited context (for example, in a single organization or for a single function), and at the other end are PKIs that attempt to provide service to a very large population for a broad set of purposes.

Finding: Many of the problems that appear to be intrinsic to public key infrastructures (as opposed to specific public key infrastructure products) seem to derive from the scope of the public key infrastructure. (5.5)

Recommendation: Public key infrastructures should be limited in scope in order to simplify their deployment and to limit adverse privacy effects. Software such as browsers should provide better support for private (versus public) certificate authorities and for the use of private keys and certificates among multiple computers associated with the same user to facilitate the use of private certificate authorities. (5.3)

Finding: Public certificate authorities and trusted third parties could present significant privacy and security concerns. (5.3)

Finding: Public key infrastructures have a reputation for being difficult to use and hard to deploy. Current products do little to dispel this notion. (5.4)

BOX ES.4
Biometrics

In addition to public key cryptography, biometrics is also often touted as an effective authentication solution. As with any authentication technology, however, the truth of this claim depends, among other things, on the context in which the biometric systems are used. "Biometric authentication" (often called biometrics) is the automatic identification or authentication of human individuals on the basis of behavioral and physiological characteristics. Biometrics has the obvious advantage of authenticating the human, not just the presented token or password. Common biometrics in use today verify fingerprints, retinas, irises, and faces, among other things. Downsides to biometrics include the fact that not all people can use all systems, making a backup authentication method necessary (and consequently increasing vulnerability); the fact that revocation is not possible for current systems (the saying goes that most individuals "have only two thumbs"); and that remote enrollment of a biometric measure (sending one's fingerprint or iris scan over the Internet, for example) may defeat the purpose and is easily compromised.

Finding: Biometric authentication technologies hold the promise of improved user convenience. Vendors of these technologies also promise reduced system management costs, but this has yet to be demonstrated in practice. Moreover, these technologies can pose serious privacy and security concerns if employed in systems that make use of servers to compare biometric samples against stored templates (as is the case in many large-scale systems). Their use in very local contexts (for example, to control access to a laptop or smart card) generally poses fewer security and privacy concerns. (5.2)

Recommendation: Biometric technologies should not be used to authenticate users via remote authentication servers because of the potential for large-scale privacy and security compromises in the event of a successful attack (either internal or external) against such servers. The use of biometrics for local authentication—for example, to control access to a private key on a smart card—is a more appropriate type of use for biometrics. (5.2)

---

tion, like security, is poor in most systems in large part because systems builders are not motivated to improve it.

There is an inherent tension between authentication and privacy, because the act of authentication involves some disclosure and confirmation of personal information. Establishing an identifier or attribute for use within an authentication system, creating transactional records, and revealing information used in authentication to others with unrelated interests all have implications for privacy. The many possible impacts of authentication may not be considered by system designers—whose choices strongly influence how privacy is affected—and they may not be appreciated by the public. Most individuals do not understand the privacy and security aspects of the authentication systems they are required to use in interactions with commercial and government organizations. As a result, individuals may behave in ways that compromise their own privacy and/or undermine the security of the authentication systems.

> **Finding: Authentication can affect decisional privacy, information privacy, communications privacy, and bodily integrity privacy interests. The broader the scope of use of an authentication system, the greater its potential impact on privacy. (3.1)**

The tension between security and privacy does not mean that they must be viewed as opposites. The relationship between the two is complex: Security is needed in order to protect data (among other things), and in many circumstances the data being protected are privacy-sensitive. At the same time, authentication may require the disclosure of personal information by a user. If many have access to that personal information, the value of the information for authentication is decreased, and the decreased privacy of the information—through others' access to personal information used in authentication—can also compromise security.

A critical factor in understanding the privacy implications of authentication technologies is the degree to which an authentication system is decentralized. A centralized password system, a public key system, or a biometric system would be much more likely to pose security and privacy hazards than would decentralized versions of any of these. The scope and scale of an authentication system also bear on these issues.

> **Finding: Scale is a major factor in the implications of authentication for privacy and identity theft. The bulk compromise of private information (which is more likely to occur when such information is accessible online) or the compromise of a widely relied on document-issuing system, can lead to massive issuance or use of fraudulent identity documents. The result would adversely affect individual privacy and private- and public-sector processes. (6.4)**

Usability is a significant concern when determining how authentication systems should be deployed and used in practice. Such systems will fail if they do not incorporate knowledge of human strengths and limitations. Users need to be aware when an authentication (and hence possibly privacy-affecting) event is taking place. In addition, user understanding of the security and privacy implications of certain technologies and certain modes of use plays a major role in the effectiveness of the technologies. For example, without a clear understanding of the security/privacy threats to the system, users may behave in ways that undermine the protections put in place by the designers.

> **Finding: People either do not use systems that are not designed with human limitations in mind or they make errors in using them; these actions can compromise privacy. (4.1)**

> **Recommendation: User-centered design methods should be integral to the development of authentication schemes and privacy policies. (4.2)**

There are ways to lessen the impacts on privacy that authentication systems have. Guidelines include the following:

> **Recommendation: When designing an authentication system or selecting an authentication system for use, one should**

> - **Authenticate only for necessary, well-defined purposes;**
> - **Minimize the scope of the data collected;**
> - **Minimize the retention interval for data collected;**
> - **Articulate what entities will have access to the collected data;**
> - **Articulate what kinds of access to and use of the data will be allowed;**
> - **Minimize the intrusiveness of the process;**
> - **Overtly involve the individual to be authenticated in the process;**
> - **Minimize the intimacy of the data collected;**
> - **Ensure that the use of the system is audited and that the audit record is protected against modification and destruction; and**
> - **Provide means for individuals to check on and correct the information held about them that is used for authentication. (3.2)**

More generally, systems should be designed, developed, and deployed with more attention to reconciling authentication and privacy goals.

> **Recommendation: The strength of the authentication system employed in any system should be commensurate with the value of the resources (information or material) being protected. (2.1)**

Recommendation: In designing or choosing an authentication system, one should begin by articulating a threat model in order to make an intelligent choice among competing technologies, policies, and management strategies. The threat model should encompass all of the threats applicable to the system. Among the aspects that should be considered are the privacy implications of the technologies. (4.1)

Recommendation: Individual authentication should not be performed if authorization based on nonidentifying attributes will suffice. That is, where appropriate, authorization technologies and systems that use only nonidentifying attributes should be used in lieu of individual authentication technologies. When individual authentication is required, the system should be subject to the guidelines in Recommendation 3.2 (above). (2.3)

Recommendation: Systems that demand authentication for purposes other than accountability, and that do not themselves require accountability, should not collect accountability information. (2.2)

Recommendation: System designers, developers, and vendors should improve the usability and manageability of authentication mechanisms, as well as their intrinsic security and privacy characteristics. (4.5)

Recommendation: Organizations that maintain online-accessible databases containing information used to authenticate large numbers of users should employ high-quality information security measures to protect that information. Wherever possible, authentication servers should employ mechanisms that do not require the storage of secrets. (6.2)

MULTIPLE IDENTITIES, LINKAGE, AND SECONDARY USE

Who do you find when you authenticate someone? There is no single identity, identifier, or role associated with each person that is globally unique and meaningful to all of the organizations and individuals with whom that person interacts.

Finding: Most individuals maintain multiple identities as social and economic actors in society. (1.1)

People invoke these identities under different circumstances. They may identify themselves as named users of computer systems, employees, frequent fliers, citizens, students, members of professional societies, licensed drivers, holders of credit cards, and so on. These multiple identities allow people to maintain boundaries and protect privacy. That capacity diminishes with the number of identifiers used.

Finding: The use of a single or small number of identifiers across multiple systems facilitates record linkage. Accordingly, if a single identifier is relied on across multiple institutions, its fraudulent or inappropriate use (and subsequent recovery actions) could have far greater ramifications than if used in only a single system. (4.3)

The networking of information systems makes it easier to link information across different, even unrelated, systems. Consequently, many different transactions can be linked to the same individual. Systems that facilitate linkages among an individual's different identities, identifiers, and attributes pose challenges to the goal of privacy protection. Once data have been collected (such as from an authentication event or subsequent transactions), dossiers may be created.

Finding: The existence of dossiers magnifies the privacy risks of authentication systems that come along later and retroactively link to or use dossiers. Even a so-called de-identified dossier constitutes a privacy risk, in that identities often can be reconstructed from de-identified data. (4.2)

Secondary use of authentication systems (and the identifiers and/or identities associated with them) is related to linkage. Many systems are used in ways that were not originally intended by the system designers. The obvious example is the driver's license: Its primary function is to certify that the holder is authorized to operate a motor vehicle. However, individuals are now asked to present their driver's license as proof of age, proof of address, and proof of name in a variety of circumstances. As discussed in *IDs—Not That Easy* and in this report, the primary use of an authentication system may require security and privacy considerations very different from those appropriate for subsequent secondary uses. (For example, a driver's license that certifies one is capable of driving a motor vehicle is a far cry from certification that one is not a threat to airline travel.) Given the difficulty of knowing all the ways in which a system might be used, care must be taken to prevent secondary use of the system as such use can easily lead to privacy and security risks.

Finding: Current authentication technology is not generally designed to prevent secondary uses or mitigate their effects. In fact, it often facilitates secondary use without the knowledge or consent of the individual being authenticated. (4.4)

Finding: Secondary uses of authentication systems, that is, uses for which the systems were not originally intended, often lead to privacy and security problems. They can compromise the underlying mission of the original system user by fostering inappropriate usage models, creating security concerns for the issuer, and generating additional costs. (4.5)

At the extreme end of the identity spectrum is the concept of anonymity. Anonymity continues to play an important role in preserving the smooth functioning of society—and it helps to protect privacy. The widespread use of authentication implies less anonymity.

Finding: Preserving the ability of citizens to interact anonymously with other citizens, with business, and with the government is important because it avoids the unnecessary accumulation of identification data that could deter free speech and inhibit legitimate access to public records. (6.7)

Linkage and secondary uses of information and systems can be lessened.

Recommendation: A guiding principle in the design or selection of authentication technologies should be to minimize the linking of user information across systems unless the express purpose of the system is to provide such linkage. (4.3)

Recommendation: Future authentication systems should be designed to make secondary uses difficult, because such uses often undermine privacy, pose a security risk, create unplanned-for costs, and generate public opposition to the issuer. (4.4)

THE UNIQUE ROLES OF GOVERNMENT

Government institutions play multiple roles in the area where authentication and privacy intersect. Their approaches to authentication and privacy protection may differ from those of private sector entities for structural and legal reasons.

Finding: Electronic authentication is qualitatively different for the public sector and the private sector because of a government's unique relationship with its citizens:

a. Many of the transactions are mandatory.
b. Government agencies cannot choose to serve only selected market segments. Thus, the user population with which they must deal is very heterogeneous and may be difficult to serve electronically.
c. Relationships between governments and citizens are sometimes cradle to grave but characterized by intermittent contacts, which creates challenges for technical authentication solutions.
d. Individuals may have higher expectations for government agencies than for other organizations when it comes to protecting the security and privacy of personal data. (6.2)

As a provider of services, the government has been seeking ways to more easily authenticate users who require such services. In some cases, interagency and intergovernmental solutions may conflict with the fundamental principles espoused in the Privacy Act of 1974.

Finding: Many agencies at different levels of government have multiple, and sometimes conflicting, roles in electronic authentication. They can be regulators of private sector behavior, issuers of identity documents or identifiers, and also relying parties for service delivery. (6.1)

Finding: Interagency and intergovernmental authentication solutions that rely on a common identifier create a fundamental tension with the privacy principles enshrined in the Privacy Act of 1974, given the risks associated with data aggregation and sharing. (6.8)

Government plays a special role in issuing identity documents (driver's licenses, birth certificates, passports, Social Security cards) that are foundational documents relied upon to establish identity in numerous authentication systems. However, the processes used to produce these foundational documents are not necessarily sufficiently secure to serve their stated function. Further, although states issue driver's licenses and the federal government issues passports, each may depend on the other for reissuance or replacement; no single entity has a complete authoritative database. While on the one hand the lack of easy linkage can be seen as a privacy boon, on the other the relative ease with which some foundational documents can be forged means that fraud is more likely and security and privacy risks (including identity theft) are great.

Finding: Many of the foundational identification documents used to establish individual user identity are very poor from a security perspective, often as a result of having been generated by a diverse set of issuers that may lack an ongoing interest in ensuring the documents' validity and reliability. Birth certificates are especially poor as base identity documents, because they cannot be readily tied to an individual. (6.3)

Recommendation: Birth certificates should not be relied upon as the sole base identity document. Supplemented with supporting evidence, birth certificates can be used when proof of citizenship is a requirement. (6.1)

MOVING FORWARD

When people express concerns about privacy, they speak about intrusion into personal affairs, disclosure of sensitive personal information, and improper attribution of actions to individuals. The more personal the information that is collected and circulated, the greater the reason for these concerns—and the proliferation of authentication activity implies more collection and circulation of personal information. There are choices to be made: Is authentication necessary? If so, how should it be accomplished? What should happen to the information that is collected? It is time to be more thoughtful about authentication technologies and their implications for privacy. Some of this thinking must happen among technologists, but it is also needed among business and policy decision makers.

The tension between authentication and privacy—and the need for greater care in choosing how to approach authentication—will grow in the information economy. In addition to the management control concerns associated with security, the economic value of understanding the behavior of customers and others is a strong motivator for capturing personal information. It is also a strong motivator for misusing such information, even if it is only captured through authentication systems.

The decision about where and when to deploy identity authentication systems—if only where confirmation of identity is already required today or in a greater range of circumstances—will shape society in both obvious and subtle ways. The role of attribute authentication in protecting privacy is underexplored. In addition, establishing practices and technical measures that protect privacy costs money at the outset. Many privacy breaches are easy to conceal or are unreported; therefore, failing to protect privacy may cost less than the initial outlay required to establish sound procedural and technical privacy protections. If the individuals whose information has been compromised and the agencies that are responsible for enforcing privacy laws were to become aware of privacy breaches, the incentive for proactive implementation of technologies and policies that protect privacy would be greater.

> **Finding: Privacy protection, like security, is very poor in many systems, and there are inadequate incentives for system operators and vendors to improve the quality of both. (4.6)**

> **Finding: Effective privacy protection is unlikely to emerge voluntarily unless significant incentives to respect privacy emerge to counterbalance the existing incentives to compromise privacy. The experience to date suggests that market forces alone are unlikely to sufficiently motivate effective privacy protection. (4.7)**

Even if the choice is made to institute authentication systems only where people today attempt to discern identity, the creation of reliable, inexpensive systems will inevitably invite function creep and unplanned-for secondary uses unless action is taken to avoid these problems. Thus, the privacy consequences of both the intended design and deployment and the unintended uses of authentication systems must be taken into consideration by vendors, users, policy makers, and the general public.

> **Recommendation: Authentication systems should not infringe upon individual autonomy and the legal exercise of expressive activities. Systems that facilitate the maintenance and assertion of separate identities in separate contexts aid in this endeavor, consistent with existing practices in which individuals assert distinct identities for the many different roles they assume. Designers and implementers of such systems should respect informational, communications, and other privacy interests as they seek to support requirements for authentication actions. (3.1)**

The federal government has passed numerous laws and regulations that place constraints on the behavior of private sector parties as well as on government agencies. Among them are the Family Educational Rights and Privacy Act, the Financial Services Modernization Act, the Health Insurance Portability and Accountability Act of 1996, and, in 1974, the

Privacy Act, which regulates the collection, maintenance, use, and dissemination of personal information by federal government agencies. Given the plethora of privacy-related legislation and regulation, making sense of government requirements can be daunting.

TOOLKIT

With a basic understanding of authentication, privacy interests and protections, and related technologies, it is possible to consider how one might design an authentication system that limits privacy intrusions while still meeting its functional requirements. This report provides a toolkit for examining the privacy implications of various decisions that must be made when an authentication system is being contemplated. As mentioned previously, most of these decisions can be made irrespective of the particular technology under consideration.

The kind of authentication to be performed (attribute, identity, or individual) is an initial choice that will bear on the privacy implications. Viewed without regard to the resource that they are designed to protect, attribute authentication systems present the fewest privacy problems and individual authentication systems the most. Despite the fact that it raises more privacy concerns, in some instances individual authentication may be appropriate for privacy, security, or other reasons.

In the process of developing an authentication system, several questions must be answered early. Decisions will have to be made about which attributes to use, which identifiers will be needed, which identity will be associated with the identifier, and how the level of confidence needed for authentication will be reached. The answers to each of these questions will have implications for privacy. Chapter 7 elaborates on four types of privacy (information, decisional, bodily integrity, and communications) and on how they are affected by the answers to each of the preceding questions. The analysis proposed is technology-independent, for the most part, and can be applied to almost any proposed authentication system.

1

Introduction and Overview

The growth of technologies that ease surveillance, data collection, disclosure, aggregation, and distribution has diminished the obscurity and anonymity that are typical of everyday interactions. From phone systems that block the calling number on outgoing calls and simultaneously identify all incoming callers,[1] to "loyalty" programs that collect data about individuals' purchasing habits,[2] to the government's use of tracking and identification technologies in an increasingly broad range of environments, records of individuals' activities are now routinely made and stored for future use. Technologies such as facial recognition and video cameras are being deployed in an attempt to identify and/or monitor individuals surreptitiously as they go about the most mundane of activities.[3] Ubiquitous computing promises to put computa-

---

[1]"Pacific Bell Offers Privacy Manager,"*RBOC Update* 12(5) (new offering for per-call control over incoming messages); Beth Whitehouse, "In Pursuit of Privacy: Phone Services Designed to Protect Can Also Be Extremely Frustrating," *Newsday*, March 26, 2001, p. B03 (problems arising from use of caller ID and call-blocking plans).

[2]See, generally, Marion Agnew, "CRM Plus Lots of Data Equals More Sales for Borders— Retail Convergence Aligns Web-based Marketing and Strategies with Those of Physical Stores," *InformationWeek*, May 7, 2001 (Borders' plan to merge online and off-line customer data and loyalty programs); Kelly Shermach, "Coalition Loyalty Programs: Finding Strength in Numbers," *Card Marketing* 5(3):1 (benefits of shared data from joint marketing card products).

[3]Lev Grossman, "Welcome to the Snooper Bowl: Big Brother Came to Super Sunday, Setting Off a New Debate About Privacy and Security in the Digital Age," *Time*, February

tional power everywhere by embedding it seamlessly and unobtrusively into homes, offices, and public spaces. The fully networked environment that ubiquitous computing is making possible raises complicated questions about privacy and identification.[4] What does it mean when data collection, processing, and surveillance—and perhaps authentication and identification—become the norm?

In applications ranging from electronic commerce to electronic tax filing, to controlling entry to secured office buildings, to ensuring payment, the need to verify identity and authorize access has driven the development of increasingly advanced authentication systems. These systems vary widely in complexity and scope of use: passwords in combination with electronic cookies are used for many electronic commerce applications, smart cards coupled with biometrics allow access to secured areas, and sophisticated public-key mechanisms are used to ensure the integrity of many financial transactions. While there are many authentication technologies, virtually all of them involve the use of personal information and, in many cases, personally identifiable information, raising numerous privacy concerns.

This report examines authentication technologies through the lens of privacy. It is aimed at a broad audience, from users (both end users and organizations) of authentication systems, to people concerned with privacy broadly, to designers and implementers of authentication technologies and systems, to policy makers.

12, 2001, p. 72 (the use of facial recognition technology by the Tampa Bay police department to search the 72,000 people in the crowd at Super Bowl XXXV); Ace Atkins, "Surveillance Tactic Faces Off with Privacy," *Tampa Tribune*, February 7, 2001, p. 1 (police might buy controversial new technology, tried out at the Super Bowl, that scans faces in public places; surveillance cameras take pictures of people in crowds and a computer compares numeric facial patterns to a databank of criminals); Katherine Shaver, "Armey Protests Cameras Sought on GW Parkway; Speed Deterrent Likened to Big Brother," *Washington Post*, May 9, 2001, p. B01 (the National Park Service tested a radar camera from August 1999 to February 2000 in two areas of the George Washington Memorial Parkway in the Washington, D.C., area, and House Majority Leader Richard Armey asked Department of the Interior Secretary Gale A. Norton to ban the cameras, calling them "a step toward a Big Brother surveillance state"); Richard Morin and Claudia Deane, "DNA Databases Casting a Wider Net," *Washington Post*, May 8, 2001, p. A21 (the national DNA database and the fact that all 50 states have passed some version of a DNA data-banking law); Ian Hopper, "New Documents Disclose Extent of FBI's Web Surveillance," *Sunday Gazette Mail*, May 6, 2001, p. P6D (the FBI's use of Internet eavesdropping using its controversial Carnivore system—a set of software programs for monitoring Internet traffic [e-mails, Web pages, chat-room conversations, and other signals]—13 times between October 1999 and August 2000 and a similar device, Etherpeek, another 11 times.)

[4]See CSTB's report *Embedded, Everywhere: A Research Agenda for Networked Systems of Embedded Computers* (Washington, D.C., National Academy Press, 2001), particularly Chapter 4, which discusses security and privacy in ubiquitous computing environments.

Notwithstanding considerable literature on privacy, the legal and social meaning of the phrase "the right to privacy" is in flux. Rather than presenting an encyclopedic overview of the various technologies or an indepth treatise on privacy, this report explores the intersection of privacy and authentication, which raises issues of identification, authorization, and security.

This introductory chapter presents definitions and terminology that are used throughout the report. It introduces four overarching privacy concerns that illustrate how privacy and authentication can interact in ways that negatively affect privacy. It also provides a "day-in-the-life" scenario to motivate a discussion of authentication and privacy. Finally, there is a brief discussion of what this report does not do, along with an outline of the rest of the report.

DEFINITIONS AND TERMINOLOGY

Throughout this report, numerous interrelated concepts associated with authentication, identity, and privacy are discussed. Several of these concepts are briefly defined below for clarity. As noted in the committee's first report, *IDs—Not That Easy*, many of these concepts represent complicated, nuanced, and, in some instances, deeply philosophical topics.[5] Note that while the definitions below refer to individuals, they should also be understood to apply, when appropriate, to nonhuman subjects such as organizations, identified computers, and other entities. Popular belief to the contrary, authentication does not necessarily *prove* that a particular individual is who he or she claims to be; instead, authentication is about obtaining a level of confidence in a claim. The concepts below are teased apart both to describe how the terms are used in this report and to highlight how ambiguous many of them remain.

- **An *identifier* points to an individual. An identifier could be a name, a serial number, or some other pointer to the entity being identified.** Examples of personal identifiers include personal names, Social Security numbers (SSNs), credit card numbers, and employee identification numbers. It is sometimes necessary to distinguish between identifiers and the things that they identify. In order to refer to an identifier in a way that distinguishes it from the thing that it identifies, the identifier is written in quotation marks (for example, "Joseph K." is an identifier—specifically, a personal name—whereas Joseph K. is a person).

---

[5]Indeed, the committee has refined and evolved its core definitions since the publication of its earlier report *IDs—Not That Easy: Questions About Nationwide Identity Systems* (Washington, D.C., National Academy Press, 2002).

• **An *attribute* is a property associated with an individual.** Examples of attributes include height, eye color, employer, and organizational role.

• ***Identification* is the process of using claimed or observed attributes of an individual to infer who the individual is.** Identification can be done without the individual's having to (or being given the opportunity to) claim any identifier (for example, an unconscious patient in an emergency room might be identified without having to state his or her name).

• ***Authentication* is the process of establishing confidence in the truth of some claim.** The claim could be any declarative statement—for example, "This individual's name is 'Joseph K.,' " or "This child is more than 5 feet tall." Both identifiers and attributes can be authenticated, as the examples just cited demonstrate.

> —***Individual authentication* is the process of establishing an understood level of confidence that an identifier refers to a specific individual.** Individual authentication happens in two phases: (1) an identification phase, during which an identifier to be authenticated is selected in some way (often the identifier selected is the one claimed by the individual), and (2) an authentication phase, during which the required level of confidence is established (often by challenging the individual to produce one or more authenticators supporting the claim that the selected identifier refers to the individual). In the information security literature, individual authentication is sometimes referred to as "user authentication." In the biometrics literature, individual authentication of an identifier claimed by the individual is often called "verification."

> —***Identity authentication* is the process of establishing an understood level of confidence that an identifier refers to an identity. It may or may not be possible to link the authenticated identity to an individual.** For example, verification of the password associated with a Hotmail account authenticates an identity (foo@example.com) that may not be possible to link to any specific individual. Identity authentication happens in two phases: (1) an identification phase, during which an identifier to be authenticated is selected in some way (often the identifier is selected by a claimant), and (2) an authentication phase, during which the required level of confidence is established (often by challenging the claimant to produce one or more authenticators supporting the claim that the selected identifier refers to the identity).

—*Attribute authentication* **is the process of establishing an understood level of confidence that an attribute applies to a specific
individual.** Attribute authentication happens in two phases: (1) an
attribute selection phase, during which an attribute to be authenticated is selected in some way, and (2) an authentication phase,
during which the required level of confidence is established, either
by direct observation of the individual for the purpose of verifying
the applicability of the attribute or by challenging the individual to
produce one or more authenticators supporting the claim that the
selected attribute refers to the individual.

• **An *authenticator* is evidence that is presented to support the
authentication of a claim. It increases confidence in the truth of the
claim.** A receipt, for example, can act as an authenticator of a claim that
an item was purchased at a specific store.[6] A driver's license can act as an
authenticator that a particular name (a form of identifier) refers to the
individual who carries the license. Knowledge of a secret or the ability to
display some distinctive physical characteristic such as a fingerprint can
also serve as the authenticators of an individual's name.

• ***Authorization* is the process of deciding what an individual
ought to be allowed to do.** Authorization is distinct from authentication
(which establishes what an individual "is" rather than what the individual "is allowed.") Authorization policies determine how authorization decisions are made. Authorization policies base decision making on
a variety of factors, including subject identifiers (such as names) and
subject attributes other than identifiers (such as employee status, credit
rating, and so on).

• **The *identity* of X is the set of information about an individual X
that is associated with that individual in a particular identity system Y.
However, Y is not always named explicitly.** An identity is not the same
as an identifier—so "Joseph K." is an identifier (specifically, a name), but
Joseph K. is a person. It is not always easy to determine which individual
an identifier refers to. For example, "George Bush, the president of the
United States, who lives in Texas and who attended Yale" is an identifier
that refers to *two* individuals. Identities also consist of more than just
names—so Richard Nixon was an individual, but his identity also includes other facts, such as that he was president of the United States and
that he resigned that office. Furthermore, identities contain statements
that are not strictly facts—a man who was stranded on a desert island in

---

[6]Confusion can arise when the same thing is used as both an authenticator and an identifier, as happens frequently with credit card numbers.

1971 and who believed in 1975 that Richard Nixon was still President would have his facts wrong but would not misidentify Nixon. Finally, people disagree about identities and about which individuals they refer to; if one believes newspaperman Bob Woodward, there was an individual who went by the code name "Deep Throat" during the Watergate investigation that led to Nixon's resignation, but different people have different opinions about who that individual is.

• **Security refers to a collection of safeguards that ensure the confidentiality of information, protect the integrity of information, ensure the availability of information, account for use of the system, and protect the system(s) and/or network(s) used to process the information.** Security is intended to ensure that a system resists attacks and tolerates failures. (See Chapter 4 for a more in-depth discussion of security and authentication.)

• *Privacy* **is a multifaceted term with many contextually dependent meanings. One aspect of the right to privacy is the right of an individual to decide for himself or herself when and on what terms his or her attributes should be revealed.** (See Chapter 3 for some historical background on privacy and a brief exploration of current privacy law and policy in the United States.)

AUTHENTICATION IN DAILY LIFE

Individuals authenticate themselves to others and to information systems in many different contexts. The identifiers and attributes that they authenticate vary, depending on the situation. Individuals may identify themselves as named users of computer systems, employees, frequent flyers, citizens, students, members of professional societies, licensed drivers, holders of credit cards, adults over the age of 18, and so on. There need not be any single identity associated with each person that is globally unique and meaningful to all of the organizations and individuals with whom that person interacts. Thus, people often assert different identities under different circumstances.

Finding 1.1: Most individuals maintain multiple identities as social and economic actors in society.

To illustrate the myriad ways in which instances of identification and authentication arise in everyday life and to highlight some of the important issues associated with new systems, the committee hypothesized scenarios in the life of Joseph K. as he goes on a business trip. The italic sentences describe Joseph's actions; the indented paragraphs that follow point out important associated issues. (Specific technologies are discussed in more detail later in the report.)

Joseph first dials in to his corporate network from home and authenticates himself to a network access server. He does so by claiming to be an employee of CompuDigi Corporation, using a name and a smart card that is read by his computer.

> Successfully completing this authentication procedure authorizes Joseph to access the corporate network. All employees have the same basic access privileges for the network, so it might seem that there is no need to authenticate each employee independently by name for log-in purposes. However, by assigning each employee a unique log-in name, CompuDigi can track Joseph's log-in sessions separately from those of other employees, enabling audit, and it can more easily revoke Joseph's access if he leaves the company or if his smart card is lost or stolen.

Joseph now accesses an airline Web site to book his flights, probably unaware that authentication of another sort is going on.

> The Web site employs Secure Sockets Layer (SSL), a security protocol, to provide confidentiality for data transmitted between Joseph's personal computer (PC) and the site. This prevents eavesdroppers on the path between the PC and the Web site from observing sensitive data. It also provides an implicit authentication of the Web site to Joseph. This authentication is based on the Internet name of the Web site, as contained in the uniform resource locator (URL) that Joseph implicitly selected from his list of commonly accessed Web sites.

Joseph is generally unaware of this authentication process unless it fails and generates a warning message. The only indication to him that the process has succeeded is the appearance of a small padlock icon in the browser window (which he may not notice). Joseph now uses his airline frequent-flyer account number to identify himself and a personal identification number (PIN) to authenticate this identifier.

> The airline is not necessarily interested in Joseph's identity as an employee of CompuDigi but rather in his identity as a customer of the airline.

Based on his frequent-flyer status, Joseph is able to request a seat with better legroom in the front section of the aircraft.

Joseph is authorized to upgrade his seat based on his frequent-flyer status (an attribute), which in turn is based on his travel history. (Joseph's frequent-flyer number may remain constant with the airline for many years, but his status and hence his authorization to upgrade to a better seat will vary depending on how often he flies.) Thus, Joseph's frequent-flyer number (an identifier) is used as a key for a database that the airline uses to determine his status and hence his authorization.

To pay for his flight, Joseph provides a credit card account number. Knowledge of the account number and expiration date serves to authenticate him as a cardholder.

Using a credit card number and expiration date as authenticators is a relatively weak form of authentication, since the account number serves as the primary identifier as well. This credit card data might be stored on the Web server; or, it might be used only for the transaction at hand and not be stored on the Web server. If there were a way for Joseph to be sure that the Web server was not storing his credit card information, it might increase his trust in the system (assuming that he had been notified of this policy).

An electronic ticket is issued for Joseph's flights. Next, he wishes to connect to the Web site of a hotel chain to book a room.

This Web site supports a feature known as client certificates, a little-used facet of SSL that can be employed to automate the user-authentication process. When Joseph initially registered on the Web site as a frequent guest of the hotel chain, the site interacted with his browser in order to issue him a public key certificate (an electronic file containing information related to Joseph's interactions with this site; see Chapter 5 for more on public key cryptography, private keys, and certificates). This certificate contains an identifier that links to Joseph's account but is otherwise not meaningful. Thus, the certificate cannot be used by Joseph to authenticate himself to any other Web sites. During the initial certificate generation process, Joseph was prompted to provide a password to be used by his browser to protect the private key associated with the certificate. This single password could protect all of the private keys stored by Joseph's browser for use with all of the certificates issued by Web sites that Joseph visits. Such use of the password would simplify Joseph's life if he had many certificates, but few Web sites make use of client certificates, so in practice Joseph would gain only a small benefit from this feature. Note that in terms of security, the private key becomes a proxy for the password(s) and is thus no more secure than the combination of that password and the physical means used to protect the encrypted private key.

When Joseph visits the hotel Web site (having registered and received a certificate earlier), his browser is queried by the Web site to send Joseph's certificate and to use the associated private key to verify Joseph's frequent-guest account identifier. Joseph is prompted by the browser to enter the password to unlock his private keys, and he is logged in to the Web site.

Again, it is Joseph's identity as a frequent client (rather than his name or other attributes) that is important. His status as a frequent guest entitles him to a free room upgrade. This is another example of authorization based on data associated with Joseph's identity in a specific context. In this context, Joseph elected to store credit card information as part of his profile with the hotel chain, so it is used automatically to guarantee his reservation in the event of a late arrival. If the Web site does not adequately protect the data that it stores, Joseph's credit card data may be inappropriately disclosed to others. The use of encryption to protect Joseph's data in transit to the site does not protect against this sort of security failure in any way.

Joseph has also elected to store several frequent-flyer numbers in his hotel profile so that he can acquire "mileage" credit for his stay.

With this action, Joseph has voluntarily elected to provide data to the hotel chain, enabling the hotel to link his (otherwise) independent hotel and airline identities. This provides the hotel marketing organization with an ability to market directly to Joseph on the basis of his travel patterns and preferences, as well as to offer amenities in a more customer-friendly fashion when Joseph stays at its hotels. It also provides an ability to sell Joseph's name, address, and possibly his e-mail address to other companies, based on the attributes in his frequent-traveler profile.

Finally, Joseph logs in to a rental car Web site and arranges for a vehicle for his trip. Here, Joseph authenticates himself using his name and his frequent-renter account number; no explicit password or PIN is required.

Joseph's profile at this Web site allows the rental car company to select automatically his favorite class of vehicle. Joseph has also provided a code that identifies him as an employee of CompuDigi, making him eligible for the special rates negotiated by CompuDigi for its employees. This code is an attribute not specific to Joseph; it is used as a basis for authorizing all employees to make use of the corporate discount program. Joseph's profile includes credit card data as well as his driver's license data, both of which are required for rental car transactions.

En route to the airport, Joseph makes use of an electronic toll tag lane, which allows him to avoid longer lines for drivers paying tolls with cash.

The toll tag device, mounted on the windshield of Joseph's car, engages in an electronic (radio frequency (RF)) challenge/response authentication protocol with a responder at each toll plaza, authenticating the toll tag device to the toll collection system. This system authenticates the tag's number, which is linked to Joseph's account identity in the toll system database. In turn, this number is linked to Joseph's bank account, enabling automatic debit of his account for each toll transaction. The toll system may be concerned only with receiving payment of the toll, so it is the identification of the bank account that is of primary interest here.[7]

Joseph arrives at the airport and makes use of a kiosk to acquire his boarding pass. To authenticate himself, he swipes the same credit card that he used to purchase the airline ticket through a magnetic-stripe reader.

In this case, possession of the credit card is viewed as authentication of identity.

At the airport security checkpoint, Joseph must present his boarding pass and a government-issued photo identification (ID) for authentication.

The name on the photo ID must match (either exactly or "closely") the name on the boarding pass, and the photo on the ID must be a good enough likeness to be acceptable to the security screening personnel.

Upon arrival at his destination airport, Joseph proceeds to the rental car area, where his car is waiting in a spot at which his name is displayed. As he exits the rental car lot, Joseph is required to present his driver's license.

---

[7]While it may be possible to link the tag to a cash account that is not linked to the driver, in many cases such systems do make explicit the linkage between the account and the (presumed) driver.

This procedure is designed to authenticate Joseph as the individual who holds the online reservation and to whose credit card the rental will be charged. In principle, the process should also verify that Joseph holds a valid driver's license, a prerequisite for car rental. In contrast to the boarding-pass check at the airport, the rental agreement has more information about Joseph, including the name of the state that issued the driver's license and the license number. Such information is nominally part of this authentication process, providing more evidence that the person presenting the license to the electronic record is connected to a printed receipt. Also, note that while a passport would be an acceptable form of photo ID for use with the boarding pass (and would be required for international flights), it is not acceptable here, because there is a requirement for a credential that demonstrates authorization to drive and that establishes accountability of a particular individual for loss of or damage to the automobile. A driver's license accomplishes both goals, because it directly asserts authorization to drive and because it contains or can be used to obtain the driver's address. The rental car agency (depending on the state in which Joseph is renting) may have reserved the right to screen Joseph's driving record, which it may access electronically using his driver's license number.

When Joseph arrives at his hotel, he presents a credit card at the front desk. The hotel matches the name on the credit card against the room-reservation database to identify Joseph.

Since the primary concern of the hotel is that it is compensated for the room rental, the presentation of a valid credit card (including verification that the credit card account is in good standing, not reported lost or stolen) is an acceptable form of authentication in this context.[8] The credit card is itself authenticated on the basis of the information contained on the magnetic stripe on the back of the card and on the basis of the appearance of the card (for example, the appearance of a standard hologram as part of the card face). If a conflict occurs—two individuals with the same name claim the same reservation at the same hotel on the same day—additional identification credentials will be required to resolve the conflict.

---

[8]Note that hotels in countries other than the United States often are required to request the presentation of a passport and sometimes even retain the document until the guest checks out.

When Joseph arrives at the CompuDigi meeting site, he uses his employee badge to gain entrance to the building. Joseph presents the card to a reader, which requires him to enter a PIN, a procedure designed to prevent unauthorized use of the card if it is lost or stolen.

Joseph's badge is a smart card, a credit-card-sized device that contains a processor, memory, and an input/output (I/O) interface. On this card is stored a public key certificate and corresponding private key. The card engages in a cryptographic challenge/response exchange with the building's physical security computer system to authenticate Joseph as a CompuDigi employee and to authorize him to enter the building.

This scenario illustrates that Joseph has many identities, not just one. These different identities represent him in his interactions with different organizations, each of which identifies him in a distinct context. In many instances, there is no need for these distinct identities to be tightly linked to one another, although there are exceptions. Sometimes Joseph makes an explicit choice to create the linkage (for example, for perceived benefits); at other times the linkage is required by the context (for example, the connection of his driver's license and his driving record). To the extent that Joseph chooses, or is allowed, to maintain separate identities in his interactions with organizations, he increases his privacy, because he discloses to each organization only the information required for interactions with that organization.

By maintaining separate and nonlinked identities, Joseph has some control over who gets which pieces of information about his activities, preferences, and lifestyle. Some of this control might be deliberate on Joseph's part, but some of it may have been the happenstance of a competitive market system in which linkages have not yet been fully unified across corporate and government databases. For Joseph to exercise proactive control over the dissemination and use of personal information about himself, he must become aware of how and where that information is being collected, linked, and used. As activities within society become increasingly automated, it becomes harder and harder for anyone to make these informed decisions.

Without informed, proactive control on Joseph's part, the various authentication events described in this scenario pose risks in terms of both security and privacy. The rest of this report elaborates on various authentication technologies and their relationship to privacy issues.

CURRENT TENSIONS

The development, implementation, and broad deployment of authentication systems require us to think carefully about the role of identity and privacy in a free, open, and democratic society. Privacy, including control over the disclosure of one's identity and the ability to remain anonymous, is an essential ingredient of a functioning democracy. It is a precondition for the exercise of constitutionally protected freedoms, such as the freedom of association.[9] It supports the robust exercise of the freedom of expression by, for example, creating psychological space for political dissent.[10] It maintains social norms that protect human dignity and autonomy by enabling expressions of respect and intimacy and the establishment of boundaries between oneself and one's community.[11]

---

[9]See *National Association for the Advancement of Colored People* v. *Alabama Ex Rel. Patterson, Attorney General,* 357 U.S. 449; 78 S. Ct. 1163 (1958); 2 L. Ed. 2d 1488 (1958) (the Court held that the immunity from state scrutiny of membership lists was so related to the right of the members to associate freely with others as to come within the protection of the U.S. Constitution); *Joseph McIntyre, Executor of Estate of Margaret McIntyre, Deceased, Petitioner* v. *Ohio Elections Commission,* 514 U.S. 334; 115 S. Ct. 1511 (1995) (statute prohibiting the distribution of anonymous campaign literature violated the First Amendment, as it was not narrowly tailored to serve an overriding state interest; the statute indiscriminately outlawed a category of speech with no relationship to the danger sought to be prevented); *Buckley* v. *American Constitutional Law Foundation; Taley* v. *California.* Also, see the work that the Electronic Privacy Information Center (EPIC) has done on anonymity, including an amicus brief in the *Watchtower Bible* v. *Stratton* case, arguing that "an ordinance requiring door-to-door petitioners to obtain a permit and identify themselves upon demand" implicates privacy as well as rights of anonymity, freedom of expression, and freedom of association. More information is available online at <http://www.epic.org/free_speech/watchtower.html>.

[10]See Martin H. Redish, "The Value of Free Speech," 130 U. Pa. L. Rev. 591, pp. 601-604 (1982) (free expression supports citizens' participation in decision making); Alexander Meiklejohn, *Political Freedom: The Constitutional Powers of the People,* New York, Oxford University Press, 1965, pp. 3-89 (free expression provides citizens with access to information necessary to formulate opinions and make decisions); Rodney A. Smolla, *Smolla and Nimmer on Freedom of Speech: A Treatise on the First Amendment,* Clark Boardman Callaghan, 1994, §13.01[3] (by allowing disempowered groups to dissent, free expression provides stability); and Julie E. Cohen, "A Right to Read Anonymously: A Closer Look at 'Copyright Management' in Cyberspace," 28 Conn. L. Rev. 981 (1996) (arguing that reading is intimately connected with freedom of speech and thought and therefore the right to read anonymously should be an understood guarantee of the First Amendment).

[11]Robert C. Post, "The Social Foundations of Privacy: Community and Self in the Common Law Tort," 77 Calif. L. Rev. 957 (1989). Post argues that the common law tort of invasion of privacy safeguards social norms—"rules of civility"—is based on the belief that personality and human dignity are injured when these rules of civility are broken. He concludes with an explanation of the role that the privacy tort plays in enabling individuals to receive and express respect, thereby enabling human dignity; in allowing individuals to receive and express intimacy, thereby enabling human autonomy; and in establishing obli-

If individuals fear unchecked scrutiny, they will be less likely to participate vigorously in the political process and in society in general.[12] If individuals are denied privacy—by the government, corporations, and other individuals—they are less able to explore ideas, formulate personal opinions, and express and act on these beliefs. At the same time, "privacy" is sometimes used as a pretext for hiding illegal activities, and society has, at times, a legitimate interest in requiring authentication or identification, either for validating claims to rights and privileges or for holding individuals responsible for their actions.

Today, when individual authentication is demanded (such as before boarding an airplane), the individual whose identity is to be authenticated is asked to participate in the process of proving who he or she is.[13] Authentication of identity generally (but not always; see Chapter 4) requires an affirmative act—the individual must affirmatively introduce herself or knowingly produce a credential containing identity information. While a third party may at times provide information about an individual's identity (such as an adult verifying the identity of a child), such information is more often a tool for confirming the identity presented by the individual being authenticated. Because authentication generally requires some affirmative act on the part of the individual, it is rare that an individual's identity is surreptitiously noted and recorded in the context of an authentication event.

The decision about where to deploy authentication systems—be it only where today verification of identity is already required or in a greater range of circumstances—will shape society in both obvious and subtle ways. Even if the choice is made to implement authentication systems only where people *today* attempt to discern identity, the creation of reliable, inexpensive systems will invite function creep—the use of authentication systems for other than their originally intended purposes—unless action is taken to prevent this from happening.[14] Thus, the privacy con-

---

gations between community members, thereby defining the substance and boundaries of community life. Id. at p. 238; Bloustein, "Privacy As an Aspect of Human Dignity: An Answer to Dean Prosser," 39 N.Y.U. L. Rev. 962, pp. 1000-1007 (1964) (arguing that the privacy torts involve the same interest in preserving human dignity and individuality).

[12]See, generally, the numerous privacy statutes that prevent the reuse of information and limit governmental access because of social interest in promoting or protecting the underlying activities (for example, related to financial information and health care), many of which are discussed in Chapters 3 and 6.

[13]The criminal justice context is an exception in which the individual's identity may be determined without their active participation.

[14]An example of secondary use is that of reliance on the driver's license for proof of age in establishments that sell alcohol. In at least one establishment in Massachusetts, licenses are swiped through a machine and all of the information contained in the magnetic stripe

sequences of both the intended design and deployment and the unintended, secondary uses of authentication systems must be taken into consideration by vendors, users, policy makers, and the general public.

FOUR OVERARCHING PRIVACY CONCERNS

While authentication systems can be used to preserve or enhance privacy, there are many ways, as described above, in which an authentication system, or even the act of authentication alone, can affect privacy; that is, privacy is involved as a consequence or corollary of authentication. Before discussing the details of authentication technologies and their impact on privacy in later chapters, several categories of privacy risk are described below. While not applicable to all authentication systems, these categories broadly characterize the risks to personal privacy that authentication systems can create.

- *Covert identification.* Some authentication systems make it possible to identify an individual without the individual's consent or even knowledge. Such systems deny the individual, and society, the opportunity to object to and to monitor the identification process. These technologies are particularly vulnerable to misuse because their use is hidden.
- *Excessive use of authentication technology.* Cost and public sensitivity have historically checked the spread of authentication systems. At the same time that technological progress has reduced the cost of these systems (along with the costs of data collection and processing generally), the public, owing to an increased sense of vulnerability and desire for security or simple familiarity, has become accustomed to demands for authentication. Together, these trends increase the likelihood that authentication systems will become more prevalent. Led by a mentality of "more is better," the public and private sectors have been quick to increase the collection of personal information where this process is supported by cheaper, easier technology.
- *Excessive aggregation of personal information.* The use of a single identifier (such as the Social Security number) or a small number of identifiers creates the opportunity for more linking of previously separate repositories of personal information. Today, different record keepers have different ways of identifying individuals (and in some cases of tying their identities to transaction histories). The many cards that people carry in their wallets reveal some of the multiple identities by which they are

---

on the back is collected. "Swipe at Your Privacy," WHDH TV, June 4, 2002. Available online at <http://www.whdh.com/features/articles/specialreport/H37/>.

known. The adoption of a single (or small number of) authentication systems across the public and private sector would greatly erode privacy by facilitating the linkage of records maintained by many disparate record keepers.[15]

• *Chilling effects.* Wherever identity authentication is required, there is an opportunity for social control. In some instances such control is a laudable goal (such as in contexts that require high security and accountability). But in other areas, there is a risk that new methods of social exclusion and vehicles for prejudicial social control will be created. For example, in a world in which a single identifier (for example, a Social Security number) is relied on by many public and private institutions, the organization in charge of issuing this identifier (the government, in this example) could interfere with a citizen's ability to engage in a wide range of legitimate private sector transactions by revoking the identifier; or, a thief could interfere with the same abilities by stealing the identifier and using it fraudulently.

While there are risks to privacy with some authentication systems, it should be noted that there are situations in which authentication provides an important method of ensuring accountability and of *protecting* privacy. For example, when specific individuals are granted access to personal or proprietary information for limited purposes, authentication can play an important role in monitoring and enforcing adherence to relevant regulations and laws limiting individuals' access to these purposes.

WHAT THIS REPORT DOES AND DOES NOT DO

This report explores the concepts of authentication, identity, and privacy. It examines various authentication technologies and describes their privacy implications. The report does not recommend specific technologies for specific purposes, nor does it provide an explicit cost analysis such as might be provided by a consultant. Instead, the report discusses the various technologies and elaborates on the trade-offs with respect to privacy that each technology permits. As the remainder of the report makes clear, analyses of specific systems or proposed systems can proceed only with an understanding of the context in which a system will be operating and an understanding of the goals that the system is trying to meet. This report provides a framework for these issues and the necessary vocabulary within which to consider them.

---

[15]See this committee's first report, *IDs—Not That Easy: Questions About Nationwide Identity Systems,* Washington, D.C., National Academy Press, 2002, for a discussion of additional questions and issues raised by large-scale, widely used identity systems.

This report seeks to identify ways in which authentication technologies are directly and indirectly affecting privacy. It recognizes that both government and commercial parties do, under many circumstances, have a legitimate need to determine with whom they are dealing. It explores ways in which current authentication systems operate without adequate heed to personal privacy. The report recommends ways in which privacy interests might be better served without compromising the legitimate interests of commercial and government entities that employ authentication technologies.

Chapters 2 and 3 elaborate on the concepts of authentication and privacy to establish the framework for the discussion in the remainder of the report. Given the historical association of authentication with security, Chapter 4 describes security concerns that motivate authentication and then discusses how usability issues matter, both for security and privacy. Chapter 5 examines particular authentication technologies and describes some of the technological issues that arise. Chapter 6 outlines some of the unique challenges facing governments and government agencies with respect to authentication and privacy. Finally, Chapter 7 presents a toolkit for thinking through the implications for privacy of the choices made with respect to how authentication systems are developed and deployed.

2

Authentication in the Abstract

B efore examining specific authentication technologies and their implications for privacy, a discussion of the terms and concepts themselves is in order. Colloquial uses of the term "authentication" are occasionally misleading; for example, authentication is neither authorization nor identification. While this report does not attempt a comprehensive examination of privacy in the context of an information-rich world,[1] this chapter and the next provide a foundation for thinking about authentication and privacy and a context for the discussions of specific technologies in later chapters.

WHAT IS AUTHENTICATION AND WHY IS IT DONE?

Authentication is the process of establishing confidence in the truth of some claim. While this report focuses primarily on authentication in the context of information and computing systems, authentication occurs outside this realm as well, as examples throughout the text illustrate. Box 2.1, for example, presents a brief discussion of authentication in the context of absentee voting. In the context of information security, the unqualified term "authentication" is often used as shorthand to mean "verification of a claimed identity," although for the purposes of this report, a slightly more nuanced meaning is assumed. (See Chapter 1 for

---

[1]Another CSTB committee is examining the broad topic of privacy in the information age; the status of this project is available online at <http://www.cstb.org/project_privacy/>.

BOX 2.1
Absentee Voting

In many places, absentee voting couples a number of mechanisms in order to achieve authentication, authorization to vote exactly once, and the confidentiality of the ballot itself. The voter's identity is checked by way of a signature, both at application time and on the outer envelope of the ballot itself. A suitable entry in some sort of recordkeeping system is used to record that this person has already been issued a ballot. But the ballot itself is sealed inside an inner, anonymous envelope; this envelope is not opened until after it has been separated from the outer, authenticated (and nonanonymous) envelope. The two events are separated temporally and spatially. Despite the authentication of the voter (by means of the signature), a measure of privacy protection is achieved through a combination of the two envelopes and rigid procedures.

---

definitions of these and related terms.) It is possible to authenticate both human users and entities that are not humans (for example, cellular telephone networks in the United States directly authenticate cell phone handsets rather than handset users[2]), and it is possible to authenticate claims that do not relate to users' personal names (for example, an individual may claim to be tall enough to enjoy a height-restricted ride at a county fair; this claim can be verified without knowing the individual's name).

Authentication is not usually an end in itself. Information systems usually authenticate users in order to satisfy security or other requirements.[3] Most commonly, security systems authenticate users in order to authorize their requests to perform actions and in order to hold them accountable for the actions that they perform. (See Figure 2.1 for a flow chart describing how the policies of the system guide whether authentication, authorization, and/or accountability are needed.)

In some instances authentication is unrelated to security; identification and authentication are sometimes used to create or expand a relationship between parties. For example, cookies[4] are sometimes used to identify

---

[2]Often, databases can be used to map from a handset identifier to the name of the individual or organization that pays the bill for the handset.

[3]In some cases, one such requirement is to protect classes of people (usually children) from material deemed inappropriate. In 2002, CSTB released a report that looked at this problem: *Youth, Pornography, and the Internet,* Washington, D.C., National Academy Press, 2002.

[4]Cookies are mechanisms used by Web browsers and Web servers to track visits and/or provide continuity of experience.

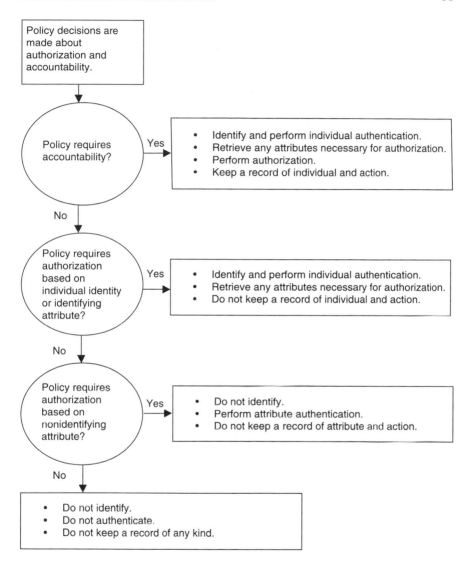

FIGURE 2.1 Authentication, authorization, and accountability. The necessity of authenticating the presenter's identity is based on the needs and policies of the system being accessed. If only authorization is sought by the system, the identity of the presenter may not be relevant.

individuals and track their browsing and purchasing behaviors. Such monitoring is undertaken to bolster personalization and marketing efforts.

The rest of this chapter describes elements of authentication systems and protocols at a high level in order to provide a foundation from which to examine specific authentication technologies. A description of the parties traditionally involved in authentication appears below, followed by a more detailed discussion of authorization and accountability.

Three Parties to Authentication

Authentication systems typically involve parties who play three roles in the authentication process. A "presenter" presents credentials (an in-depth discussion of the nature of credentials in general is provided in Chapter 6) issued by a third-party "issuer" to a "verifier" who wishes to determine the veracity of those credentials. In some cases, one party may play two roles. For example, the verifier and issuer roles are often combined.

The issuer usually[5] uses a separate system to perform an initial authentication of prospective credential holders prior to issuing credentials, to ensure that they are issued only to legitimate parties. Consider the case of a department of motor vehicles (DMV), which issues an important credential, the driver's license.[6] The DMV often relies on another credential, such as a birth certificate or a passport, to identify applicants for licenses. This reliance comes with its own risks, in that birth certificates, for example, are not strongly linked to the individuals whom they identify and are so diverse in their format that it is difficult for DMV employees to authenticate them. (The security and integrity problems associated with documents such as birth certificates are discussed in Chapter 6.)

When analyzing different authentication systems, it is important to look at how a system implements all three roles. One needs to look at the security and privacy issues and the risks for each role and the processes that the system performs and consider who has a vested interest in the success (or failure!) of the authentication event.

---

[5]Not all credentials require presenting supplementary forms of identification prior to issuance. For example, one may acquire a free e-mail account from one of several services, which then acts as a legitimate e-mail address, anonymously.

[6]The original motivation for driver's licenses was to document authority to operate a motor vehicle. However, today they are used more often as a primary identity credential in many unrelated transactions, such as boarding an airliner or cashing a check. (This is an example of the secondary use of a credential overwhelming the primary use; see Chapter 4 for more discussion of secondary uses.)

Authorization can be attained by ascertaining attributes of the user, the system, or external conditions. However, ensuring accountability often requires that a particular individual be linked to a transaction.[7]

Authenticating to Authorize

Authorization is the process of ensuring that the rules governing who may do what to which resources are obeyed. Authorization works by asking an appropriate authority (referred to herein as a "policy decision point") for an authorization decision every time an individual[8] submits a request to the system to access resources. If the policy decision point decides to grant the request, the individual is allowed to access the resource; if the policy decision point decides to deny the request, the individual is not allowed access.

The International Organization for Standardization (ISO) Standard 10181-3 defines a standard model and standard terminology for authorization in an information technology and communications context.[9] In the ISO model, authorization decisions are based on authorization policy, resource attributes (such as sensitivity of the data), context attributes (such as time of day), request attributes, and subject attributes. Subject attributes might include the requester's name and privilege attributes, such as job role, group memberships, or security clearance.

In order to make a determination, the policy decision point needs to know something about the subject it is dealing with. Since subjects might try to impersonate one another, the verifier will want to make sure that the subject attributes that it uses to make its decision have been authenticated. Policy decision points do not necessarily need to know anything about a subject's *name* or any other particular claimed identity in order to authenticate the attributes that are relevant to the policies they enforce. Two examples from Disney World illustrate this point:

---

[7]Anonymous accountability mechanisms exist. Consider, for example, a cash security deposit for using a set of billiard balls. If the user steals or damages the balls, he or she forfeits the deposit (which is then used to finance the purchase of a new set). The user who returns the balls in good condition gets the deposit back. The user is held financially accountable for loss or damage to property (the billiard balls) with no record of identity being required. Of course, this is anonymous only to the extent that anyone participating in or witnessing the transaction may know the user's identity.

[8] In this case, the individual is the initiator of an operation that involves an authorization decision. The individual is the entity whose privileges are examined to determine if he or she should be allowed to complete the requested operation.

[9]This definition is adopted because it is the international standard for terminology in this area.

• Disney World restricts access to some rides on the basis of physical height of the rider. The policy that enforces this restriction authenticates the rider's height (an attribute) by requiring riders to walk past a sign that has a picture of a hand positioned at the required height. If the rider's head is higher than the hand, the rider's height is authenticated, and the rider is allowed onto the ride. This system does not *identify* individual riders at all, but it still enforces the desired policy. It authenticates the relevant attribute (in this case, height greater than the required minimum value) of each rider. It does not collect extraneous information about the individual.

• Disney World also uses a system that is designed to prevent a single-entry pass from being used by multiple users. Disney World issues each passholder a card at the time the pass is purchased. The name of the passholder is not recorded on the card, and, in fact, the card can be transferred freely from user to user until the first time it is used. At the time of first use, information about the passholder's finger geometry (not related to the passholder's fingerprint) is linked to the card. Any time after the first use of the pass, the person presenting the pass must authenticate ownership of the pass using a finger geometry verification check (by holding his or her hand up to a measuring device). If the check fails, the person presenting the pass is denied access to the park.

Finger geometry is not distinctive enough to identify the passholder uniquely; therefore, verifying finger geometry does not provide sufficient certainty for accountability (see below). However, finger geometry varies sufficiently from person to person so that a randomly selected individual who is not the passholder is not likely to match the finger geometry linked to the card. Therefore, this system works well enough to prevent multiple users from using the same pass in most cases—an acceptable level of risk, given what the system is protecting. This system uses a loose form of biometric authentication to protect against fraud (here defined as multiple users) without collecting information that *identifies* the legitimate owner of the pass. (See Chapter 5 for further details on various biometrics technologies.)

Authenticating to Hold Accountable

Accountability is the ability to associate a consequence with a past action of an individual. To hold individuals accountable it must be possible retrospectively to tie them to the actions or events for which accountability is desired, or to be able independently to detect and respond to inappropriate behavior. Especially for purposes of after-the-fact accountability, information from the authentication event must unambiguously identify one and only one individual, who will be held responsible for the event.[10] An authentication event that identifies a group of people but not a single individual within the group cannot easily support individual accountability.[11]

Accountability usually *eventually* requires personal identification of individuals (unlike authorization, which can often be done without identifying individuals). Accountability processes are used to generate the evidence needed to punish the guilty when something is done in violation of policy or law. Even so, the identifiers used need not always be in the form of the name of the individual or even something that can be used to find the individual of interest; they only need to be able to confirm that a suspect is the individual actually responsible. What is needed for this purpose is something that can be linked to the individual with some level of assurance. A fingerprint or DNA sample, for example, can be used to establish accountability. Neither of these two types of evidence names the individual—nor does either provide a mechanism for finding him or her—but both provide means to verify (after the individual is located through other means) that the suspect probably is or is not the accountable individual.

Accountability in information systems usually works by allowing a process for observing and recording users' actions in a log. The log can later be searched (as part of an investigation into wrongdoing, for example).[12]

While authentication (whether of an individual's name or of an attribute) is often *necessary* for accountability, authentication by itself is not always *sufficient* to support accountability. Authentication is a key to attributing actions and allocating punishments to the correct individuals.

---

[10]In some cases, it may be possible to impose a certain kind of "accountability" without requiring the authentication of an identity. For example, some technologies are designed to prevent unauthorized duplication of digital media (such as CDs). In instances in which this technology works, there is no accountability that requires identity authentication; instead the CD (or the machine) might just stop functioning.

[11]It is important to note that accountability is not the only mechanism for righting wrongs. Legal and other systems sometimes address wrongs without directly holding accountable the individual responsible for the wrong—for example, by providing for redress. Accountability and redress are separate concepts. One can have redress for a harm without holding the perpetrator of the harm accountable. For example, in disputes involving alleged violations of copyright, the Digital Millennium Copyright Act of 1998 provides for redress by providing copyright holders with a method of having material removed from Web sites. This form of redress prevents future harm but does not punish previous bad acts.

[12]Note that this is conceptually distinct from the notion of auditing for the purposes of system maintenance and/or troubleshooting. Auditing may or may not require recording individualized user activity. While the mechanisms can be similar, the purposes of these two kinds of log-based monitoring are distinct.

If identities in the log are not well authenticated, a user who falls under suspicion of wrongdoing will dispute the validity of the log by claiming that the actions attributed to him or her were really performed by someone else—someone else who fooled the authentication system and impersonated the suspect.[13]

Accountability is not always a requirement in information systems (or elsewhere), and even where it is, collecting and storing information about individuals is not always necessary for accountability. In order to establish accountability, systems often collect and store information about who did what, where, and how. For example, financial markets support payment mechanisms with and without accountability. In a cash-for-goods transaction, the buyer and seller often divulge no information to one another. In contrast, credit card transactions are information-rich: A record is created that captures both the identity of each party and the details of the transaction. Credit records support accountability by uniquely mapping to an individual (except perhaps in the case of family members who share a single account and thus share each other's accountability or in situations involving powers of attorney) or to an organization.

The inability to reconstruct a transaction from records retrospectively (that is, one may not be able to identify the other party or to prove that the transaction occurred) is the norm in cash transactions. This is at least in part due to the fact that the exchange is complete when the parties separate (goods have been exchanged for cash), so there is little need to make provisions for future accountability for payment. In a credit transaction, by contrast, one party has goods, another has a *promise* of payment, and a third has a record of the transaction directing the purchaser to make payment. The incomplete nature of the transfer and the ability of a buyer or seller to deny or fabricate an exchange have resulted in the creation of identity-based audit logs that support accountability. These are needed in order to complete the payment and therefore the transaction as a whole.

These examples illustrate that anonymous, instantaneous liability-transfer mechanisms (such as cash) can reduce or even eliminate the need for accountability in some transaction-based systems. An example of an anonymous liability-transfer mechanism that is not instantaneous is a security deposit. A security deposit is an up-front payment equal to or exceeding the value of an item that is rented or borrowed (for example, a

---

[13]Where authentication of individual identities is required, the individual identities in the log will not necessarily be easily accessible to just anyone who looks into the log. It is possible to design an audit system that puts a nonidentifying unique identifier (essentially a pseudonym, sometimes called an audit ID) into the log and allows specially authorized users to link these audit IDs to personal identities only after due-process rules have been observed.

cash deposit that is made for the billiard balls used at a bar or for checking in at a hotel without a credit card).

Cash is an extremely efficient mode of commerce in part because it does not require us to know or seek to know anything about the party on the other side of the transaction.[14] Other forms of payment are less efficient, because creditworthiness, identity, or other attributes of one or more parties to the transaction need to be established before the transaction is completed, records of the transaction need to be kept, and settlement procedures need to be executed. This suggests that where accountability (and therefore authentication) can be dispensed with, transactions can be made simultaneously more efficient and more protective of privacy.[15]

WHAT DO WE AUTHENTICATE?

Earlier, authentication was defined as the process of establishing confidence in the truth of some claim, often a claimed identity. The next obvious question is, What kinds of claims are verified? Individuals might make a variety of claims that would help to support the goals of authorization and accountability.

When the goal that motivates authentication is to hold an individual accountable, it is useful to verify some piece of information that is strongly linked to or that uniquely identifies the individual—for example, an identifier (such as a personal name) or a very distinctive attribute (such as a DNA profile). It may also be useful in these cases to verify some piece of information that will help contact or locate the individual—for example, a residence address or e-mail address.

When the goal that motivates authentication is to authorize individuals' actions, it is useful to verify some piece of information that will be useful to the policy decision point in making its authorization decision. This information may be a property of the individual (such as the fact that an individual has paid for entrance to an event), or it may be a statement about the individual by some authoritative party (such as when a credit transaction is authorized by the issuing bank).

---

[14]If the cash itself is authentic, then we trust in the issuing government to make good the promise of payment, perhaps in precious metal, and we trust that there will always be an exchange market for precious metal. Most currencies now skip the precious-metal connection; governments back the currency instead with the direct promise of market stability.

[15]Of course, providing records of transactions can be important for reasons other than accountability. For example, information systems often maintain transaction logs for the purpose of diagnosing and correcting system failures. In addition, the "anonymity" of cash creates challenges for law enforcement.

Presentation of a passport to an immigration agent authenticates the passport holder for the purpose of authorizing entry into a country. The individual presents the passport, which claims his or her name and country of residence. The immigration agent verifies the claim by examining the picture in the passport to verify that the individual is the legitimate holder of the passport and possibly by doing some kind of authenticity check on the passport document itself.

In summary, authentication is the process of verifying a claim. A claim asserts that an individual has some attribute. An attribute may be an identifier, a property, or a statement about the individual by a third party. Below is a discussion of these various kinds of attributes.

Identifiers

Recall from Chapter 1 that an identifier points to an individual. An identifier could be a name, a serial number, or some other pointer to the entity being identified. An identifier can be strong in the sense that it allows unique mapping to a specific individual in a population, or it can be weak, in that it could be correctly applied to more than one individual in a population. Whether an identifier is strong or weak will depend upon the size of the population and the distinctiveness of the identifying attribute. However, multiple weak identifiers can, when combined, uniquely identify a specific individual and therefore serve as the functional equivalent of a single strong (unique) identifier. Multiple weak identifiers may lead to unique identification.[16] Some identifiers, such as pseudonyms, require a list of correspondences between pseudonyms and individuals (often called a look-up table) for unique mapping back to an individual, thus allowing only the holder of the list to identify the action with the individual. Some identifiers, such as common names, allow any observer to map an action back to an individual (though not always with 100 percent confidence). Authorization, in contrast, may require no identifier at all. Systems that use multiple weak identifiers can be made just as secure for the verifier as systems that use, for example, personal names, but the former may have the privacy advantage of not as easily identify-

---

[16]Interestingly, while the use of multiple weak identifiers may enable a certain level of security through authentication, these identifiers can also be used to create unforeseen linkages and therefore pose a risk to privacy (even while, individually, very weak identifiers might pose a minimal risk to privacy). Work done by Latanya Sweeney suggests that very little information is needed to uniquely identify a particular individual in even an ostensibly anonymized database, suggesting that creating linkages between databases—even without biometric data tying individuals to their data—may not be difficult (see <http://lab.privacy.cs.cmu.edu/people/sweeney/confidentiality.html>).

ing individuals to third parties who do not have access to the information that links the weak identifiers.

A unique identifier refers unambiguously to one and only one individual in the population. Legal personal names are commonly used identifiers for human individuals, despite the fact that they are not usually unique except in very small populations. In this case, additional identifying information, perhaps limiting the population, is often implicitly required for identification (e.g.,"Bob Smith of Centerville"). However, individuals can be identified by things other than names. Many corporate systems, for example, use employee ID numbers rather than personal names as identifiers. In large organizations, this is commonly done because ID numbers (unlike personal names) are unique.

Names that are not personal names (such as pseudonyms and e-mail addresses) can also be used as identifiers. An entity issuing or relying on such an identifier may wish to correlate it to a unique individual; individuals using these identifiers may wish to prevent such correlation. Identifiers that are not personal names can be designed to protect individuals' privacy by limiting or preventing correlation of the identifier to a specific individual by limiting access to the look-up table (in a way that personal names cannot).

In general, the strength of the identification system is related to how distinctive the combined identifiers are across the population in question. "Bob Smith" might be a strong identifier in Centerville, but quite weak across the population of the entire country. Identifying a person uniquely across the entire population of the United States might require a name and considerable additional data, such as a phone or Social Security number.

Attributes

Authorization policies are often based on attributes that do not inherently identify an individual. An attribute can be inherent (height, for example) or assigned (vice president, for example); it can be permanent or dynamic. As an example, access to confidential company information in a corporate intranet may be granted to any employee of the corporation. The relevant attribute would be status as an employee.

Some attributes can be granted to individuals with virtually no claim on the part of the individual being authorized. The most common use of this type of attribute is in granting guest access to a system. Since by definition anyone can be a guest, it is unnecessary to authenticate an individual's identity in order to determine that he or she is entitled to the guest attribute. Obviously, this attribute is not very discriminating, so one might ask why it is used at all. The answer is that authorization systems are normally set up to authorize every access to every resource—

so even publicly available resources need to be governed by a policy that says, "grant access to the public," where the public is defined as anyone who has the guest attribute.

Some attributes can be observed directly by the information system. For example, an individual's location can be determined if the system can tell that the individual is using a terminal that is known to be on the business's premises. Gender and race are in many instances observable attributes. Authentication of such attributes does not require prior authentication of an identifier for the individual.

It is sometimes possible to manifest attributes that ordinarily would not be directly observable. Bars do this when they stamp the hands of patrons who are older than the minimum legal drinking age; this allows people of legal age to enter and leave the bar without having to reauthenticate their age by showing ID cards each time they enter.

Some attributes cannot be observed directly by information systems. For example, an individual's employer or department number cannot be determined by examining the individual or his or her surroundings. Systems normally deal with such attributes by creating a process for *registering* individuals, *assigning* attributes to registered individuals, *storing* each individual's assigned properties, and *retrieving* an individual's attributes when needed for an authorization decision.

In order to retrieve a specific individual's attributes from storage (or from a third party), the system must have an identifier for the individual, which it can use to refer to the individual whose attributes it wants to look up. Furthermore, this identifier must be authenticated, so that the system can have confidence that it is talking not to an impostor but in fact to the individual whose attributes it is going to look up.

Systems usually require individuals to authenticate themselves (using a unique identifier) and subsequently to be assigned other attributes that are then stored in an attribute database. Then, at some later time, the individual reauthenticates the same unique identifier to the system, and some observer function in the system uses the unique identifier to look up the assigned attributes in the database and to make an access decision.

Statements

A statement records a belief or claim about an individual by an identifiable party.[17] Authorization decisions may in some cases be based on attestations or assertions of authorities. For example, a bank's decision to

---

[17]That is, it is possible to determine who the party is and hence whether the party is authoritative for the statement.

extend credit to an individual may be based on a credit rating asserted by a credit agency. The individual's credit rating is an attribute that is assigned by the credit agency to the individual. In this case, the party making the statement is an authority, and the party that uses the statement to make an authorization decision is a relying party.

Third-party assertions generally provide attribute information that cannot be directly observed by the relying party. In the example above, an information system cannot observe an individual's credit rating—it must instead query the credit agency to provide the rating. In order to retrieve accurately an individual's attributes from the authority, the relying party must have an appropriate identifier for the individual, which it can correlate to the individual's identity and corresponding statements in its database.

HOW DO WE AUTHENTICATE?

John Locke, in his "Essay Concerning Human Understanding,"[18] distinguished two types of identity—physical identity and psychological identity:

> [T]he identity of the same *man* consists . . . in nothing but a participation of the same continued life, by constantly fleeting particles of matter, in succession vitally united to the same organized body.

> Any substance vitally united to the present thinking being is a part of that very same self which now is; anything united to it by a consciousness of former actions, makes also a part of the same self, which is the same both then and now. *Person*, as I take it, is the name for this self. Wherever a man finds what he calls himself, there, I think, another may say is the same person.

> It is by the consciousness it has of its present thoughts and actions that it [i.e., a person] is *self to itself* now, and so will be the same self, as far as the same consciousness can extend to actions past or to come; and would be by distance of time, or change of substance, no more two persons, than a man be two men by wearing other clothes to-day than he did yesterday.

Locke also identifies the association of a set of past actions with a present actor as being critical to the notion of personal identity, and he associates identity with law and accountability:

> [A]s to this point of being the same self, it matters not whether this present self be made up of the same or other substances—I being as

---

[18]John Locke. *An Essay on Human Understanding*, Part II, Chapter 27. 1690. Available online at <http://www.ilt.columbia.edu/publications/ locke_understanding.html>.

much concerned, and as justly accountable for any action that was done a thousand years since, appropriated to me now by this self-consciousness, as I am for what I did the last moment.

In this personal identity is founded all the right and justice of reward and punishment.

The distinction between physical and psychological identity is critical to the understanding of authentication systems, because authentication systems use features of both types of identity, and they differ in their properties and application depending on which type of identity they authenticate. Password- and key-based authentication systems, for example, can be used to make individuals express intent (because such systems authenticate psychological identity), but they are prone to the theft of authentication secrets. Some biometrics, on the other hand, can be used to identify individuals without those individuals' active participation and awareness, so care needs to be taken when using biometrics in authentication systems designed to ensure accountability.

Some authentication systems also authenticate claims not on the basis of physical or psychological identity but instead on the basis of the possession of an artifact.

Thus there are three generic approaches to authentication. They are often described as "something you know," "something you have," and "something you are."[19] The properties of each approach are discussed below.

Authentication systems often combine two or all three of these approaches. This is what is done at a typical automated teller machine (ATM). Both "something you have" (the bankcard) and "something you know" the personal identification number or PIN are required to access account information or to make changes to the account. A combination of approaches (sometimes referred to as multifactor authentication) generally provides more security than do single approaches alone, because the strengths of one approach can be used to compensate for the weaknesses of another. At the same time, depending on implementation and other systems choices, multifactor authentication may raise more privacy considerations than single-factor authentication.

---

[19]The National Institute of Standards and Technology articulated these principles as related to computer security in the 1970s (D.E. Raphael and J.R. Young, *Automated Personal Identification*, SRI International, 1974; National Bureau of Standards, *Evaluation Techniques for Human Identification*, FIPSPUB-48, April 1977).

Authenticating Physical Identity

Authentication systems based on physical characteristics (something you are) authenticate individuals by observing physical characteristics of the body of the individual; these systems are often called biometric authentication systems. The physical characteristics used differ from system to system; some use fingerprints, others use the geometry of the human hand, others use the pattern of tissues in the iris of the eye, and so on.

A person wishing to be authenticated by means of a biometric mechanism need not remember anything, nor does he or she need to remember to carry an object. Unlike passwords, properly chosen biometrics cannot be readily shared in normal use.[20]

Authenticating Psychological Identity

Authentication systems based on covert knowledge (something you know) authenticate users by requiring the individual to recite a secret (sometimes personal information). These systems rely on what Locke would consider the identity of a "person"—that is, they depend on the psychological continuity of a person's memory.[21] The benefit of this

---

[20]While a number of effective techniques for attacking biometric systems have been published, the majority of users, who are neither malicious nor technologically sophisticated, will not use these techniques to circumvent protections against sharing for casual reasons— e.g., to share biometric identifiers with family members, colleagues, and so on (T. Matsumoto, H. Matsumoto, K. Yamada, and S. Hoshino, "Impact of Artificial Gummy Fingers on Fingerprint Systems," *Proceedings of SPIE* 4677 (January 2002), available online at <http://research.nii.ac.jp/kaken-johogaku/reports/H13_overview/A04-00-1.pdf>; L. Thalheim, J. Krissler, and P. Ziegler, "Biometric Access Protection Devices and Their Programs Put to the Test," *C't Magazine* 11 (May 21, 2002):114, available online at <http://www.heise.de/ct/english/02/11/114>; T. van der Putte and J. Keuning, "Biometrical Fingerprint Recognition: Don't Get Your Fingers Burned," *Proceeding of the IFIP TC8/WG8.8 Fourth Working Conference on Smart Card Research and Advanced Applications*, Kluwer Academic Press, 2000, pp. 289-303, available online at <http://www.keuning.com/biometry/Biometrical_Fingerprint_Recognition.pdf>; and D. Blackburn, M. Bone, P. Grother, and J. Phillips, *Facial Recognition Vendor Test 2000: Evaluation Report*, U.S. Department of Defense, January 2001, available online at <www.frvt.org>).

[21]Another way of thinking about identity continuity is to consider the case where two different names (or instances of the same name) correspond to the same principal (this is known in the distributed systems literature as an "indirect name" or "symbolic link"). The classic example comes from the registration of title to real estate. It is very common that someone who wishes to sell a house uses a name different from his or her name at the time the house was purchased: the person might have changed their name in marrying, or after a criminal conviction. A classic identity problem is knowing that the "Mrs. Janet Rogers" wishing to sell property at 1423 Constitution Avenue is the same person as the "Miss Janet Foster Smith" who purchased it 11 years ago.

approach is that it does not require a person to remember to carry a particular object and is in general one of the simplest forms of authentication. However, what is known can be forgotten, shared, guessed, or just plain stolen by being overheard or from the noting of written reminders. There are at least two types of covert knowledge: synthetic secrets and private secrets.

Synthetic secrets are items of information created specifically for the purpose of authentication; they typically have no relation to characteristics of the individual or to events in the (human) individual's life. Passwords are a type of synthetic secret (when used properly) and the classic example of the "something you know" approach to authentication.

The principal problem with using a synthetic secret for authentication is that because it is unrelated to the individual's life in any meaningful way, it is often difficult to remember. A joke in the security community illustrates the point: "There are two rules for choosing a good password: (1) pick something you can't remember and (2) don't write it down." This problem arises because synthetic secrets that are easy to remember are also usually easy for others to discover or guess.[22]

Private secrets are items of information that are so intimately associated with an individual or with events in the (human) individual's life that no other person (or few others) would be expected to know about them.

The use of private secrets for authentication causes several problems. People resist the use of private secrets for authentication on the grounds that they *are* private and should not have to be revealed to third parties (even to third parties who wish to authenticate us). Private secrets are rarely completely private.[23] This leads to another problem: Any item of information that is used as a private secret to authenticate an individual will typically be shared with all the people and organizations that want to authenticate the individual (technical measures exist that could prevent sharing this, but they are not widely used). Each party who authenticates the individual therefore comes to know the information that is supposed to be a private secret, and thus the information becomes less private and less secret as time goes by.

---

[22]One approach that makes passwords more difficult to share or guess is to require people to memorize images instead of sequences of words, letters, numbers, and/or characters. See "In a User-friendly World, One Picture's Worth 1,000 Passwords: Image-Driven Log-ons Are Easier to Use and More Secure, High-Tech Researchers Claim," by Michael J. Kennedy in the *Los Angeles Times*, June 4, 2002, for a description of this technology and some of the companies exploring its use.

[23]For example, a DMV and its clerks can find out driver's license numbers. An individual's mother knows her own maiden name, and so do other members of the family. Many people know or can find out Social Security numbers.

Not only do these problems compromise the individual's privacy, but they also gradually destroy the usefulness of the information as an authenticator. When the information's value as an authenticator has been substantially degraded, another piece of (private) information will have to be chosen as a new basis for the private-secret authentication process. If this sequence of events is repeated enough times, many of the individual's private secrets will have been revealed to large numbers of other parties. The individual's privacy will have been put at considerable risk, as will the ability of other parties to authenticate the individual. Social Security numbers are an excellent case study in this phenomenon, as a recent incident involving the Princeton University admissions office illustrates. Both Princeton University and Yale University use Social Security numbers as student identifiers. Yale's admissions office used the Social Security number as an authentication key to allow students to access the status of their applications for admission via a Web browser. A member of the Princeton University admissions office staff discovered this and apparently used Social Security numbers obtained from the records of applicants to Princeton in order to access the Yale admissions Web site and learn about Yale's admissions decisions.[24]

Authenticating Possession of an Artifact

Another traditional approach to authentication is the possession of a unique object. A typical house key is an example of the "something you have" approach. (Box 2.2 describes authentication by means of a car key fob.) The object should be hard to duplicate, at least by simple observation by a third party. In other words, it is possible to duplicate a house key, but merely observing a key being used does not allow the observer to duplicate the key.

The object that is possessed may have a range of functionality. It may be as simple as a traditional house key, whose shape defines it. It may be a credit card with raised lettering and a magnetic stripe for storing information. It may also be a smart card, with an embedded processor that may be used to store information or to act as a cryptographic processor.

These different types of objects have different levels of resistance to tampering and duplication. A house key is readily duplicated, if desired, by the person in possession of it. A credit card also may be duplicated, provided the person in possession of the card has the appropriate equipment. Smart cards, particularly those that perform cryptographic opera-

---

[24]See "Ivy Imbroglio: Princeton Says It Spied on Yale," *Wall Street Journal,* July 26, 2002, p. B1.

BOX 2.2
Car Key Fobs

Remote car door key fobs and garage door openers work by way of radio signals. Very early units sent a constant signal, which is clearly insecure. Later versions used an 8-bit key to distinguish among different transmitters. Again, this was inadequate; thieves learned to record and retransmit the signals. Many modern units use a so-called *rolling code*, which is generated from a pseudo-random number generator. Eavesdropping on a few code transmissions should not provide enough information to predict the next code. To avoid problems from the loss of synchronization, a range of codes is accepted by the receiver. A mechanism is also provided to resynchronize the transmitter and the receiver. No identification signal per se is transmitted by such devices. Many new cars use a radio transponder embedded in the keys themselves to unlock the ignition. Some of these use rolling codes; others use challenge/response technologies. Key fobs contain a modest amount of storage and computational ability. Specialized equipment is required to copy them, but they are easily stolen.

---

tions, are in theory harder to duplicate, because they do not ever disclose during normal operation the secret information that would be required to duplicate them.

The "something you have" approach has the advantage that the holder does not need to remember a password. The object that is used can be designed to be hard to copy, so it cannot be readily used by more than one person at a time, although it could be loaned (in which case the original person loses access to it while it is on loan). However, objects can easily be lost or stolen, and sometimes people are not in a position to carry an item when they want to use a system.

IDENTIFICATION

The processes of authentication and identification are related but distinct. While the former may require the verifying party to authenticate an identifier that refers to the individual, the *identification* of an individual is distinct from the authentication of the individual's *claimed* identity. Some authentication technologies (particularly biometric technologies) are used in both processes. Identification associates an identifier with an individual without the requirement of a claim on the part of the subject.

More specifically, identifying an individual refers to the process of examining and/or interrogating an individual (usually an individual who has been encountered before) with the objective of determining which identifier refers to that individual. In contrast, authenticating an identifier refers to the process of verifying the linkage between an identifier (usually claimed by the individual, but sometimes observed) and the individual.

THE RELATIONSHIP BETWEEN AUTHENTICATION AND IDENTIFICATION

Given that authentication and identification are distinct but related concepts, it is important to understand the interplay between them. While authentication for accountability almost always eventually requires identifying an individual at some point (as discussed previously), authentication for authorization does not always require this. In the first place, authorization does not always require authentication. When authorization does require authentication, as discussed previously, it does not always require individual authentication. Even when authorization requires individual authentication, it often does not require the authenticated identifier to be a personal name. The common use of credit cards is an example. The credit card number is the unique identifier. If the card has not been reported lost or stolen, it is assumed that the holder of the card is authorized to use it. For credit card purchases made by phone or over the Internet during which the physical holding of the card cannot be observed, a secondary piece of information from the card, such as an expiration date or additional code number, is requested.[25]

It is essential to develop authentication systems whose strength (and often therefore whose intrusiveness into privacy) is in line with the security needs of and threats to the resources being protected. In some cases it may be appropriate to require users to forgo some privacy when they are authenticated for purposes of accessing very sensitive or very valuable resources. Note that the information being protected may itself be privacy-sensitive, and thus may merit strong authentication on that basis alone.

Recommendation 2.1. The strength of the authentication system employed in any system should be commensurate with the value of the resources (information or material) being protected.

Authorization systems usually do identify individuals' personal names, even when it is not necessary to do so to meet the required secu-

---

[25]Of course, the second piece of information from the card is valid the first time it is ever used and becomes less valuable with each additional use.

rity goals. The main reason for this is convenience: Even for authorization policies that do not use them directly, personal names are familiar, sufficiently differentiable to discriminate among user populations of modest size, and convenient to use as a way to look up other individual attributes. They are therefore often used as the "label" on the "file folder" that contains the individual's other attributes. Of course, *some* authorization policies actually do require the use of personal names, and some authorization systems collect personal names up-front—that is, preventively—instead of waiting until it is clear that personal names are necessary before collecting them.

> **Finding 2.1. Authorization does not always require individual authentication or identification, but most existing authorization systems perform one of these functions anyway. Similarly, a requirement for authentication does not always imply that accountability is needed, but many authentication systems generate and store information as though it were.**

> **Recommendation 2.2. Systems that demand authentication for purposes other than accountability, and that do not themselves require accountability, should not collect accountability information.**

> **Recommendation 2.3. Individual authentication should not be performed if authorization based on nonidentifying attributes will suffice. Where appropriate, authorization technologies and systems that use only nonidentifying attributes should be used in lieu of individual authentication technologies. When individual authentication is required, the system should be subject to the guidelines in Recommendation 3.2 (see Chapter 3).**

The CSTB report *IDs—Not That Easy* raised a number of questions that should be addressed before the implementation of any large-scale identity system. These same questions apply generally to authentication systems, given that authentication and identity are often closely connected. While smaller-scale authentication systems may imply decreased urgency (that is, a system to restrict access to a hotel swimming pool, in which the attribute necessary for authorization is "current hotel guest," may require less rigorous attention to these questions than a system that would track the enrollment status of all foreign students in the United States on the basis of their visas or other IDs), the principles outlined in *IDs—Not That Easy* still hold, especially with regard to understanding the goals of the system and minimizing unnecessary data collection and retention. The questions are reprinted here from *IDs—Not That Easy*[26] for reference.

- What is the *purpose of the system*? Possible purposes of an identity system include expediting and/or tracking travel; prospectively monitoring individuals' activities in order to detect suspicious acts; retrospectively identifying perpetrators of crimes.
- What is the *scope of the population* to whom an "ID" would be issued and, presumably, recorded in the system? How would the identities of these individuals be authenticated?
- What is the *scope of the data* that would be gathered about individuals participating in the system and correlated with their system identity? "Identification systems," despite the name, often do much more than just identify individuals; many identity systems use IDs as keys to a much larger collection of data. Are these data identity data only (and what is meant by identity data)? Or are other data collected, stored, and/or analyzed as well? With what confidence would the accuracy and quality of this data be established and subsequently determined?
- *Who would be the user(s)* of the system (as opposed to those who would participate in the system by having an ID)? If the public sector or government will be the primary user, what parts of the government will be users, in what contexts, and with what constraints? In what setting(s) in the public sphere would such a system be used? Would state and local governments have access to the system? Would the private sector be allowed to use the system? What entities in the private sector would be allowed to use the system? Who could contribute, view, and/or edit data in the system?
- What *types of use* would be allowed? Who would be able to ask for an ID, and under what circumstances? Assuming that there are datasets associated with an individual's identity, what types of queries would be permitted (e.g., "Is this person allowed to travel?" "Does this person have a criminal record?"). Beyond simple queries, would analysis and data mining of the information collected be permitted? If so, who would be allowed to do such analysis and for what purpose(s)?
- Would participation in and/or identification by the system be *voluntary or mandatory*? In addition, would participants have to be aware of or consent to having their IDs checked (as opposed to, for example, being subjected to surreptitious facial recognition)?

---

[26]Computer Science and Telecommunications Board, National Research Council. *IDs—Not That Easy: Questions About Nationwide Identity Systems.* Washington, D.C., National Academy Press, 2002, pp. 9-11.

• What *legal structures* protect the system's integrity as well as the data subject's privacy and due process rights, and which structures determine the liability of the government and relying parties for system misuse or failure?

The next chapter explores the history and meaning of privacy, concluding with a recommendation for the development of authentication systems modeled on these questions.

3

Privacy Challenges in Authentication Systems

Ⅰn principle, authentication technologies can both advance and undermine privacy interests. In practice, however, a combination of forces, including the following—

- The influence of the prevalent security paradigm of fully mediated access,
- The desire of businesses to collect personal information cheaply and unobtrusively,
- The pressure on governments and businesses to streamline their interactions and reduce costs, and
- The resiliency of digital information—

is more likely to lead to authentication systems that

- Increase requests for identification,
- Increase the collection of personal information,
- Decrease the ability of individuals to understand and participate in data collection decisions,
- Facilitate record linkage and profiling, and
- Decrease the likelihood that individuals will receive notice of or have the right to object to third-party access to personal information.

While authentication systems can undermine privacy in these ways, they can also be used in privacy-enhancing or privacy-preserving ways, primarily by securing personal data and preventing unauthorized access to the data. The privacy-enhancing benefits of authentication systems are derived from the security features of the overall systems in which they are deployed and are not intrinsic to the authentication components themselves.

As with any technology, careful consideration of the privacy risks, benefits, and trade-offs involved must be considered before authentication systems are designed and deployed. To some extent, tension between authentication and privacy is inherent, because the act of authentication often requires some revelation and confirmation of personal information.[1]

PRIVACY IMPACT OF THE DECISION TO AUTHENTICATE

First, let us look in broad terms at what an authentication system requires and examine how the collection, retention, reuse, and linkage of personal information might affect privacy interests:

• Establishing an initial identifier or attribute for use within the system may require an individual to reveal personal facts or information (such as name, address, fingerprints). A requirement to reveal identifying personal information may inhibit participation in certain activities (such as medical tests).

• The act of authentication itself may cause the creation of records of individuals' actions (such as where they shop, what they read, and when they come and go) that are linkable to one of three entities: a specific individual (individual authentication); a (possibly pseudonymous) identity that may or may not be linked to an individual (identity authentication); or, an attribute that applies to a specific individual (attribute authentication).

• In addition, transactional information revealing details of an event (purchase, building entry) may be created as a result of or subsequent to authentication and can then be linked back to the identity or individual and be retained in the relevant record.

• The requirements of the authentication or initial identity-establishment process may impose objectionable requirements (for example, they might conflict with religious beliefs[2] or impose on bodily integrity).

---

[1]In fact, some private sector and public sector policies impose requirements on those who collect data related to the protection of those data.

[2]In June 2002, CNN reported "Muslim Woman to Challenge Ban on Veil in Driver's License Photo," available online at <http://www.cnn.com/2002/LAW/06/27/license.veil.ap/index.html>. For religious reasons, a woman wanted to wear a veil for her driver's license photo in spite of objections from the State of Florida that allowing it would jeopardize public safety.

- Personal information or data may be exposed at multiple points and to multiple entities during the operation of an authentication system: They may be revealed during the authentication process, created during the authentication process, and/or retained as a result of the authentication process, all of which affect privacy. Personal information may also remain within a device possessed by the individual, reside in a system run by a single entity, or enable many entities to observe and/or collect personal information.

- Authentication may require the use of an identifier that, even if not personally identifiable per se, can be used to compile a dossier of facts (records of use of the identifier) that otherwise would be difficult or impossible to correlate. This collection of discrete facts may lead to a revelation of the individual's identity.

- Depending on where the user's identity and other authentication-related data are stored, they may be accessible to a variety of individuals within one or more institutions, and they may be more or less susceptible to access by hostile third parties through technical exploits or legal processes.

This general examination of authentication systems and the personal information practices that result from such systems harks back to the several general privacy risks created or increased by authentication systems, as described in Chapter 1 of this report: covert identification, excessive use of authentication technology, excessive aggregation of personal information, and chilling effects.

Given this categorization of privacy risks, an examination of relevant privacy interests will provide a better understanding of the foundations and contours of such interests, the values they protect, and the challenges that authentication technologies pose to privacy interests.

ACCESS CONTROL AND INFORMATION SYSTEMS

Access policies are a defining aspect of information systems. In a networked environment, the mediation of absolutely every user interaction with the system and its resources is a first step in enforcing access-control policies, identifying misuse, and investigating breaches. The Internet, perhaps the canonical example of a large, networked information system and a vast network of networks, while in many respects "open," is a highly mediated environment. Standards and protocols establish the who, what, when, where, and how of information exchanges.[3]

---

[3]As Larry Lessig (in *Code and Other Laws of Cyberspace*, New York, Basic Books, 1999) and Joel Reidenberg (in "Lex Informatica: The Formulation of Privacy Rules Through Technology," *Texas Law Review* 76(1998):553-593) argue, these standards establish the code by which online behavior is regulated.

Decisions about whether a given user may communicate with a resource, whether a given computer may communicate with another, whether a given network may communicate with another, and what extent of information exchange is allowed in each instance dominate the Internet. This is in part because the Internet exists at the collective will of individuals, private parties, and government entities to allow information to flow across their systems. Without these agreements to support the exchange of bits, there would be no Internet.[4]

These agreements also conceal the organizational boundaries and institutional rules that users traverse when they access a site. Users are generally unaware of the intricacies established by their Internet service provider (ISP) or of the communication requirements for moving around on the Internet. The reality is that what users experience as a library or a public space is in fact a mixture of public and private networks. Not only are users generally ignorant of the jurisdictional boundaries they cross, but they are also usually oblivious of the presence of other users. One commentator said that being on the Internet is "like being in a movie theater without a view of the other seats. . .[where] masses of silent, shuffling consumers . . . register their presence only by the fact of a turn-stile-like 'hit' upon each web page they visit. . ."[5] These characteristics of the online world are in stark contrast with the physical world in three important respects:

1. In the physical world there are many clearly defined public spaces and many privately owned spaces in which access control is nonexistent or minimal;

2. In physical space, relatively few actions are mediated; and

3. In the off-line world, if mediation occurs it is typically evidenced by a physical sign.

In the off-line world, individuals and institutions make decisions about whether or not to mediate interactions between individuals and resources. For example, a university may decide not to control who walks across the campus but to control who enters certain buildings. Similarly, libraries and bookstores generally do not exert control over who enters the premises or what materials they access, but they do exert control over

---

[4]For a detailed look at the technological underpinnings of the Internet, see Computer Science and Telecommunications Board, National Research Council, *The Internet's Coming of Age*, Washington, D.C., National Academy Press, 2001.

[5]Jonathan Zittrain. "The Rise and Fall of Sysopdom." *Harvard Journal of Law and Technology* 10(1997):495. Available online at <http://jolt.law.harvard.edu/low/articles/10hjolt495.html>.

the terms on which individuals may remove things from the premises. In contrast, in a networked environment—that is, an engineered system— the answer to the question Should we mediate access? is almost always yes; the inquiry begins with the questions How much do we mediate? With what mechanism?

With increasing frequency, authentication systems are being deployed to control access and movement in physical spaces as well as to control access to networked systems themselves. The increase in the scope of authentication and identification supported by networked systems is extending the scope of recorded interactions. The systems and the hardware that interacts with them are changing the information that can be collected during interactions and the extent to which it can be reused. As discussed below, these changes challenge the privacy of individuals in four significant respects.

1. *Computer technology reduces the costs of record keeping.* The reduction in costs has escalated the data collection and retention associated with authentication events. Increased data collection and retention exacerbate the privacy consequences of authentication events. Flashing one's driver's license in a corner store is qualitatively different from providing a digital copy of one's driver's license to an online merchant. In the latter case, the driver's license information is provided to the merchant in a format that encourages capture and allows for retention and reuse. One potential outcome of this change is that identity authentication (or the authentication of a relatively unique attribute or set of attributes with the same effect) is more likely to result in a personally identifiable stored record than was the case in earlier environments. A recent example illustrates this point. Using a scanner that allows him to read and capture data from the magnetic stripes on the back of Massachusetts driver's licenses, a barkeep in Boston has built a database of personal information—including driver's license number, height, weight, date of birth, eye and hair color, address, and, in some instances, Social Security number—on his patrons.[6] Without the state-issued driver's license, collecting such data on individuals would be expensive and cumbersome and would meet with privacy objections. The introduction of machine-readable cards and the market availability of readers have increased the chances that personal information would be captured, reused, and potentially sold. The introduction of technology—without any change in policy—has led to practices that are more invasive of privacy.

---

[6]Jennifer Lee. "Finding Pay Dirt in Scannable Driver's Licenses." *New York Times,* March 21, 2002.

2. *Once data are collected, computerized record-keeping facilitates record linkage.*[7] Distributed relational databases allow diverse records with a common attribute or attributes to be more readily combined. This ability to link and profile record subjects supports the secondary use of information. To build on the driver's license example above, stores across the country are making similar use of scannable driver's license data.[8] As customer records across various sectors of the economy become tied to driver's license data, it becomes markedly easier to share and merge for different purposes the data collected by different establishments. And it is not only the private sector that makes use of the scannable licenses to control access. Some government buildings are also using these scannable licenses to record information about visitors.

3. *Rules codified for use in computerized systems are generally less flexible (for both good and bad uses) than policies implemented by humans.* Businesses and other entities often treat long-time customers and first-time customers differently.[9] A long-time customer may not need to provide the same level of authentication before engaging in an interaction or transaction. Information systems, while they can be programmed to treat different people differently, generally apply authentication rules designed for the worst-case scenario (in this instance, the new customer). In other words, unless otherwise directed, the system will demand the same information from a repeat visitor as from a newcomer and will retain that information. Therefore, the baseline data collected in information systems transactions tends to be richer than that collected in manual systems.

4. *Information technology enables covert identification and possibly overt identity authentication on a large scale.* The covert nature of some information systems used for identification and identity authentication (such as the driver's license scanners discussed above) denies individuals full information about the transaction and impedes oversight and accountabil-

---

[7]See the 1993 report of the Committee on National Statistics, *Private Lives and Public Policies: Confidentiality and Accessibility of Government Statistics*, Washington, D.C., National Academy Press, 1993, as well as the same committee's 2000 workshop report *Improving Access to and Confidentiality of Research Data*, Washington, D.C., National Academy Press, 2000, for more on issues surrounding data collection, linkage, and confidentiality. Available online at <http://www7.nationalacademies.org/cnstat/>.

[8]The Driver's Privacy Protection Act of 1994 prohibits states from disclosing this information, except in limited circumstances, without individual consent. While the law does not prohibit the creation of such databases by the private sector, it is clear that scannable licenses undermine congressional policy to limit the use of driver's license data for non-driving-related purposes.

[9]The downside of this practice is discrimination. Without accurate data, rules about who is a risky customer are more likely to be influenced by the biases of the business or individual. Accurate data can check these tendencies.

ity through the political process. While individuals are aware that the license is being scanned, they are not necessarily informed that information from it may be retained, reused, exchanged, or used to link with other systems. Indeed, individuals are unlikely to know what information can actually be retrieved from scanning the back of the license. Even if people were to learn over time the data collection possibilities inherent in a driver's license, there will always be circumstances in which nondisclosure of those possibilities can cause problems.

There are other systems that, while discussed prior to implementation or debated by the public after the fact, nevertheless provide little signal to the individual at the time that identification occurs. For example, many cities have installed cameras to detect drivers running red lights. In locations where such cameras have been proposed or implemented, initial opposition has often generated community discussion about what information is collected, what decisions can be made on the basis of it, and what recourse is available to individuals.[10] While this public debate increases the general awareness of the individuals who reside in an area (but not necessarily those who pass through), the collecting of information in this way is more covert than the scanning of driver's licenses described above. An individual gives over a driver's license. Here, an individual drives through an intersection—hardly an activity that signals an identification or authentication event. While the cameras are more easily understood by individuals as identification (surveillance) tools than is the driver's license reader, it is less likely that the presence of a camera will be noticed.

The increasing use of the Internet and other networked systems to support access to information, deliver services, and communicate raises questions about the access-control policies governing these interactions and their impact on individual privacy. Similarly, the use of information systems and networking to control access to and movement in physical spaces and to support attribute- and identity-based service and sales decisions off-line raises questions about the authentication systems that support these interactions and their privacy implications. Ubiquitous computing, sensor-equipped buildings, and smart highways are the direction of the future. They raise important questions about what kind of authentication occurs, how the data used and generated during authentication events are handled, and how the answers to these questions support or

---

[10]William Matthews. "Battle Lines Form over Red-Light Cameras." *Federal Computer Week* (September 3, 2001). Available online at <http://www.fcw.com/geb/articles/2001/sep/geb-comm2-09-01.asp>.

undermine individual privacy, access to information, freedom of association, and other democratic values.

A highly mediated environment of networked systems requires system owners to choose between attribute authentication and identity authentication. This choice and the decisions about retention, reuse, and disclosure that flow from it influence the degree of privacy that individuals using the system enjoy. To the extent that individuals are aware of the chosen policies and their implications, the privacy provided by the system will in turn influence individuals' decisions about how and in what circumstances to interact with it.

THE LEGAL FOUNDATIONS OF PRIVACY

Privacy is a fundamental tenet of legal systems and political philosophies that value individual freedom, autonomy, and political participation. Privacy has many and varied definitions and is evoked in many contexts to achieve differing results. It has important political, emotional, social, and legal dimensions. It protects against intrusions in physical places, interference with personal decisions, misuse of personal information, and various interests similar to property interests. The underlying values that privacy protects include individuality and autonomy; intimacy; fairness; and limited, tolerant government.

Early legal definitions of privacy center on the notion of being left alone. Phrases such as "a man's home is his castle"[11] and "the right to be let alone"[12] capture this notion of privacy, which encompasses the ability of individuals to retreat to the safety of home, pull the shades, and lock the doors, freeing themselves from prying neighbors and state surveillance. While a powerful and important element of privacy, this right to seclusion became increasingly incapable of protecting individuals as society became more interdependent and as interactions became more information-rich. Social and technological changes in the 1960s and 1970s generated renewed interest on the part of philosophers and lawyers in defining and conceptualizing privacy.[13] From their analyses and writings emerged an appreciation for a more complex and multifaceted concept of privacy and its legal foundations.

---

[11]". . . [T]he house of every one is to him as his castle and fortress." Semayne's Case, 5 C. Rep. 91a, 77 Eng. Rep. 194 (K.B. 1603).

[12]"They conferred, as against the Government, the right to be let alone—the most comprehensive of rights, and the right most valued by civilized men." Justice Brandeis dissenting in *Olmstead* v. *United States*, 277 U.S. 438, 478 (1928).

[13]See, for example, Edward J. Bloustein, "Privacy as an Aspect of Human Dignity," *New York University Law Review* 39 (December 1964): 962-1007; Charles Fried, "Privacy," *Yale Law*

Privacy law in the United States derives from many sources, including common law, the U.S. Constitution and state constitutions, and state and federal statutes. As the values that it protects suggest, privacy law comprises several branches. This report examines the potential privacy impact of authentication technologies on four areas of privacy, each of which has a constitutional basis in the United States:

1. *Bodily integrity*, which protects the individual from intrusive searches and seizures;
2. *Decisional privacy*, which protects the individual from interference with decisions about self and family;
3. *Information privacy*, which protects the individual's interest in controlling the flow of information about the self to others; and
4. *Communications privacy*, a subset of information privacy that protects the confidentiality of individuals' communications.

As discussed above, authentication technology can intrude on each of these privacy interests. Authentication methods may require contact with or close proximity to the body, potentially raising concerns under the "bodily integrity" branch of privacy law. Authentication may introduce new opportunities to collect and reuse personal information, intruding on "information privacy." Authentication systems may be deployed in a manner that interferes with individuals' "decisional privacy" by creating opportunities for others to monitor and interfere with important expressive or other personal activities. Authentication methods may raise new opportunities to intercept or monitor a specific individual's communications, revealing the person's thoughts and the identities of the individuals with whom he or she communicates. This section provides some historical context for the privacy interests listed above.

Constitutional Roots of Privacy

The word "privacy" is notably absent from the U.S. Constitution. However, the values and interests that privacy protects are explicitly expressed in various amendments and have been held by the U.S. Supreme Court to be implicit in other amendments. For example, the Fourth Amendment prohibition against unreasonable searches and seizures and the Fifth Amendment prohibition of compelled self-incrimination explic-

---

Journal (January 1968): 475-493; Judith Jarvis Thompson, "The Right to Privacy," *Philosophy and Public Affairs* 4 (summer 1975): 303; James Rachels, "Why Privacy Is Important," *Philosophy and Public Affairs* 4 (summer 1975): 323-333; William M. Beaney, "The Right to Privacy and American Law," *Law and Contemporary Problems* 31 (1966): 357.

itly protect privacy interests in personal papers and effects and in personal thoughts and beliefs, respectively,[14] while the First Amendment prohibition against the suppression of speech and assembly has been found to implicitly include the right to speak and to assemble anonymously. The Supreme Court has interpreted the First, Third, Fourth, Fifth, Ninth, and Fourteenth Amendments as providing protection for different aspects of personal privacy. Although it is important to note that constitutional claims arise only in cases in which some state action interferes with privacy, the values represented by these constitutional claims resonate broadly throughout society.

First Amendment Interest in Privacy and Anonymity

The First Amendment guarantees the freedoms of speech, association, and access to information. Numerous Supreme Court cases document the right of individuals to speak, associate, and receive information without having their identities revealed. The ability to speak anonymously is rooted not only in the Constitution but also in the actions forging a consensus for its ratification. The Federalist Papers were penned under several noms de plume. The Supreme Court has affirmed the right of anonymity in political speech and the right to solicit door to door without registering or identifying oneself.[15] Similarly, the Court has recognized the chilling effect that the disclosure of membership lists would have on the freedom to associate, and therefore it has shielded such lists from government scrutiny.[16] The ability to receive information anonymously, the corollary of the right to speak anonymously, while less clearly

---

[14]"When the Fourth and Fifth Amendments were adopted, 'the form that evil had theretofore taken' had been necessarily simple. Force and violence were then the only means known to man by which a Government could directly effect self-incrimination. It could compel the individual to testify—a compulsion effected, if need be, by torture. It could secure possession of his papers and other articles incident to his private life—a seizure effected, if need be, by breaking and entry. Protection against such invasion of 'the sanctities of a man's home and the privacies of life' was provided in the Fourth and Fifth Amendments by specific language." Justice Brandeis dissenting in *Olmstead* v. *United States*, 277 U.S. 473, quoting *Boyd* v. *United States*, 116 U.S. 616, 630.

[15]See *McIntyre* v. *Ohio Elections Commission*, 514 U.S. 334 (striking down a state statute requiring political leafleteers to identify themselves on their leaflets). Recently the Supreme Court upheld a similar challenge to a local ordinance requiring all individuals petitioning door to door to register and identify themselves (*Watchtower Bible and Tract Society, Inc.* v. *Village of Stratton*, 00-1737). Also see *Watchtower Bible and Tract Society of New York, Inc., et al.* v. *Village of Stratton, et al.* (00-1737) 240 F.3d 553, reversed and remanded; available online at <http://supct.law.cornell.edu/supct/html/00-1737.ZS.html>.

[16]*NAACP* v. *Alabama*, 357 U.S. 449 (1958) (striking down a state statute that required organizations to disclose their membership to the state).

articulated by the Court, can be found in cases forbidding the government from requiring individuals to affirmatively register to receive certain kinds of information[17] and affirming the right of individuals to possess for in-home consumption "obscene" materials that could not legally be sold.[18] Recently the Colorado Supreme Court held that the First Amendment to the U.S. Constitution and the state constitution "protect the individual's right to purchase books anonymously, free from governmental interference."[19]

Third Amendment Privacy Protection

The Court has found protection of a right to privacy against unreasonable surveillance and compulsory disclosure in the Third Amendment's protection against quartering soldiers. This protection has generally been viewed as secondary to the broader protection of the Fourth Amendment.

Fourth Amendment Roots of Privacy Law

The Fourth Amendment to the U.S. Constitution protects individuals against unreasonable searches of their persons and places and against unreasonable seizures of their property. Fourth Amendment jurisprudence articulates limits on government searches of individuals, residences and other private places, and communications. The principle on which the Fourth Amendment is based derives from an even older tradition in British common law. As early as the early 17th century, British courts were placing limits on the power of the Crown to enter anyone's home. Though the power of the monarch was still substantial, Semayne's Case[20] in 1603 says that "the house of every one is to him as his castle and fortress." Over time, this basic limitation on entry into the sanctity of one's home has been stated with more precision. The state may not enter

---

[17]See *Lamont* v. *Postmaster General*, 381 U.S. 301 (1965) (striking down a postal regulation requiring individuals to register a desire to receive communist propaganda).

[18]See *Stanley* v. *Georgia*, 394 U.S. 557 (1969) (striking down a state statute criminalizing in-home possession of obscene material); *Denver Area Educational Telecommunications Consortium, Inc.* v. *FCC*, 518 U.S. 727 (striking down cable statute requiring individuals to request in writing segregated, patently offensive cable programming as overly restrictive in light of alternatives that protected the anonymity of viewers).

[19]*Tattered Cover, Inc.* v. *City of Thorton*, Colo. Sup Ct 2002 Colo. LEXIS 269, April 8, 2002; see also Julie E. Cohen, "A Right to Read Anonymously: A Closer Look at 'Copyright Management' in Cyberspace," 28 Conn. L. Rev. 981 (1996) (arguing that the right to read anonymously is protected by the First Amendment).

[20]See *Semayne's Case*, 5 C. Rep. 91a, 77 Eng. Rep. 194 (K.B. 1603).

without a reason and a warrant issued by a court; in addition, the state must "knock and announce" the search. Announcing the search and presenting the target of the search with a copy of the warrant for inspection is critical to assure that the state does not enter without a warrant and that the reasons for which the warrant were issued can be challenged, at least after the fact. These procedural safeguards have been found necessary to guard against abuse of the invasive searching power granted to the state.

Searches conducted without simultaneous notice are considered secret searches and generally prohibited under U.S. constitutional law. For obvious reasons, wiretapping and other types of electronic surveillance are, by definition, secret. A telephone wiretap that first announces to the parties being tapped that their voices are being recorded is not likely to yield any useful evidence. Yet, courts have allowed that wiretapping, though generally violating the rule against secret searches, may be allowed in limited circumstances. Historically, electronic surveillance was only allowed for a limited class of serious crimes, and only after other investigative means had failed.[21] In recent years the list of crimes has grown. In addition, the statutory protections for electronic communications such as e-mail do not directly parallel those established for voice communications in the wake of Supreme Court rulings, not to mention that the effects of the USA PATRIOT Act of 2001 (Public Law 107-56, Uniting and Strengthening America by Providing Appropriate Tools Required to Intercept and Obstruct Terrorism Act of 2001) on opportunities for surveillance and accountability are still to be determined. (See the sections below entitled "Statutory Privacy Protection" and "Privacy of Communications.")

Fifth Amendment Protection of Privacy

The protection against self-incrimination also serves as a basis for a type of privacy protection, including primarily decisional privacy and, somewhat more weakly, bodily integrity. Although the principle of the Fifth Amendment—that no person shall be compelled to be a witness against himself or herself—may be relevant in many contexts, its application is limited to criminal cases or other government proceedings. The Court has adopted a rather narrow view of the coverage of the Fifth Amendment by making a distinction between testimonial evidence, involving communication by the individual and thus falling under the Fifth Amendment, and physical evidence, entailing the taking of something

---

[21]Recent developments may be changing this baseline, however. For a general discussion of the law, see Computer Science and Telecommunications Board, National Research Council, *Cryptography's Role in Securing the Information Society*, Washington, D.C., National Academy Press, 1996.

from an individual and thus falling outside the protection of the Fifth Amendment. This distinction was made most clearly in *Schmerber* v. *California*,[22] in which the Court ruled that there was no Fifth Amendment protection against blood tests, viewed as physical evidence, to determine blood alcohol content following a car accident. The Court distinguished between situations in which a defendant was forced verbally to incriminate himself or herself and situations in which marks or material were taken from him or her for identification purposes (fingerprints, photographs) or for purposes of preventing the dissipation of evidence (blood test). Although the latter situations would not be covered by the Fifth Amendment, the Court indicated that the Sixth Amendment protection of counsel, the Fourth Amendment protection against unreasonable searches and seizures, and the due process clause[23] would provide protection against the state's overreaching in such situations.

Ninth Amendment Penumbras, Fourteenth Amendment Due Process Clause, and Decisional and Informational Privacy

As mentioned above, privacy has been invoked to protect the individual's right to make decisions about important aspects of life without government interference. A line of Supreme Court cases starting with *Griswold* v. *Connecticut*[24] in 1965 began to establish such a right, although various justices viewed the source of the right differently. Justice Douglas believed the privacy right emanated from the First, Third, Fourth, Fifth, and Ninth amendments, which created "penumbras" of privacy protection. Other justices preferred to lodge the right in the Ninth Amendment. In *Roe* v. *Wade*,[25] the Court held that the right to privacy was founded in the Fourteenth Amendment's liberty clause and restrictions on state action. The right to privacy protected in this line of cases has been primarily limited to reproductive and family interests, including the individual's right to make choices with respect to childbearing, child rearing, and the use of contraceptives.[26] In *Whalen* v. *Roe*,[27] the Court articu-

---

[22]*Schmerber* v. *California*, 384 U.S. 757 (1966).

[23]In *Rochin* v. *California*, 342 U.S. 165 (1952), Justice Frankfurter, writing for the majority, said that the forced regurgitation of stomach contents was conduct that "shocks the conscience" and violates the due process clause of the Fourteenth Amendment.

[24]*Griswold* v. *Connecticut*, 381 U.S. 479 (1965).

[25]*Roe* v. *Wade*, 410 U.S. 113 (1973).

[26]In *Paul* v. *Davis* (424 U.S. 693 (1976)), the Supreme Court refused to expand the areas of personal privacy considered "fundamental" to include erroneous information in a flyer listing active shoplifters. The court limited these fundamental privacy areas to "matters relating to marriage, procreation, contraception, family relationships, and child rearing and education" (713).

[27]*Whalen* v. *Roe*, 429 U.S. 589 (1977).

lated a constitutional basis for a right of information privacy, arguing that the constitutionally protected "zone of privacy" protects both an interest in avoiding disclosure of personal matters and an interest in independent decision making. Although recognizing an expanded privacy interest, the Court unanimously found that the New York law in question, which required the maintenance of computerized records of prescriptions for certain drugs, did not pose a significant constitutional threat to either privacy interest, in part because of the security of the computer system and the restrictions on disclosure. In subsequent cases, the Court has not expanded constitutional protections for information privacy.

The Common Law Roots of Privacy Law

As mentioned above, constitutional privacy protections limit state action; they do not protect against intrusion by private individuals or entities. Historically, tort law has provided protection for some aspects of personal privacy. English and early American case law provides examples of the use of tort law to protect against trespass into private spaces, unwanted knowledge of private events, and unwanted publicity of private matters. In 1890, concerned with tabloid journalists' and photographers' intrusion on private matters, Samuel D. Warren and Louis D. Brandeis, in "The Right to Privacy,"[28] set forth the "right to an inviolate personality." American courts and legislatures adopted various expressions of the new privacy tort throughout the early 20th century. In 1960, William L. Prosser structured and defined these various tort law privacy protections into four separate privacy torts:

1. *Intrusion upon seclusion:* objectionable intrusion into the private affairs or seclusion of an individual,
2. *Public disclosure of private facts*: publication of private information that a reasonable person would object to having made public,
3. *False light:* publication of objectionable, false information about an individual, and
4. *Misappropriation of name or likeness:* unauthorized use of an individual's picture or name for commercial advantage.[29]

The 1964 Restatement of Torts (a clarification and compilation of the law by the American Law Institute) adopted the Prosser framework.[30]

---

[28]Samuel D. Warren and Louis D. Brandeis. "The Right to Privacy." *Harvard Law Review* 4 (December 1890):195.

[29]William L. Prosser, "Privacy," 48 Cal. L. Rev. 383 (1960).

[30]Restatement of Torts (2d) 1964.

Together, these torts provide a basis for privacy suits against those who publish embarrassing false information or intimate information about an individual, peep or spy on an individual, or commercially exploit an individual's picture, name, or reputation. Today privacy torts provide limited protection for individuals. As torts, they are unlikely to directly shape the design and use of authentication systems. However, the principles behind the intrusion-upon-seclusion, public-disclosure-of-private-facts, false-light, and misappropriation-of-name-or-likeness torts are useful reminders of some of the things that privacy is designed to protect against—intrusion into personal affairs, disclosure of sensitive personal information, and improper assignment of actions to individuals. Each of these is relevant to the discussion of authentication systems.

Statutory Privacy Protections

In recent years, the Federal Trade Commission (FTC) Act of 1914[31] has become a tool for enforcing privacy statements—whatever they may be—made by commercial actors to the public. Section 5 of the FTC Act gives the FTC jurisdiction over "unfair and deceptive trade practices." Importantly, while the statute clearly provides an enforcement opportunity where statements about data collection practices are made, it alone provides no independent basis for compelling such statements, or for driving their contents.[32] A series of workshops, industry-developed self-regulatory guidelines, and enforcement actions by the FTC and offices of the states attorneys general have provided some check on objectionable or questionable private sector practices.

Over the years, Congress has enacted a number of privacy statutes. Most have come in response to changes in technology, to market failures, or to narrow interpretations of the Fourth Amendment. Market failures have led, as one would suspect, to statutes that primarily regulate private sector behavior. Narrow rulings on the protections afforded by the Fourth Amendment have led to statutes regulating government access to information. Finally, statutes that address both market failures and narrow constitutional interpretations have most often resulted from advances in technology that cause civil libertarians and industry to push for new privacy protections against the expansion of governmental and private sector authority to collect and use private information.

---

[31]15 U.S.C. §§ 41-51.

[32]Jeff Sovern has articulated the position that the FTC actually has the authority to go after various unsavory data practices under its current legislation and mandate. See Jeff Sovern, "Protecting Privacy with Deceptive Trade Practices Legislation," *Fordham Law Review* 69(4):1305.

The existing federal and state statutory privacy protections are often described as piecemeal or patchwork.[33] Personal information contained in "systems of records" held by the federal government are covered by the Privacy Act of 1974,[34] the Freedom of Information Act of 1967,[35] and other federal statutes dealing with particular records or record keepers.[36] Statutes of many states on access to information contain privacy exceptions, and some states have "mini" privacy acts. In general, rules governing access to and use of state and local records containing personal information are less stringent. Personal information held by the private sector is afforded the weakest statutory protections. While 11 federal statutes currently provide some form of privacy protection for records held by specific private sector entities[37] and a set of statutory-like regulatory protections applies to health information,[38] much detailed personal information in the hands of businesses is available for reuse and resale to private third parties and available to the government with little in the way of legal standards or procedural protections. (Chapter 6 in this report goes into more detail about some of these statutes and the roles that government plays in the privacy and authentication sense.)

Business records are subject to few privacy regulations. While recent statutes have increased the privacy regulations in the private sector, the

---

[33]See Colin J. Bennett, *Regulating Privacy: Data Protection and Public Policy in Europe and the United States,* Ithaca, N.Y., Cornell University Press, 1992; David Flaherty, *Protecting Privacy in Surveillance Societies,* Chapel Hill, University of North Carolina Press, 1989; Priscilla M. Regan, *Legislating Privacy: Technology, Social Values, and Public Policy,* Chapel Hill, University of North Carolina Press, 1995; and Paul Schwartz and Joel Reidenberg, *Data Privacy Law,* Charlottesville, Va., Michie, 1996.

[34]5 U.S.C. § 552a.

[35]5 U.S.C. § 552.

[36]Driver's Privacy Protection Act of 1994, 18 U.S.C. § 2721 (1994); Family Educational Rights and Privacy Act of 1974, 20 U.S.C. § 1232g.

[37]Right to Financial Privacy Act of 1978, 12 U.S.C. § 3401; Electronic Communications Privacy Act of 1986, 18 U.S.C. § 2510 (1995); Communications Assistance and Law Enforcement Act of 1994, PL 103-414, 108 Stat. 4279 (1994) (providing heightened protections for transactional data); Cable Communications Act of 1984, PL 98-549, 98 Stat. 2779 (1984) (codified as amended in scattered sections of 47 U.S.C.); Video Privacy Protection Act of 1988, 18 U.S.C. § 2710 (1994); Consumer Credit Reporting Reform Act of 1996, 15 U.S.C. 1681 § 2 (1997); Telemarketing and Consumer Fraud and Abuse Prevention Act of 1994, 15 U.S.C. §§ 6101, 6108; Privacy of Customer Information (Customer Proprietary Network Information Rules of the Telecommunications Reform Act of 1996), 47 U.S.C. § 222 (c), (d) (1996); Fair Credit Reporting Act of 1970, 15 U.S.C. § 1681 et seq.; Children's Online Privacy Protection Act (1998), 16 U.S.C. §§ 6501 et seq; Financial Services Modernization Act (1999), 15 U.S.C. § 6801 et seq.

[38]On April 14, 2001, privacy regulations were issued by the Department of Health and Human Services by authority granted under the Health Insurance Portability and Accountability Act of 1996 (see Chapter 6 for more information on HIPAA).

U.S. legal and regulatory approach continues to be driven by concerns about a given sector or a narrow class of information (see Chapter 6). In addition to piecemeal rules governing private sector use of personal information, the general rule established in two 1970s cases leaves personal information "voluntarily" provided to businesses without Fourth Amendment protection.[39] The rationale espoused in these two cases dramatically shaped privacy case law and led to statutory protections for privacy. The principle that in general individuals have no constitutionally based privacy interest in information about them contained in the routine records of a business has specific consequences for individual privacy in authentication systems that routinely collect information about an individual during the course of an authentication event that precedes a transaction.

INFORMATION PRIVACY AND
FAIR INFORMATION PRACTICES

Statutory protections for personal information all rest on the same core set of "fair information practices," which were developed in response to the move from paper to computerized records. The first "code of fair information practices," developed in 1973 by an advisory committee in the then-Department of Health, Education, and Welfare (HEW), provided a core statement of principles that may be enforced either by statute or voluntarily.[40] These principles set out basic rules designed to minimize the collection of information, ensure due-process-like protections where personal information is relied upon, protect against secret data collection, provide security, and ensure accountability. In general, the principles emphasized individual knowledge, consent, and correction, as well as the responsibility of organizations to publicize the existence of a record system, to assure the reliability of data, and to prevent misuse of data. Although the practices cited in the HEW code have been broadly accepted, slightly different iterations of fair information practices have been offered by different bodies.[41,42] Because of the broad recognition accorded the

---

[39]In 1976, in *United States* v. *Miller*, the Supreme Court held that individuals had no constitutionally protected privacy interest in checks held by a bank. Shortly thereafter, in 1979, in *Smith* v. *Maryland*, the Court ruled that because the numbers dialed by a telephone subscriber were routinely collected business records of phone companies, subscribers had no Fourth Amendment privacy interest in them and therefore no right to receive notice of or to object to their disclosure to the government.

[40]Secretary's Advisory Committee on Automated Personal Data Systems. U.S. Department of Health, Education, and Welfare. *Records, Computers and the Rights of Citizens*, Washington, D.C., 1973. Available online at <http://aspe.os.dhhs.gov/datacncl/1973privacy/tocprefacemembers.htm>.

[41]When discussions of online privacy began in the early 1990s, the concept and prin-

fair information practice principles, they are explained in detail in Table 3.1 and used later in this report for analyzing the privacy impact of different authentication systems. In general, though, the individual principles have not been implemented with uniform rigor. Limitations on the collection of information have not been widely adopted, consent has been largely renounced in favor of choice, and access has been harder to achieve.

The concept of notice is in some respects a simple idea: people are to be informed about how personally identifiable information is collected, used internally, and disclosed or exchanged. An organization's information practices should be, in theory, transparent. In practice, there are questions about how complete notices need to be without either compromising the proprietary interests of the organization or confusing people. Additionally, what really constitutes effective notice?[43]

---

ciples of "fair information practices" provided the foundation for policy discussions. Two executive branch study commissions—the Information Infrastructure Task Force (IITF) and the National Information Infrastructure Advisory Council (NIIAC)—developed privacy principles for the National Information Infrastructure (NII). In both cases, these study commissions echoed many of the traditional principles developed earlier, often modifying, and in some cases weakening, some of the core principles, such as consent and redress. But both commissions also struggled with questions about fair information practice that are new in the online environment. The IITF and the NIIAC recognized emergent principles, including the need to provide some opportunity for individuals to use technical controls, such as encryption, to protect the confidentiality and integrity of personally identifiable information. Both acknowledged that individuals should be able to remain anonymous as they conduct some online activities. The importance of educating the public about the privacy implications of online activities was highlighted in the codes developed by the IITF and the NIIAC. Although these early online privacy study commissions advocated a fairly detailed list of fair information practices, by 2000 the various iterations of fair information practices for online privacy discussed by the Federal Trade Commission and others largely focus on four: notice, choice, access, and security. Efforts to articulate more clearly the essence of information privacy were not limited to the United States. Indeed, the most comprehensive of these codes of fair information practices is the one crafted by the Organization for Economic Cooperation and Development (OECD) in 1980. The OECD code emphasized eight principles: collection limitation, data quality, purpose specification, use limitation, security safeguards, openness, individual participation, and accountability.

[42]Different countries have adopted these principles to varying extents. Canada, for example, has developed a national privacy code, the Model Code for the Protection of Personal Information. This code was developed through a consensus process that included representation from Canada's Direct Marketing Association. More information is available online at <http://www.csa.ca/standards/privacy/>.

[43]Other problems with the effectiveness of notices are illustrated by experience with the Financial Services Modernization Act of 1999 (commonly referred to as the Gramm-Leach-Bliley Act), discussed in more detail in Chapter 6, which requires financial institutions to give notice to customers regarding the sharing of personal information with a third party. Financial institutions have complained about the expense incurred in sending notices. Consumers have complained that notices are incomprehensible and unhelpful. See Mark Hochhauser, *Lost in the Fine Print: Readability of Financial Privacy Notices,* July 2001. Available online at <http://www.privacyrights.org/ar/GLB-Reading.htm>.

TABLE 3.1   Fair Information Principles and Practices

Principle	Practice/Meaning
Collection limitation	Collect the minimum amount of information that is needed for the relationship or transaction at issue——By lawful and fair means.—With the knowledge and consent of the individual.
Data quality	Information should be relevant, accurate, timely, and complete.
Purpose specification	Use of data should be specified at the time that data are collected.
Use limitation (restriction on secondary uses)	Data should only be used for the specific purpose for which they are collected and for which the individual understands they will be used, except under two conditions:—With the prior consent of the individual, and—With the appropriate legal authority.
Security	The integrity of the information and the system should be maintained to ensure against loss, destruction, unauthorized access, modification, unauthorized use, or disclosure.
Openness/notice	There should be no secret data systems. People should be able to ascertain the existence of data systems and their purposes and uses.
Individual participation	An individual has rights to—Know if he or she is a subject of a system,—Access information about him- or herself,—Challenge the quality of that information, and—Correct and amend that information.
Accountability	The organization collecting and using information can be held responsible for abiding by these principles through:—Enforcement and/or—Redress.

Federal agencies comply with notice provisions of the Privacy Act of 1974 by publishing requests for comments in the *Federal Register* when they plan to create "systems of records"—those information systems that contain personally identifiable information such as a name or Social Security number. Few individuals read the *Federal Register* to see whether a federal agency that maintains data on them in a system of record has announced in a routine use notice changes in the way that the agency intends to use those data.

The concept of "consent," or the less stringent "choice," is a more complex idea. In theory, individuals are to be given some power or control over how personally identifiable information about them is used. In practice, the primary question is whether such control comes from giving the individual the opportunity to opt in by giving prior permission or the opportunity to opt out by allowing them to say no. Privacy advocates argue that "opt in" is more consistent with the idea of consent, while "opt out" erroneously assumes that individuals tacitly give consent to secondary uses. Organizations argue that "opt out" gives individuals adequate opportunity to choose and does not overburden consumers or industry.

Recognizing the complexity and importance of access and security in the online environment, the FTC convened an advisory committee to examine and advise on these subjects.[44] With regard to access, the committee addressed four questions: (1) What is the meaning of access (merely view or view and modify)? (2) Access to what? (3) Who provides access? and (4) How easy should access be? The Advisory Committee on Online Access and Security was unable to agree on a clear recommendation and instead presented a range of access options. In part, the committee recognized that the dilemmas presented by the need to authenticate for access purposes complicated access options and necessitated an evaluation of the particular circumstances.

The Advisory Committee on Online Access and Security recognized that security likewise is contextual, that costs and inconveniences affect the level of security that administrators are willing to set and users are willing to bear, and that the establishment of a security system should begin with a risk assessment. The committee outlined five options for achieving security and recommended a solution including these three principles: (1) every Web site should have a security program, (2) the

---

[44]Federal Trade Commission (FTC). *Final Report of the FTC Advisory Committee on Online Access and Security.* Washington, D.C., May 15, 2000. Available online at <http://www.ftc.gov/acoas/papers/finalreport.htm>.

elements of the security program should be specified, and (3) the security program should be appropriate to the circumstances.

However, in the absence of the comprehensive adoption of statutes based on fair information practices, much personal information remains vulnerable to misuse, abuse (including the potential for identity theft), and unfettered government access. This situation poses serious privacy threats to authentication information held by private sector entities.

PRIVACY OF COMMUNICATIONS

Concern about the privacy of individual communication has grown as society comes to depend more and more on electronic and networked communications. While the privacy of communications is only one aspect of the larger privacy policy framework, the evolution of the law of communications privacy provides useful insights for policy makers and system designers considering the privacy implications of authentication systems. The development of communications privacy law illustrates that as technology reaches farther and farther into sensitive, protected areas of human activity, a legal response can guarantee that this sensitive information, which may not have previously been revealed, accessible, or even in existence, will be protected in accord with basic constitutional values. At the same time, lawmakers and courts have recognized that along with protecting the privacy of communications, laws also need to provide for law enforcement access to confidential information where necessary, consistent with basic Fourth Amendment protections. Debates over the appropriate balance between individual privacy interests and law enforcement power revolve around the proposition that increasingly powerful technologies demand increasingly strong privacy protections. While the privacy issues raised by authentication technologies encompass more than the communications inside or associated with those authentication systems, new privacy protections are indeed needed for these emerging technologies.

Communications privacy law has generally governed law enforcement access to interpersonal communications (wiretapping), but it also covers access by unauthorized private third parties. The expressive nature of communications has resulted in legislative and judicial recognition of the sensitivity of personal communications through special procedures controlling law enforcement access to communications. In general, advances in communications technology precipitate debates about the appropriate level of Fourth Amendment protection. These debates reveal an evolving notion of what information is sensitive and thus deserving of protection from both governmental and commercial intrusion.

As advanced communications technologies such as the Internet (e-mail, the World Wide Web, and so on), wireless phones, and other devices complement and in some cases replace telephone communications, the United States as a nation has generally recognized the need to create privacy protections similar to those established for voice communications by the Supreme Court.[45] From telegraph to telephone, wireline phone to cell phone, e-mail to the World Wide Web, users of the major new communication technologies have acquired privacy protections for their communications. Thus far in the history of electronic communications, policy makers, commercial providers, and even those in the field of law enforcement have come to agree that new technologies demand privacy protections,[46] both out of faithfulness to basic constitutional values and to assure the commercial viability and acceptance of the latest communications technologies. However, the scope of such protections has consistently fallen short of the standards, based on the Fourth Amendment, that govern real-time voice communications. At the same time, the range of information and communications flowing through these new communications technologies has dramatically increased. Thus today, many kinds of information are potentially accessible under the secret searches of wiretap law. In addition, in light of recent events, there is an expanding sense of what government may legitimately need to access to meet national security and law enforcement requirements.

Most recently, Congress has struggled with the question of the protection of online transactional records such as logs tracking the Web pages viewed by individual users and records of electronic mail messages sent and received. Though law enforcement argued that these logs revealed little information and should be easily available for any investigative purpose at all, the legislature found that this information is sufficiently sensitive to warrant extra protection.

Electronic communications have required the expansion of privacy protection commensurate with new technology capabilities (see Box 3.1). The Electronic Communications Privacy Act (ECPA) of 1986 was supported by a coalition of businesses and privacy advocates who understood that protections similar to those for first-class mail were a necessary precursor to business and individual adoption of e-mail as a communica-

---

[45]See *Katz* v. *United States*, 389 U.S. 347 (1967); Available online at <http://laws.findlaw.com/us/389/347.html>.

[46]In *Kyllo* v. *United States*, Justice Scalia, writing for the majority, noted "We think that obtaining by sense-enhancing technology any information regarding the interior of the home that could not otherwise have been obtained without physical 'intrusion into a constitutionally protected area' (*Silverman*, 365 U.S., at 512) constitutes a search—at least where (as here) the technology in question is not in general public use"; see <http://supct.law.cornell.edu/supct/html/99-8508.ZO.html>.

BOX 3.1
Expansion of Fourth Amendment Protection and
Technological Capabilities

In their early stages, important new communications technologies such as the telephone and electronic mail were not accorded the privacy protections that are now taken for granted. In each case, the application of Fourth Amendment protections was unsettled, so the legislative branch had to step in to provide some level of protection. When the telephone first came into use, law enforcement was able to conduct unfettered surveillance of private conversations because the U.S. Supreme Court ruled telephone calls to be beyond the protection of the Fourth Amendment. Though telephone callers never invited law enforcement officers to listen in on their calls, the Court held that Fourth Amendment protections only applied to intrusions on one's property (either physical or real). As conversations had no property interest attached to them, they merited no privacy protection. Later, however, the Supreme Court reversed itself and declared that "the Fourth Amendment protects *people, not places*."[1]

Early electronic mail systems also lacked clear legal protection. To some, the fact that an e-mail message passed through the hands of third parties (Internet service providers or other operators of electronic mail systems) meant that the sender and the recipient had forfeited their privacy rights by handing over the message to others. At the urging of the nascent electronic mail industry and privacy advocates, however, Congress extended privacy protection to e-mail and set clear rules governing law enforcement access. These rules are now in some flux owing to the passage of the USA PATRIOT Act of 2001 and uncertainty about how it will be applied and enforced.

---

[1]See *Katz* v. *United States*, 389 U.S. 347 (1967), which states "Because the Fourth Amendment protects people rather than places, its reach cannot turn on the presence or absence of a physical intrusion into any given enclosure. The 'trespass' doctrine of Olmstead v. United States, 277 U.S. 438, and Goldman v. United States, 316 U.S. 129, is no longer controlling." Available online at <http://laws.findlaw.com/us/389/347.html>.

---

tions tool for sensitive information.[47] Similarly, the privacy amendments to ECPA in 1994 creating a higher level of protection for transactional information generated in Web-based interactions recognized that this information was more sensitive than the numbers dialed on a phone, and consequently that public use of the Web would be aided by creating more stringent protections against access.

---

[47]See Electronic Communications Privacy Act of 1986 (PL 99-508). Available online at <http://www.cpsr.org/cpsr/privacy/wiretap/ecpa86.html>.

CONCLUDING REMARKS

Authentication technologies, like other technical advances, renew the debate about how much privacy protection should be provided to personal information generated in the authentication process. As with other advances, in order to speed adoption, policy makers, industry, law enforcement, and privacy advocates should identify the privacy-sensitive features of these technologies and develop appropriate protections.

Finding 3.1: Authentication can affect decisional privacy, information privacy, communications privacy, and bodily integrity privacy interests. The broader the scope of an authentication system, the greater its potential impact on privacy.

Recommendation 3.1: Authentication systems should not infringe upon individual autonomy and the legal exercise of expressive activities. Systems that facilitate the maintenance and assertion of separate identities in separate contexts aid in this endeavor, consistent with existing practices in which individuals assert distinct identities for the many different roles they assume. Designers and implementers of such systems should respect informational, communications, and other privacy interests as they seek to support requirements for authentication actions.

In terms of developing an actual system, and considering fair information principles and practices as described in this chapter, as well as how authentication works in the abstract (as discussed in Chapter 2), the following guidelines are offered for the development of authentication systems that would protect privacy interests as much as possible.

Recommendation 3.2: When designing an authentication system or selecting an authentication system for use, one should:

- **Authenticate only for necessary, well-defined purposes;**
- **Minimize the scope of the data collected;**
- **Minimize the retention interval for data collected;**
- **Articulate what entities will have access to the collected data;**
- **Articulate what kinds of access to and use of the data will be allowed;**
- **Minimize the intrusiveness of the process;**
- **Overtly involve the individual to be authenticated in the process;**

- Minimize the intimacy of the data collected;
- Ensure that the use of the system is audited and that the audit record is protected against modification and destruction; and
- Provide means for individuals to check on and correct the information held about them that is used for authentication.

4

Security and Usability

Previous chapters describe abstract notions of authentication and privacy. Fully understanding the implications of authentication for privacy requires considering authentication systems as a whole. No working authentication technology exists in a vacuum. How is the technology deployed? What policies are in place with respect to its use? Which resources is the system meant to protect? What are the goals of the system? Understanding the technology as part of a larger system is key to evaluating its privacy implications. In this chapter, authentication is examined within a broader systems context. Two important systems-level characteristics of authentication systems are discussed: security and usability.

As noted previously, security is a primary reason for the deployment of authentication systems. Security is also vital to the preservation of privacy in that one must make use of security technology in order to protect privacy-related information. It is not simply the technical mechanisms of security that matter but also the processes and policies governing who has access (and how) to sensitive data. It is therefore essential to understand the security requirements and properties of both the authentication system itself and the resources it is protecting. To that end, a discussion of threat models and how to think about security risks is presented. The people using these systems are an important component of them, and their needs and behaviors must be taken into account. Accordingly, the committee develops the notion of user-centered design, with particular emphasis on the authentication context. Finally, it remarks on and makes recommendations about secondary and unplanned-for uses of authentication systems.

THREAT MODELS

As noted previously, a significant motivator for authentication technologies is increased system security. Ultimately, understanding the context in which the system will be deployed and the threats likely to be faced will enable determining whether authorization, accountability, and/or identification (as well as authentication) will be required. While authentication technologies are generally used to increase system security, security is not a binary property of a system.[1] A system is secure, or insecure, only relative to a perceived threat.[2] To understand this concise characterization, some definitions are required.

Threats

The terms "attack" and "threat" are often used interchangeably in security discussions, and in informal discussions this is an acceptable practice. However, in this report the committee adopts more precise definitions for these terms and other, related security terms to facilitate an understanding of the security issues related to authentication systems:

- A *vulnerability* is a security-relevant flaw in a system. Vulnerabilities arise as a result of hardware or software bugs or procedural, personnel, or physical security problems.
- An *attack* is a means of exploiting a vulnerability. Attacks may be

---

[1]As part of overall system security, the security of the authentication component itself (separate from broader system security issues) is crucial, because without it, a primary purpose of the authentication process is undermined. For any authentication technology, the possible vulnerabilities, present and future, must be evaluated. Apart from flaws particular to a given method, there are several questions that can be asked of any scheme, such as whether the authentication credentials can be shared (and if so, whether the original owner still retains the ability to use them), whether the credentials can be forged, and which sorts of errors can be due to human limitations (such as forgetting a secret or losing a token). Another question that bears on the security of the authentication system is whether a secret value is transmitted to or stored by the verifier. In some sense, a proper understanding of the vulnerabilities is even more important than the vulnerabilities themselves. Do system security administrators understand the failure modes? Do users understand the weak points?

[2]For an in-depth discussion of computer and information security, see Computer Science and Telecommunications Board, National Research Council, *Trust in Cyberspace*, Washington, D.C., National Academy Press, 1999. Available online at <http://cstb.org/pub_trust/>.

technical, procedural, physical, and so on, corresponding to the type of vulnerability being exploited. Passive wiretapping, buffer overflows, and social engineering (for example, deceiving individuals such that they reveal privileged information) are examples of attacks.

- An *adversary* is an entity (an individual or an organization) with hostile intent. Hackers, criminals, terrorists, and overly aggressive marketers are examples of adversaries.

- A *threat* is a motivated, capable adversary. The adversary is motivated to violate the security of a target (system) and has the ability to mount attacks that will exploit vulnerabilities of the target.[3]

- A *countermeasure* is a security mechanism or procedure designed to counter one or more types of attack. A countermeasure does not remove a vulnerability but instead prevents some types of attack from effectively exploiting one or more vulnerabilities. Secure Sockets Layer (SSL), for example, can be used to encrypt communication between a browser and a server in order to counter passive wiretapping attacks that could disclose a static password.[4]

In practice, every system contains vulnerabilities of some sort, when viewed in a broad context. The existence of a vulnerability does not in itself make a system insecure. Rather, a system is insecure only in the context of a perceived threat, because that threat is motivated and capable of exploiting one or more vulnerabilities present in the system. For example, in order to exploit a vulnerability in an implementation of a user-authentication system, an adversary might have to possess a very sophisticated technical capability. If likely adversaries do not possess that capability, then the system may be considered adequately secure for an intended application context. Of course, the adversary could also bribe one or more insiders. All vulnerabilities must be considered.

To understand threats, one usually begins with a list of common adversaries and a discussion of their possible motivations, capabilities, and degree of aversion to detection. The following examples illustrate this notion:

- *Hackers* represent a class of adversaries who tend to be opportunistic. That is, a target often is selected because of its vulnerability rather than for its strategic value. Hacker capabilities are primarily in the form of attacks launched via network access, as opposed to the exploitation of

---

[3]This definition is consistent with the use of the term in political and military contexts, such as references to the "Soviet threat" during the Cold War.

[4]Of course, this protection does not address other fundamental vulnerabilities of static passwords, such as ease of guessing.

physical or personnel vulnerabilities. Often these attacks are not stealthy, and many hackers do not seem to be especially averse to detection. Individual hackers do not tend to possess significant resources, but groups of them may collaborate to bring to bear significant computing resources against a target (some distributed denial-of-service attacks are an example, although such attacks may also be carried out by individuals). A small number of hackers are highly skilled, and these individuals create attack tools that are distributed to a much larger, less-skilled hacker community. Because of the opportunistic nature of hackers and because the hacker community is so large, all systems with network connectivity should consider hackers as threats. Many hackers seem to place little value on their time, and thus may be willing to expend considerable personal time on what might seem a trivial target, perhaps motivated more by the desire for bragging rights than by the value of the data accessed.

- *Insiders* are authorized users in some organizational context. Thus, they have legitimate access to some set of computers and networks within that context and usually have physical access to computers employed by other users in that context. The threat from insiders can arise in one of two ways. First, benignly intended insiders may behave inappropriately out of either curiosity or error, causing damage. Second, malicious insiders may intend to cause damage. In both cases, the set of things that could be damaged or taken usually is constrained by the organizational context in which an insider operates. Insiders are usually averse to detection, although a disgruntled employee who is being fired may be less so. Malicious insiders typically have limited resources, but their intimate knowledge of systems and physical access to them give malicious insiders advantages relative to external attackers.

- *Industrial spies*, in contrast to hackers, select targets on the basis of the perceived value of some aspect of the target (for example, content), and they are highly averse to detection. They tend to employ stealthy online attacks to reduce the risk of detection, but they also may employ attacks (for example, bribery) against personnel. Because these adversaries are paid to conduct attacks, their methods take personnel and materiel costs into account. Industrial spies may also take jobs in order to acquire insider access (see above).

- *Criminals* often select targets for financial gain and thus often prefer stealthy attacks that minimize the risk of detection. (An exception might be denial-of-service attacks used to extort.) They may be willing to exploit personnel or physical security vulnerabilities as well as to engage in technical attacks. They may employ considerable financial resources.

- *Activists* launch attacks whose goal might be to generate publicity (for example, by disrupting services) to serve a more subtle purpose (for example, to acquire data used to embarrass the target). They are not especially averse to detection, nor do they generally possess significant resources, but they may exploit ideological biases in personnel (insiders) and may engage in physical attacks.

• *Nation-state spies and terrorists* typically select targets with great care and employ very stealthy techniques to avoid detection and attribution. They may bring significant financial and technical resources to bear against the target. They may employ a full range of attacks to exploit physical, procedural, and personnel vulnerabilities. Even state-sponsored espionage budgets are not infinite, so the cost of attacking a target is balanced against the expected gains.

In the context of user-authentication technologies, it is important to understand the threats against which the technologies are effective and under what circumstances the technologies will fail.[5] If security is compromised, privacy is likely to be compromised as well. In addition, as the rest of the report describes, even with sufficient security there still may be threats to privacy. Choices about which kinds of authentication systems to deploy need to take these factors into account.

> **Recommendation 4.1: In designing or choosing an authentication system, the first step should be to articulate a threat model in order to make an intelligent choice among competing technologies, policies, and management strategies. The threat model should encompass all of the threats applicable to the system. Among the aspects that should be considered are the privacy implications of using the technologies.**

Dealing with Threats

Assuming (perhaps unrealistically) that a serious and explicit evaluation of the security of a system relative to a perceived threat model has been carried out, the next question is what to do in response: How should one protect the system? The answer will depend on the potential losses (including the potential damage to reputations) if attacks were to succeed, as well as on the risk-management strategies adopted by those making the decisions. Several fundamental approaches to securing systems have been adopted over time, and multiple approaches usually are employed that complement one another.[6]

---

[5]For example, an authentication technology that uses a one-time password list may be very effective against hackers using network-based attacks but ineffective against an insider who might have ready access to the list taped to a monitor.

[6]The concise mantra adopted by the Department of Defense in the 1990s, "Prevent, de-

If a vulnerability cannot be eliminated, security countermeasures are often deployed to mitigate the risk that the vulnerability will be exploited. Countermeasures usually thwart some specific, known class of attacks and thus may not offer protection against new attacks that exploit the vulnerability. Although deploying countermeasures is not as attractive as eliminating underlying vulnerabilities, it is an essential part of the security technology arsenal, since countermeasures can be added into an existing system to complement the security capabilities of that system.

The minimization of vulnerabilities and deployment of countermeasures generally will improve system security, but rarely will they ensure system security in the face of a wide range of attacks. Thus, it is also prudent to engage in monitoring in order to detect traffic patterns or system behavior that may be indicative of an attack. This process is referred to as "intrusion detection" and is commonly employed in many environments today. Of course, it implies being able to differentiate the behavior of intruders from that of normal authorized users. Even if an intrusion-detection system detects an attack only after the attack has been successful, the detection can be useful for evaluating the extent or mode of the attack.

Responses to attacks usually take the form of applying new software releases or updates, deploying new countermeasures, or adjusting intrusion detection systems to better monitor newly discovered vulnerabilities. Rarely is it practical to engage in any form of retaliatory action against an attacker; this is true for several reasons, including the difficulty of locating the source of an attack and legal constraints on such activities.

Once a sufficient threat analysis has been undertaken, the security requirements of the system should be more explicit.[7] It is at this point that decisions can be made about whether authentication is necessary and

---

tect, respond," reflects this multifaceted theme. Another commonly accepted approach to security is captured by the phrase "defense in depth." The notion here is that multiple, independent security mechanisms provide greatly improved security, since all must be circumvented in order to breach security. Defense in depth is compatible with efforts to "prevent, detect, respond," though it also can be pursued independently. Preventative measures attempt to prevent attacks from succeeding. For example, it is obviously desirable to remove vulnerabilities from a system whenever that proves feasible. The security patches (security-relevant software updates) issued by vendors are an example of this process. Applying security patches generally is viewed as a preventative measure since it prevents later exploitation of a vulnerability. But in many cases a patch is remedial—that is, the patch is distributed after an attacker has already exploited a vulnerability.

[7]One of the reasons that e-commerce has blossomed is that banks assume the risk of bad credit card transactions (perhaps passing some portion of this risk on to merchants). Risk analysis and apportionment must therefore be part of a careful threat and security requirement analysis.

what requirements the authentication subsystem would need to satisfy. The overall security requirements of the system will determine whether an authentication component is required, and, as indicated previously, the authentication system itself will have its own security needs. Finally, the perceptions and actualities of ease of use and usefulness (in this case, the prevention of perceived harm) play important roles in how secure systems of countermeasures are in practice. This is discussed further in the next section.

AUTHENTICATION AND PEOPLE—USER-CENTERED DESIGN

Authentication and privacy schemes will fail if they do not incorporate knowledge of human strengths and limits. People cannot remember all of their passwords, so they write them down (typically under the keyboard or on their handheld computers) or make them easy to remember (using pets' names or their own birth dates) and consequently easy to guess. People do not change passwords, because it makes them too hard to remember. Furthermore, people do not want to delete a file containing pages and pages of characters such as " X ÿÿÿÿÿÿ°ÿ ö:I†ÿÿÿÿ H   ." Its purpose is unclear, and there is a fear of disabling some application on the computer. Similarly, although much private information is stored in the cookies on computers—information about personal identification numbers, preferences, and time-stamped indicators of which Web sites were visited—people do not remove these after every transaction, even in cases where the cookies provide no real benefit to the user.[8] Two possible reasons for this are that since there are no visible traces of their existence and use, people forget that the cookies are there, and if they do remember, it is too hard to find and delete them. Similarly, people find it difficult to read the "fine print" of privacy notices that companies are now required to send out, both because the print itself may be too small and because the notices are usually written in obfuscated style.[9]

Therefore, in order to work effectively, authentication and privacy schemes need to be designed with the same consideration of human strengths and limits as for any other technology, maybe more. To do this, one can borrow heavily from the practice of user-centered design and

---

[8]Rarely are there negative consequences from cookie contents, so people continue to trust the system. This potentially misplaced trust leads to other vulnerabilities and raises a philosophical problem. Like civil liberties, society gains from an atmosphere of trust. Is the desire to preserve that atmosphere enough to accept a few vulnerabilities, or is it so important to prevent the vulnerabilities that the atmosphere of trust will be sacrificed?

[9]The problem of providing effective privacy notice is appreciated by consumer protection experts.

from some additional aspects of psychology. The following section outlines the practice of user-centered design and discusses how it applies to the design of authentication and privacy schemes. Some other facts about human behavior that are relevant to these issues are noted. A suggested design and evaluation process is presented for considering various alternatives for authentication and privacy that are proposed in this report.

Lessons from User-Centered Design

User-centered design puts the user's needs and capabilities at the forefront. Much of today's technology is driven by the pursuit of a technology solution, without regard to whether the technology provides the full functionality that the user needs in the context of its use or whether it is learnable, usable, and pleasant. After the failure of a number of products and systems—notably the Apple Newton, the Mars orbiter, and the Florida 2000 election ballot—more and more software engineers are putting "user-experience engineers," or people with human factors experience, on their teams.[10]   User-experience engineers use various methods to understand the user's needs and to design an interface that is easy to learn, usable, and enjoyable. There is evidence that the software is measurably better and the products more successful in the marketplace when these methods are used.

User-experience engineers rely on a number of design principles that are based on the known strengths and limits of human cognition. Cognitive psychologists have known for years, for example, that human short-term memory is limited and fragile, that learning takes time, and that people make moment-by-moment decisions about cost or effort and perceived benefit. However, people are also remarkably perceptive, in both the literal and conceptual sense. Humans have great powers of understanding visual input, particularly if it follows certain principles of grouping and use of color and dimension. People make errors by misremem-

---

[10]Extracted from several articles by user-experience expert Donald Norman. Norman provides the example of the Soviet Union's Phobos 1 satellite in a 1990 article in *Communications of the ACM*. The orbiter was lost on its way to Mars not long after launch. Later, it was found that the cause of the error was an operator who sent a sequence of digital commands to the satellite but mistyped a single character. Unfortunately, this error triggered a test sequence stored in the read-only memory that was supposed to be executed only when the spacecraft was on the ground. The wrong sequence set the satellite in rotation, and it was no longer possible to resume control over it; it was lost in space (D.A. Norman, "Commentary: Human Error and the Design of Computer Systems," *Communications of the ACM* 33(1990): 4-7.) Norman commented on the 2000 Florida ballot in an interview with Kenneth Chang of the *New York Times* ("From Ballots to Cockpits, Questions of Design," *New York Times*, January 23, 2001).

TABLE 4.1   Key Design Principles in User-Centered Design

Principle	Practices
Build on what the user knows.	Do not tax the memory of users by having them learn too many new things. Use their words. Build the system interaction with a story or metaphor in mind that the user will easily understand.
Simplify.	Do not add features that aren't useful. Package large feature sets in terms of clusters of things for a particular task, not jumbled together to cover all possibilities.
Allow users to do things in the order in which they think of them.	Do not make users do things in the order that the computer needs if it is different from what users would do naturally. (The computer can keep track of things better than the user can.)
Display information in clustered, meaningful visual displays.	Place things that go together conceptually near each other in the display and in an order that fits what users are trying to achieve.
Design for errors.	People make errors. Design so that errors are not costly to the user or difficult to correct. Allow each action to be undone once the user has seen the consequence of the error.
Pace the interaction so that the user is in control.	The user can be slow, but the system shouldn't be. Slow reaction to a user action discourages acceptance of a technology.

bering, by not attending to signals, and by simple mistaken acts such as hitting a key adjacent to the one intended.

On the basis of knowledge accumulated from decades of research in cognitive psychology, user-experience engineers have developed a core set of design principles, a common set of which are shown in Table 4.1. How these lessons apply to systems employing authentication and privacy schemes is explored next.

Issues of Limited Memory

The issue of forgetting passwords is clearly an issue of limited memory and of the first two principles shown in Table 4.1. Learning and recall are hard and take time. Because of this limitation, people will augment their memories by writing things down. Recently, new services have been offered on the Internet and in some operating systems to alleviate the problem that many people have with many different passwords—for example, one for ordering tickets online, one for access to digital libraries, and others for getting financial information online. This type of service will build for a person a single portal to which he or she signs on with one password. It stores all of that person's passwords and automatically accesses the services for which he or she has signed up. Many of the user's resources are consequently subject to theft with the loss of a single password—the one used to access such a resource.

Simplicity

There are systems that have the desired functionality of allowing the user fine-grained control but that tend to be far too complicated to use. Some e-mail systems, for example, allow the user to formulate rules to sort incoming e-mail into folders for examination later in some order of priority. There are two major problems with these systems. First, people find that the rules that they have to write are maddeningly difficult because they must specify their preferences in very specific terms having to do with searchable fields in e-mail. For example, when a correspondent has more than one e-mail account, the rule writer must remember not just a particular person's name, but all of the character strings that might appear in that person's e-mail "From" line. Second, if the rules designate things to be automatically deleted, the user may have no trace of unintended consequences. Similar effects follow when users attempt to program their telephones to deny calls from telemarketers. They must specify their rules not by naming people from whom they want to hear but by designating telephone numbers. The system was designed without regard for the difficulty that the user will incur at the interface.

Technologies that are difficult to learn will exclude people who are not willing to or cannot expend the effort needed to learn them. Of note, a recent study of people's understanding of Pretty Good Privacy (PGP), a communications encryption technology, showed that many users failed outright to understand what they were supposed to do and made catastrophic errors, such as sending the private key instead of the public key.[11]   However, criticisms of user-interface problems are usually more accurately applied to an implementation than to a building-block technology per se.

Making Things Visible

Associated with people's ability to understand complex visual displays is their inattention to things not visible: "Out of sight, out of mind." The example of cookies earlier in this report is an instance of invisibility. Things invisible are often not attended to. The files in "temp" folders similarly fail with regard to visibility and readability. But, since the possible consequences of the loss of privacy are not brought to the user's attention on a daily basis, it can be easy to forget about their possible harm. The fact that people ignore things that are not visible may explain why they claim to be concerned with privacy and then do not protect their privacy when given the opportunity.

Indirect Effects of Bad User-Centered Design

Poorly designed systems can also have indirect effects on privacy, accuracy, and control. Many of the databases in use at large financial companies, motor vehicle bureaus, social service agencies, and so on are legacy systems with badly designed interfaces and poor checks on the accuracy of data entered, resulting in errors in database records. Many of these errors are caused by poorly designed interfaces, poor training for the high-turnover workforce (high turnover caused by the boredom of such a low-level job), and low motivation. And, since it costs an organization money to ensure accuracy (for example, verifying by doubly entering the data and finding mismatches, or building algorithms that will check on accuracy and duplication, and so on), errors are accepted. It is the victim of an error who seems to have to bear the cost of correction.

Lessons from Cognitive and Social Psychology

Other aspects of human behavior, including the following, affect the success of authentication and privacy schemes:

- How people make decisions,
- The basis on which they trust other people and institutions,

---

[11]A. Whitten and J.D. Tygar. "Usability of Security: A Case Study." *Proceedings of the 9th USENIX Security Symposium.* August 1999.

- Their assumption that the physical world does not apply to the virtual world, and
- How a person's behavior changes when that person is not visible to others.

These aspects of human behavior are all relevant to the design of authentication and privacy schemes.

Decision Making

Throughout daily life, people make small decisions about whether to take actions or not. Often such decisions are based on simple calculations of cost and benefit. In making decisions, people frequently overvalue things that have immediate value and undervalue actions that may have a long-term payoff. And, sometimes the cost is clear and the benefit unknown. This tendency causes people to not make the effort to do something that would protect their long-term interests.

For example, knowing that people do not like having their private information accessible to others unknown to them, some entrepreneurs have built software called "cookie cutters" that automatically preserves the cookies a person chooses to preserve and flushes the rest when a Web session is over. Unfortunately, not only are such programs generally expensive, but they also require a particular level of skill for installation and require users to specify their preferences in much the same way as e-mail filtering programs and telephone screening devices do. The cost is high, both in time and in the effort to understand and specify things, and the benefits are really unclear. It is hard to articulate the benefit of keeping this information private, both now and in an unforeseen future.

The fact that people often see immediate benefits but not long-term consequences also explains why they are willing to divulge private information for short-term freebies. For example, some people will allow their Web activity to be monitored if they are given a free e-mail account.

Trust

Much of our society is based on trust. People take actions that make them vulnerable, believing that others will do them no harm. They accept payment in checks or credit cards assuming that the payer has the resources and will pay when asked. They follow traffic rules in general, expecting others to do so as well. People buy things sight-unseen on the Web, expecting delivery of the goods and/or services as advertised. People believe, often wrongly, that when they share their e-mail address or Social Security number, this information will not be sold to third parties who will either solicit them to buy unwanted things or defraud them in some way (steal from their accounts). In normal, everyday behavior, people do not authenticate one another. They spend little effort and make assumptions based on commonly available data. Furthermore, people are usually not proved wrong after doing this, so their experience with the system encourages them to behave this way.

On what information do people base their judgments with respect to trust and lying? The best information that someone is trustworthy comes from direct experience: A person was trusted in the past and all behavioral evidence is that he or she caused the trusting person no harm or, better yet, looked after his or her interests. The second source of information when making such judgments is a set of physical and behavioral attributes that suggest someone is similar to the trusting person. The chain of reasoning goes like this: If I am trustworthy and you are like me, then you must be trustworthy, too. The third source is endorsements, either from someone a person knows, such as a friend who has had direct experience with the person or institution in question, or from some famous person who would lose reputation if he or she lied about another's trustworthiness. The fourth source is assessment of reputation directly—for example, the reputation of a person in a powerful position could be lost if he or she were not trustworthy or an organization that has been around for a long time might not continue to exist if it was less trustworthy.

Knowing how people make decisions, some people and institutions hide behind false information. Some individuals might buy from a Web site that has an endorsement symbol from the Better Business Bureau, even though there is not necessarily an immediate way to authenticate the valid use of the symbol. It could simply have been copied from another site. Some people might choose to enter credit card information into a site that seems to be designed well and not into one that seems to be slapped together, making the assumption that a well-designed site costs money and could not have been afforded by a fly-by-night vendor. Because people do not spend the time and effort to investigate authenticity and the shortcut attributes that they use are well known, they are left open to fraud at many levels.[12]

---

[12]The Federal Trade Commission is charged with consumer protection broadly and has been investigating conduct on the Web. More information on the FTC, privacy, and fair information practices is presented in Chapter 3.

Assumptions from the Real World That Do Not Transfer to the Virtual

In our social interaction in the physical-spatial world, some behaviors are correlated—for example, when I see you, you can see me. When I get closer to you, you get closer to me; when I hear you, you can hear me. The digital world has uncorrelated these attributes. With Web cameras or one-way videoconferencing, I can see you, but you *can't* see me. A whole host of surveillance devices allows detection without obvious detectability. What used to be reciprocal is now one-way. However, people behave as if the virtual world had the same reciprocity as the real world. One day, for example, as a demonstrator was explaining online video-conferencing on a public site, she was startled when someone she could not see spoke to her. That person, in turn, could see her, but, because of the camera angle, could not see that she had an audience of high-level executives. Thinking that she was alone, he made several lewd remarks. The demonstrator and the executives were surprised and offended by the encounter. They had wrongly assumed that the only others online were those they could see.

There are a number of cases today in which the person using a service or technology is told the conditions (for example, that others may monitor an interaction or that the numbers a person types in will be used for other purposes), but they forget. The many years that humans spend learning physical reality are hard to dismiss when one is merely told that things might be otherwise.

Accountability A related issue is accountability. There is mounting evidence that when people are anonymous or hidden, they will behave in ways that are very different from normal. For example, when feedback for a product or service is anonymous, people are more likely to say negative things, knowing that they are not held accountable for their behavior. They can get away with more. A similar effect comes into play in e-mail flaming. When the recipient is not visible to the writer of the e-mail, the writer tends to say more emotionally charged things, things that he or she would soften if the recipient were visible. There is evidence from experiments on trust that if people cannot be seen by others, they will behave in a more self-serving, as opposed to a cooperative and trusting way.

Actions There are at least two approaches to accommodating the known limits of human behavior when considering authentication and privacy schemes: designing to fit those known limits and training people to be cautious when caution is warranted.

**Finding 4.1: People either do not use systems that are not de-
signed with human limitations in mind or they make errors in
using them; these errors can compromise privacy.**

**Recommendation 4.2: User-centered design methods should be
integral to the development of authentication schemes and privacy policies.**

Training, Public Education Campaigns, and Regulations

It is unlikely that technologies and the policies associated with them
will be transparent to everyone. People have a hard time changing expectations and assumptions in a world that is invisible to them. Consequently, some protective measures may have to be put in place to make
up for these human shortcomings. In many cases, it is not apparent to the
user what information is being given to the verifier. Most users do not
know what information is on magnetic-stripe cards, smart cards, and bar-
coded cards. Printed information on the cards is more apparent to the
user, but information learned by way of back-end processes (for example,
a check of a credit report) can be invasive of privacy, yet invisible to the
user. As for protective measures at a micro level, Web sites could have
visible statements of the sort heard in many recorded messages on customer service hotlines—namely, that the conversation (site use) may be
monitored to ensure quality. Similarly, small explanatory or warning
signs might appear when one moves the mouse pointer over a field that
asks for information from the user. More broadly, a public education
campaign may be necessary to keep people from unknowingly making
themselves vulnerable, just as people are warned of new scams. The goal
of such education should not be to cause people to mistrust others but to
train them to understand the nature of information systems and how they
can and should protect themselves.

Ultimately, most individuals do not understand the privacy and
security aspects of the authentication systems that they are required to
use in interactions with commercial and government organizations. As
a result, they may behave in a way that compromises their privacy and/
or undermines the security of the authentication systems. To remedy
these problems, system interfaces should be developed that reveal the
information collected and how it is used. Research is needed to explore
how to do this effectively. In addition, as part of the deployment of any
new system that includes the collection of privacy-sensitive data, individuals should be educated about the privacy and security aspects of
the authentication systems that they use, including the risks associated
with the systems.

FACTORS BEHIND THE TECHNOLOGY CHOICE

A crucial factor that will encourage or discourage the use of any authentication technology is ease of deployment. A scheme that relies on something that users already have (or already "are") is easier to deploy than one that requires shipping (and perhaps installing) new equipment. Smart cards are relatively hard to deploy, however, since few people have the smart card readers and associated software on their computers. In addition, most card issuers insist on owning their own cards, which is why cards that could technically "share" issuers (for example, a payment card that is also an airline affinity-program card) have not been successful in the market. With respect to possession of the correct hardware, however, most computers sold in the past several years have Universal Serial Bus (USB) ports; a USB-based token that functioned like a smart card might require less effort to deploy, although the software barrier would still exist. This observation is not an endorsement of USB tokens but rather points out how many factors, cost among them, may inhibit or facilitate the deployment of hardware-based authentication technologies.

The building blocks from which different authentication systems are constructed may be used to protect or invade privacy. Among the privacy issues that arise are what data are revealed to the issuer upon initial interaction with the system and what data are created and stored at that time, as well as when authentication events occur. A system in which personal data are retained after an authentication transaction is more intrusive of privacy than one in which no data are collected or retained. One of the most crucial issues with respect to privacy and authentication systems, as discussed in Chapter 2, is *linkage*: Can the results of an authentication process be linked to other sets of data? If the same individual uses cash for two activities, those activities are not linkable through the cash that was used; however, two uses of a stored-value card are linkable even if the card itself was purchased anonymously.

Cost is another factor in deciding which authentication technologies to deploy. Authentication can be expensive. There may be hardware, software, and procedural-development costs for the presenter, the verifier, and the issuer. Integrating authentication procedures into existing systems and procedures may be expensive as well. Data collection and verification, both for initial registration and for recovery from lost credentials, can impose additional overhead. After deployment, authentication systems have ongoing costs. New users must be added to the system and old users deleted. Hardware and software require maintenance and upgrades. Procedural updates and user and administrator training and education are important (and costly) too; many systems fail not for technical reasons, but because someone did not follow proper procedures.

That, in turn, raises the issue of skills: What does it cost to obtain the services of enough people with appropriate abilities to deploy and operate an authentication system? Finally, costs have to be apportioned. Who pays for all of this? What is the balance of costs between the user, the issuer, the verifier, and any back-end systems?

Balanced against the costs of using an authentication system are the perceived and actual gains from deploying the system. Since vulnerabilities are hidden and threats are generally not observable except to those who have done ample analysis of the particular system and its context, people using the system may underestimate the benefit of risk mitigation. This can result in inappropriate choices of authentication systems or in inappropriate usage models that defeat the purpose of the system. For example, a recent study found that many users did not adhere to the rules about not making their passwords guessable, or about keeping them secret and changing them often. People had a number of excuses for ignoring such rules: they were not the kind of people who keep secrets, they shared passwords because doing so showed how they trusted other people, they thought they were not targets because they had nothing of value, and so on.[13]

Other factors besides cost and security have a bearing on technology choices. Not all authentication systems work for all population sizes. Some are too expensive on a per-user basis to work with large numbers of users; others have too high an up-front cost to be suitable for small populations. Furthermore, all systems have error rates encompassing false positives and/or false negatives. The likelihood and cost of each type of error, along with a priori estimates of the number of potential imposters, must be assessed to determine what trade-offs should be made.[14] In addition, the consequences of privacy invasions represent costs that may be hard to monetize (absent actual damages) and may be incurred by someone other than the system owner.

Finally, an authentication system must be matched to the needs of the context in which it is employed, keeping in mind that authentication may be excessive if simple authorization will suffice. Notwithstanding that stronger authentication is often suggested as an initial step to improve security, the issues are often much subtler. Deciding whether and how to employ authentication systems (or any other security technology) requires

---

[13]D. Weirich and M.A. Sasse. "Persuasive Password Security." *Proceedings of CHI 2001 ACM Conference on Human Factors in Computing Systems.* Seattle, Wash., April 2001.

[14]Creation of exception-handling procedures for dealing with incorrect decisions opens up additional vulnerabilities for the system, as imposters might claim to have been falsely rejected and request handling as an exception.

careful thought and decisions about what types of risk-management strategies are acceptable. Avoiding expedient responses and knee-jerk choices is critical, both for security and for privacy protection. This complexity, the multitude of contexts in which authentication systems could be deployed, and the ultimate need for someone to make policy decisions about security and privacy requirements are why simple cost-benefit analyses are unlikely to be effective in guiding the needed choices.

A final factor that must be considered when deciding how to proceed—namely, the recognition that authentication systems must be adequate to protect the resources they are guarding against the perceived threats, while at the same time remaining simple enough for administrators and others to use. This important point is often overlooked when developing technologies. Authentication systems will ultimately be used by people, so—as described in the previous section—their ease of use and understandability will have a major impact on their effectiveness.

SYSTEMS AND SECONDARY USE

Understanding only the underlying technologies is insufficient for appreciating the ramifications of authentication systems. It is important to know how the systems will work in context to determine their security and privacy implications. As discussed previously, some of the gravest privacy violations come about because of the inappropriate linking of data within or across systems. This can happen because the same identifier is used in multiple systems, because efforts were made to correlate data that has had the identification information removed, or for other reasons. Once data have been collected about an individual, dossiers (anonymous or identified) can be created. The creation of dossiers coupled with an authentication system may pose a privacy risk. Avoiding this risk requires awareness of the broader context in which the authentication systems and the data associated with authentication events will be used.

> Finding 4.2: The existence of dossiers magnifies the privacy risks of authentication systems that come along later and retroactively link to or use dossiers. Even a so-called de-identified dossier constitutes a privacy risk, in that identities often can be reconstructed from de-identified data.

> Finding 4.3: The use of a single or small number of identifiers across multiple systems facilitates record linkage. Accordingly, if a single identifier is relied on across multiple institutions, its fraudulent or inappropriate use (and subsequent recovery ac-

tions) could have far greater ramifications than if it is used in only a single system.

Recommendation 4.3: A guiding principle in the design or selection of authentication technologies should be to minimize the linking of user information across systems unless the express purpose of the system is to provide such linkage.

In addition to dossier creation through planned-for uses of authentication systems, secondary use and unplanned-for uses increase the risk of privacy violations. Unintended uses of a given technology or information system can always have inadvertent side effects, and there are numerous examples in the literature of a system meeting its design specifications but failing in the field because it was used in ways not anticipated by its designers. In the realm of authentication technology and individual privacy, unplanned-for secondary uses can have grave consequences for users. Arguably, much identity theft is accomplished through secondary uses of authentication or identification data. See Box 4.1 for a more in-depth discussion of identity theft.

An authentication system could be designed and deployed in a secure, privacy-sensitive fashion. However, if some aspect of the system were to be used in ways not originally intended, both security and any privacy protection available could be at risk. The driver's license is a canonical example of inappropriate secondary use. Its primary function is to identify those authorized to drive motor vehicles. It is quite unlikely that the designers of the original processes by which driver's licenses are issued anticipated they would be used as a security document needed to board a commercial airliner or drink in bars.

Most information systems, including authentication systems, do not explicitly guard against secondary uses, although occasionally there are contractual relationships that limit secondary use (such as credit card agreements). In some cases, the credential presented may be used for additional verification purposes in contexts unrelated to the original purpose (such as with a driver's license or when an e-commerce Web site gives permission for the cookies that users have allowed it to place on their hard drives to be used by other entities). In other instances, the data collected prior to, during, or subsequent to authentication may be used in ways that have little to do with the authentication step itself. A simple example would be when information used to register at a Web site in order to access content that is later used for marketing purposes by that Web site. A more insidious form of unplanned-for usage would involve a technology designed for a certain security context, user population, and so on that is later (intentionally or unintentionally) used in a new context

BOX 4.1
Identity Theft

Identity theft occurs when someone usurps a portion of another person's personal identifying information in order to pose as that person. The information usually includes some combination of name, address, Social Security number, mother's maiden name, password, credit card number, date of birth, driver's license number, and employer. With this information the "thief" can open new accounts, order products, rent apartments, take out a mortgage, and/or borrow money, all under the identity of the first party. Identity theft goes beyond the theft of a credit card to the misappropriation of a person's very identity. It constitutes fraud. From the victim's perspective, there is no easy way to develop an audit trail that proves who actually made the transaction. Was it the person who owns or is authorized to use the account, or was it the person who appropriated the account? Note that a significant part of the problem is that nonsecret data are used by many entities for authentication purposes. An additional problem is the difficulty in revoking authenticators and identifiers when they are misused. In essence, the level of confidence required, in the vocabulary introduced in Chapter 1 of this report, is not high enough. As Chapter 7 describes, the choice of identifier and authenticator is crucial for privacy protection and better security.

Reports of identity theft have increased over time. In March 2002, the General Accounting Office (GAO), acknowledging that there are no comprehensive statistics on identity theft, reviewed data from a number of sources—including consumer reporting agencies, the Federal Trade Commission (FTC), the Social Security Administration (SSA), and federal law enforcement—all of which indicated that the prevalence of identity theft was growing.[1] Victims of identity theft pay dearly; in 1997, the Secret Service estimated that victims lost an aggregate $745 million. But victims also face nonfinancial hardships, including criminal records, difficulty finding a job, and inability to get mortgages or credit. Sallie Twentyman, a victim of identity theft, testified before the Senate Committee on the Judiciary that the confusion and frustration that resulted felt like a "financial cancer." In Ms. Twentyman's case, her renewal credit card was stolen before it reached her, and the thief changed "her" address and opened more accounts in "her" name.[2]

A survey conducted by Privacy Rights Clearinghouse and the California Public Interest Research Group found that the average victim of identity theft did not find out that he or she was a victim until 14 months after the identity theft occurred and that it took the victim an average of 175 hours to resolve the problems that occurred as a result of the identity theft.[3] In January 2002, the FTC announced that identity theft was the top consumer fraud complaint in 2001, accounting for 42 percent of the complaints in the Consumer Sentinel database.

---

[1]General Accounting Office. *Identity Theft: Prevalence and Cost Appear to Be Growing*, GAO-02-363. Washington, D.C., Government Printing Office, pp. 3-5, March 2002.

[2]Sallie Twentyman (witness), "Identity Theft: Restoring Your Good Name," testimony before the Senate Committee on the Judiciary, March 20, 2002.

[3]CALPIRG (Sacramento, Calif.) and Privacy Rights Clearinghouse (San Diego, Calif.), *Nowhere to Turn: Victims Speak Out on IdentityTheft*, May 2000.

(continues)

BOX 4.1 Continued

Although identity theft existed before the Internet, there is concern that it will escalate even more in the digital world. The Internet has given identity thieves easier access to more sources of information. With e-signatures and digital certificates, it will be imperative to ensure that the digital representation is authentic, or associated with the correct individual, and that the transaction can be audited. There is a dual need: to determine who the consumer is and to ensure that the personal information of the consumer is protected.

In 1998, Congress passed the Identity Theft and Assumption Deterrence Act, which legally recognized that the victims of identity theft were the individuals whose identities were stolen and not the financial institution that lost money; made it illegal to steal another person's personal information (not necessarily documents) with the intent to commit a violation; and increased potential sentencing for violators. The act also required the FTC to establish a national clearinghouse for identity theft complaint data and to educate consumers about how to protect themselves.[4] The FTC has held workshops on the subject. Other government agencies have also taken action regarding identity theft. For example, the Treasury Department sponsored an ID Theft Summit in March 2000. Finally, most states have passed laws that criminalize identity theft.

In response to the human and financial costs of identity theft, a variety of policy responses have been proposed. Most recognize the necessity of a multipronged effort involving the public and private sectors and employing legal and technological tools. The education of consumers is essential to ensure that they take steps to minimize the possibility of identity theft and to alert them to signs of possible theft. Public and private organizations can help prevent identity theft by reducing the amount of data that is exposed, limiting the release of information that is given at the point of service, and enhancing the security of data that are collected. Additionally, aggressive criminal investigations, prosecution, and punishment are seen as critical.

In the 107th Congress much attention was focused on identity theft. A number of bills were introduced. In the House, these include the Identity Theft Protection Act of 2001 (H.R. 220), the Social Security Number Protection Act of 2002 (H.R. 4513), the ID Theft Loophole Closure Act (H.R. 2077), and the Protect Victims of Identity Theft Act of 2001 (H.R. 3368). In the Senate, bills include the Restore Your Identity Act of 2001 (S. 1742), the Social Security Number Misuse Prevention Act of 2001 (S. 848), and the Identity Theft Prevention Act of 2001 (S. 1399).

---

[4]See the Web site <http://www.consumer.gov/idtheft>.

without a determination as to whether the security and privacy safeguards still hold.

Abstractly, the difficulties that arise from secondary use are primarily due to incorrect assumptions. Secondary uses are implicitly relying on whatever assurances, security models, and privacy protections the original designers and implementers were working with. These may not align well with the needs of the secondary user. In addition, the original system was probably designed with a particular threat model in mind. However, that threat model may not be appropriate for secondary uses. This incongruity can make it difficult to respond to an attack on the primary system, since with widespread secondary use, the universe of motivations behind the attack is much larger. Another problem is that the data collected for primary purposes may not be the data that are needed by secondary uses, or, they may not be of appropriate quality or reliability. In addition, secondary uses can facilitate information leakage from the original system, which can cause both security and privacy problems. As noted in the committee's first report,[15] understanding and clearly articulating the goals of the system is crucial and may help mitigate any problems that might arise from secondary uses. Nonetheless, the risks of secondary use are significant and must be considered.

> **Finding 4.4: Current authentication technology is not generally designed to prevent secondary uses or mitigate their effects. In fact, it often facilitates secondary use without the knowledge or consent of the individual being authenticated.**

> **Finding 4.5: Secondary uses of authentication systems, that is, uses for which the systems were not originally intended, often lead to privacy and security problems. They can compromise the underlying mission of the original system user by fostering inappropriate usage models, creating security concerns for the issuer, and generating additional costs.**

> **Recommendation 4.4: Future authentication systems should be designed to make secondary uses difficult, because such uses often undermine privacy, pose a security risk, create unplanned-for costs, and may generate public opposition to the issuer.**

CONCLUDING REMARKS

As is evident from this and preceding chapters, neither authentication nor privacy is a simple issue. Instead, the issues interact in complex ways with the total system. This is seen clearly in the case of knowledge-based authentication, which relies on some prior history of contact and on reasonably private and unguessable knowledge that the authentic client

---

[15]Computer Science and Telecommunications Board, National Research Council. *IDs—Not That Easy: Questions About Nationwide Identity Systems.* Washington, D.C., National Academy Press, 2002.

will nevertheless have access to. Seen from this perspective, password-based authentication is popular because it demands so little up-front—initial passwords can easily be chosen or assigned without any need for history, special hardware, custom software on the client's computer (if any), and so on. By the same token, the weaknesses of passwords—guessability, the cost of recovering forgotten passwords, and so on—stem from many of the same roots.

Privacy has similar attributes. Many organizations that rely on identity-based authorization do so not because they wish to, but because it is easy: they can rely on an infrastructure that someone else has built. This accounts for the ubiquity of driver's licenses as a de facto "official" identification and age-authorization card: The departments of motor vehicles (DMVs) are paying the cost of issuing the cards; everyone else can ride free. Furthermore, it is precisely this overloading of function that gives rise to privacy violations: Many different transactions can be linked back to the same individual. Switching to better—and privacy-protecting—technologies is thus not an easy task.

Finally, computer security in many organizations is not as strong as it could be or needs to be.[16] In the federal government, there are numerous efforts to document federal agency computer security plans and practices and some that find glaring weaknesses in these plans and practices.[17] Many reports over the years have described security issues, concerns, and research challenges.[18] While security and privacy are often discussed as though they were in opposition to one another, in many ways adequate security is a prerequisite for privacy. If data are not well protected, they may compromise the privacy of the individual to whom they pertain. However, achieving information security sometimes requires the disclosure of personal information (for example, by requiring authentication). At the same time, insufficient privacy protection may mean that personal information about others is easily discovered, calling into question the reliability of authentication systems that depend on such information. While this report urges that care be taken to avoid unnecessary authentication and identification (and therefore avoid unnecessary privacy risks),

---

[16]See Computer Science and Telecommunications Board, National Research Council, *Cybersecurity Today and Tomorrow: Pay Now or Pay Later*, Washington, D.C., National Academy Press, 2002.

[17]See Representative Stephen Horn's report card on federal agency computer security efforts as one measure of the state of preparedness in this area; available online at <http://www.house.gov/reform/gmit/hearings/2000hearings/000911computersecurity/000911reportcard.htm>. Another measure is the Office of Management and Budget's scorecards, available at <http://www.whitehouse.gov/omb/budintegration/scorecards/agency_scorecards.html>.

[18]See CSTB's reports on security at the Web site <http://cstb.org/topic_security/>.

the interplay between achieving privacy protection and security in the development of information systems should be carefully considered. Privacy and security, while often in tension, are complementary as well. Security can protect private data, and maintaining privacy can aid in avoiding security breaches. Usability is a key component of this mix, since hard-to-understand or hard-to-use systems will be prone to errors and may drive an individual to work around either the security mechanisms or the mechanisms that would protect privacy. Lessons learned in trying to create secure, usable systems therefore apply when seeking to develop systems that protect privacy.

> **Finding 4.6: Privacy protection, like security, is very poor in many systems, and there are inadequate incentives for system operators and vendors to improve the quality of both.**

> **Finding 4.7: Effective privacy protection is unlikely to emerge voluntarily unless significant incentives to respect privacy emerge to counterbalance the existing incentives to compromise privacy. The experience to date suggests that market forces alone are unlikely to sufficiently motivate effective privacy protection.**

> **Recommendation 4.5: System designers, developers, and vendors should improve the usability and manageability of authentication mechanisms, as well as their intrinsic security and privacy characteristics.**

5

Authentication Technologies

T his chapter describes the basic technologies used as building blocks for authentication systems, especially those employed in computer and network environments. First, it describes technological choices that determine a dimension of authentication separate from the different kinds of authentication described in Chapter 2. Then, technological instantiations of the three main authentication mechanisms (something you know, have, are) are described. Multifactor authentication is considered, and decentralized and centralized systems are compared. Finally, security and cost considerations for individual authentication technologies are discussed. Throughout, this chapter also touches on the privacy implications of specific technologies in the context of authentication systems, as appropriate.

TECHNOLOGICAL FLAVORS OF AUTHENTICATION

"Individual authentication" is defined in Chapter 1 as the process of establishing an understood level of confidence that an identifier refers to a specific individual. In an information systems context, it often is useful to distinguish among several types or modes of authentication, both for individuals (often referred to as "users") and for devices (such as computers). This is a dimension distinct from the individual/attribute/identity authentication types discussed in Chapter 2. In the security literature, these modes are often referred to as one-way as opposed to two-way authentication, initial versus continuous authentication, and data origin versus peer-entity authentication.

Much individual authentication in an information system takes place in a client/server context, in which the individual user is the client (a "presenter" in the terminology introduced in Chapter 2) and some computer is a form of server (the "verifier"). A user is required to authenticate his or her identity to a computer, usually as a prerequisite for gaining access to resources (access control or authorization). This is typically an explicit one-way authentication process; that is, the user authenticates himself or herself to the computer. If the user is authenticating to a computer directly (for example, when sitting at a desktop or laptop computer), there is an implicit two-way authentication; the user sees the computer with which he or she is interacting and presumably knows that it is the one he or she wishes to use.[1]

However, if the user is authenticating to a computer accessed via a communication network, there is often no way to verify that the computer at the other end of the communication path is the one that the user is trying to contact. The user typically relies on the communication infrastructure operating properly and thus connecting him or her to the intended computer. This assumption may be violated by any of a number of attacks against the communication path, starting with the computer that the user is employing locally. This lack of explicit, secure, two-way authentication can subvert many types of individual authentication mechanisms. If a presenter provides an identifier and authenticator to the wrong verifier, both security and privacy are adversely affected. Thus, two-way authentication is preferred so that a presenter can verify the identity of the verifier to which a secret may be disclosed.

Initial authentication takes place when an individual first establishes a connection of some sort to a system. This may be a direct, very local connection, such as logging in to a desktop or laptop computer, or it may be a remote connection to a computer via a communication network. In either case, there is an assumption that future communication, for some period of time, is taking place between the two parties who were initially authenticated. For a direct connection, as defined here, this assumption usually relies on physical and procedural security measures; there is an assumption that the user will log out when leaving the computer unattended and in a place where others might access it. This is a form of implicit, continuous authentication. This assumption may not always be

---

[1]Looks can be deceiving, and even visual inspection of a proximate device is not always sufficient to authenticate it.

valid, and sometimes users are required to reauthenticate themselves explicitly to the computer periodically, to verify that they are still present. This periodic reauthentication requirement is an explicit attempt at continuous authentication, although it is not really continuous. Periodic reauthentication is also burdensome for the user and thus not commonly employed.

When the connection between the user and a computer is through a network, there are many more opportunities for the connection to be "hijacked"—that is, for an attacker to inject traffic into the connection or to seize the connection from the legitimate user. In remote-access contexts, it is appropriate to employ explicit measures to ensure continuous authentication. Typically, this continuity is effected using cryptographic means, based on a secret (a cryptographic key) shared between a local computer employed by the user and a remote computer being accessed by the user, for the life of the connection. In this latter context, the technical term for the security service being provided is "data origin authentication." Continuous authentication is generally a result of a transition from initial, individual authentication to data origin authentication. It is the source (origin) of the data sent between two systems—for example, between a user's desktop and a server—that is being authenticated rather than the user per se. A further technical distinction is sometimes applied. If the authentication mechanism ensures the timeliness of the communication and thus provides protection against attacks that replay old messages, the service is referred to as "peer-entity authentication."

Individual authentication increasingly takes place in the context of information systems, and thus all of the flavors of authentication described above are relevant to this discussion of individual authentication technologies.

BASIC TYPES OF AUTHENTICATION MECHANISMS

By the mid-1970s, three basic classes of authentication technologies for use with information systems had been identified.[2] They are colloquially characterized as "something you know, something you have, and something you are" and were discussed abstractly in Chapter 2. This section focuses on specific technological examples of each of these basic classes. In the first class are authentication technologies based on what an individual can memorize (know). Passwords and personal identifica-

---

[2]D.E. Raphael and J.R. Young. *Automated Personal Identification*. Stanford Research Institute International, 1974; National Bureau of Standards. "Evaluation Techniques for Human Identification." FIPSPUB-48, April 1977.

tion numbers (PINs) are the canonical examples of such technology. In the "something you have" class are physical objects that are (assumed to be) hard to forge or to alter, such as magnetic-stripe cards, smart cards, SecurID cards, and so on. The object is issued to an identified individual and retained by the individual, so that possession of the object serves to identify the individual. In the last class are biometric authentication technologies, which measure physical and behavioral characteristics of an individual. Each of these classes of authentication technologies has advantages and limitations with regard to security, usability, and cost.

Something You Know

Simple, password-based authentication is the most common form of initial, one-way authentication used in information systems. A user remembers a short string of characters (typically six to eight) and presents the character string to a system for verification when requested. The string of characters is reused many times in authenticating to the same system; hence the passwords are usually referred to as "static." This sort of system is susceptible to many forms of attack. Because users have trouble choosing and remembering values with a significant number of "random" bits, passwords generally are vulnerable to guessing attacks. Unless passwords are protected (usually this means encrypted) for transmission over communication paths, they are subject to interception and subsequent use by a wiretapper. The lack of two-way authentication means that a user can be tricked into revealing a password if he or she connects to an attacker instead of to the desired system.

Password-based authentication is cheap to implement; it may not require any explicit software purchases. It is easy for users and developers to understand, so training costs are low. But, on a life-cycle basis, passwords are expensive for an organization to administer, largely because of the costs of help-desk support for users who forget passwords. Users find passwords difficult to manage as they deal with a growing number of systems that require them. This leads to password reuse (that is, using the same password for multiple systems) and insecure storage of passwords (for example, in unencrypted files on computers). Both of these practices undermine the security of password-based systems. In the former case, if one system is compromised and the passwords used in it become known, other systems in which the user employs the same passwords could be compromised. That is, compromise of the user's desktop or laptop or personal digital assistant (PDA) compromises all of the passwords employed by that user to access many other systems.

Many of the common recommendations for improving the security of passwords without changing the fundamental mechanisms involved trade one form of insecurity for another. For example, if users are encouraged to choose passwords that are hard to guess, they will probably have to record the passwords somewhere (because these passwords are not easily remembered), making them vulnerable to attacks against the stored passwords. Users are encouraged to change passwords periodically, which also increases the likelihood of recording the passwords in vulnerable locations.

Passwords are easily shared. A user can tell others his or her password; in many situations this is common and even encouraged as a sign of trust.[3] Passwords can also be shared inadvertently, as they are often written down in semipublic places.[4] This is not always a serious problem if the threat model focuses primarily on outsiders, but insiders represent threats in many contexts, and users often do not consider this type of threat when sharing passwords or recording them.

In principle, passwords can offer a great deal of anonymity. In practice, however, most people cannot remember many different passwords, and they tend to reuse the same passwords for different purposes. Moreover, if allowed to select an identifier as well as a password, the user may choose to use the same values for multiple systems. This makes it potentially easy to link multiple accounts to the same user across system boundaries, even though the base technology does not necessarily impose such linkages. Additionally, the recovery mechanisms for lost passwords generally require one's mother's maiden name, an e-mail address, or some other form of personal information. Thus, the infrastructure for password maintenance often requires sharing other forms of information that is personal and so presumed to be less likely to be forgotten (see Box 5.1). This, too, potentially undermines privacy.

> **Finding 5.1: Static passwords are the most commonly used form of user authentication, but they are also the source of many system security weaknesses, especially because they are often used inappropriately.**
>
> **Recommendation 5.1: Users should be educated with respect to the weaknesses of static passwords. System designers must consider trade-offs between usability and security when deploying authentication systems that rely on static passwords to ensure that the protections provided are commensurate with**

---

[3]D. Weirich and M.A. Sasse. "Persuasive Password Security." *Proceedings of CHI 2001 Conference on Human Factors in Computing Systems,* Seattle, Wash., April 2001.

[4]J. Nielsen, "Security and Human Factors," Useit.com's Alertbox, November 26, 2000. Accessed on March 26, 2002, at <http://www.useit.com/alertbox/20001126.html>.

BOX 5.1
Knowledge-Based Authentication

A form of authentication with similarities to both passwords and challenge/response is knowledge-based authentication. In this case, users present data elements that the verifier can approve on the basis of previous transactions and registration activity. For example, the Internal Revenue Service (IRS) and a number of state revenue agencies have implemented an electronic signature and authentication technique that relies on a taxpayer's presenting data from the previous year's transaction. In addition to checking traditional identifying information presented on a tax return, such as the tax identification number and date of birth, these tax authorities have the taxpayer sign a tax return by entering data from the previous year's tax return. For instance, at the federal level, the IRS electronic authentication program for tax year 2001 allowed the taxpayer to sign his or her return with a self-selected PIN. The IRS verifies the identity of the taxpayer using the self-selected PIN when the taxpayer provides the adjusted gross income (AGI) for tax year 2000. In subsequent years, the taxpayer has the choice of using the same or a different PIN, but must update the AGI data for each previous tax year. By using the data from the previous year's return, the IRS is able to authenticate the transaction on the basis of knowledge that presumably only the IRS, the taxpayer, and whoever might have prepared the return for the taxpayer possesses. This type of authentication relies heavily on the data in question being kept secure. (Chapter 6 in this report provides more information on electronic authentication in the IRS e-file program and the distinction between electronic signatures and authentication.)

Similarly, the popular online payment site paypal.com deposits a small amount into a user's bank account and asks the user for the amount deposited. In effect, so-called knowledge-based authentication is a form of password. The crucial difference is that it is communicated to the user via some out-of-hand mechanism to which an imposter is presumed not to have access. Additionally, it is assumed that the legitimate user will look up the authenticator rather than know it; this is no different from a conventional password that is written down. The crucial distinction is that knowledge-based technology generally relies on a prior history of contact between the client and the verifier.

the risk and harm from a potential compromise of such an authentication solution. Great care should be taken in the design of systems that rely on static passwords.

More secure authentication technologies can be based on password technology at some levels. For example, schemes such as encrypted key exchange (EKE)[5] and Kerberos (a network authentication protocol)[6] also

---

[5]S. Bellovin and M. Merritt. "Encrypted Key Exchange: Password-Based Protocols Secure Against Dictionary Attacks." *Proceedings of the IEEE Symposium on Security and Privacy.* Oak-

make use of static passwords. These schemes employ sophisticated cryptographic mechanisms and protocols to counter many of the attacks that are effective against static passwords. They typically provide one-way, initial authentication, which may transition to two-way, data-origin and peer-entity authentication for subsequent communication. These are not, per se, password-based authentication technologies. The section "Multifactor Authentication" discusses in more detail authentication protocols of this sort.

Something You Have

The "something you have" class of authentication technologies is based on the possession of some form of physical token that is presumed to be hard to forge or alter. Many forms of physical tokens are used for authentication and for authorization outside the context of information systems, and they exhibit varying degrees of resistance to forgery and alteration. For example, many driver's licenses and credit cards make use of holograms as a deterrent to forgery, relying on visual verification by a human being when they are presented. Yet credit cards are now used extensively for purchases by mail or telephone or over the Web. In these contexts, there is no visual verification of the credential, so the antitamper security mechanisms are ineffective. In information systems, the security of hardware tokens, to first order, is usually based on the ability of these devices to store, and maybe make direct use of, one or more secret values. Each of these secrets can be much larger and more random than typical passwords, so physical tokens address some of the vulnerabilities, such as guessability, cited above for passwords. Nonetheless, the simplest forms of tokens share some of the same vulnerabilities as passwords—that is, they both deal with static, secret values.

A magnetic-stripe card is an example of a simple physical authentication token. Tokens of this sort offer the primary benefit of storing larger secrets, but they offer almost no protection if the token is lost or stolen, because readers are readily available and can extract all data (secrets) from the magnetic stripe. After a secret is read from the card (even in the context of a legitimate authentication process), the secret is vulnerable in the same ways that a password is (for example, it can be intercepted if transmitted via an insecure communication channel or compromised

---

land, Calif., May 1992, pp. 72-84. Available online at <http://citeseer.nj.nec.com/bellovin92encrypted.html>.

[6]More information on Kerberos is available online at <http://web.mit.edu/kerberos/www/>.

BOX 5.2
New York City Transit Metrocard

The New York Metropolitan Transportation Authority uses a magnetic-stripe fare card called a Metrocard. The Metrocard is accepted on all New York City buses and subway trains. A magnetic stripe on the card holds the stored value information; however, the same information is recorded on a central computer system. Thus, although the card appears to be an anonymous-bearer instrument, transactions charged to a particular card are logged. While this feature is primarily an antifraud device, it has in fact been used by police agencies to verify suspects' movements. Furthermore, since cards may be purchased by credit card, the potential exists to track an individual even without possession of the individual's physical card.

Tho privacy implications of this system have been known for some time. A 1997 study[1] on multipurpose fare media not only discussed the privacy issue but also found that it was indeed a major concern of consumers. Fare cards have a modest amount of storage and no computational ability. Because they are copyable, there is a need for consultation with the central site.

---

[1] *Transit Cooperative Research Program Research Results Digest,* June 1997, available online at < http://gulliver.trb.org/publications/tcrp/tcrp_rrd_16.pdf>.

---

while held in storage in a computer[7]). When a magnetic-stripe card is swiped, all the data can be read from the card and become accessible to malicious software in the system. This possible misuse argues against storing the secrets used to authenticate multiple, distinct identities on one card. (The storage space on cards of this sort also is very limited.) Conversely, requiring a user to carry multiple physical cards to maintain multiple secrets is inconvenient for the user and adds to overall costs. Although magnetic-stripe cards and their readers are not very expensive, computer systems (other than in retail sales contexts) generally do not offer readers as standard equipment, so there are cost barriers to the use of such cards for individual authentication in home or corporate environments. This is a good example of trade-offs among competing goals of security, user convenience, and cost. Sometimes applications for magnetic cards focus on authorization rather than authentication, as in the case of transit fare cards (see Box 5.2).

---

[7]In a well-designed system, a secret read from a card would not be retained in storage on the system for very long, and the vulnerability here would be much less than when passwords are stored in a file.

A not-so-obvious form of "something you have" authentication is a Web cookie. The need for cookies arises because the protocol used for Web access, hypertext transfer protocol (HTTP), is "stateless"; HTTP does not provide a reliable way for a server to know that a particular request is coming from the same user as a previous request.[8] Pure stateless operation would make it difficult to provide functions such as browsing through an online catalog and collecting a "shopping cart" full of items that the user has decided to purchase. Also, if the user is browsing through information that needs authentication (such as information about the user's bank account), it would be inconvenient if the user had to type a name and password each time a different page was viewed.

The solution to this problem, designed by Netscape, is called a "cookie." A cookie is data given by a Web server to the client to maintain state. Each time a client makes a request to a server, any cookies provided to the client by that server are sent to the server along with the request. Thus, for example, the identifier and password provided by a user for initial authentication may be transformed into a cookie to facilitate continuous authentication of the HTTP session. Sometimes a cookie is a bigger secret than an individual could remember. It may be like a secret stored in a token; in this case, the token is the user's computer, with all the attendant security problems that arise from storing secrets in a file on a computer and the problems that arise if the secret is transmitted across a communication network without encryption. Sometimes a cookie is used to track an individual's authorization in the context of an HTTP session. In such cases, the cookie itself may be a cryptographically protected value in order to prevent a user from tampering with it and thus fooling the Web server.

The use of cookies is often criticized as a mechanism that violates privacy, but it depends on how they are used. If they are used solely to effect session continuity, overcoming the limitations of HTTP, and if the server does not maintain information about the user, they can be a privacy-neutral or even privacy-enhancing technology. But cookies are sometimes used to track a user's movements through multiple sites. Many sites that do not require authentication will set a cookie on the first visit. This lets the site track return visits by presumably the same user, even though the site operators do not know who that person is in a larger context. Often, this technique is employed by third-party advertising

---

[8]The statelessness of the HTTP protocol implies that each request sent for a page is completely independent of any requests that came before. Thus preserving information from one click to the next requires additional technology (D. Kristol and L. Montulli, "HTTP State Management Mechanism," Request for Comments (RFC) 2965).

sites; this use of cookies permits tracking users (and their interests) across multiple Web sites. This is a form of covert identification (see Chapter 1); the user's identity as a Web site visitor and a dossier of his or her activity are compiled and retained, and an identifier in the form of the cookie is assigned. It is not necessary to use cookies to track user activity, however. Even if cookies were banned, it would still be possible to track a user's Web history through other mechanisms such as log files, browser caches, and browser history files.[9]

Smart cards are credit-card-size tokens that contain memory and, often, a processor. Smart cards that act only as memory devices are essentially as vulnerable as magnetic-stripe cards in terms of extracting the secrets stored on the cards, because readers are widely available, and malicious software can extract stored values from the card. The costs for these cards is somewhat higher than those for magnetic-stripe cards, and smart card readers are more expensive as well, but smart storage cards offer more data storage than magnetic-stripe cards do, and they resist wear better.[10] Universal Serial Bus (USB) storage tokens are another hardware storage token format. They have a potential advantage in that many PCs offer USB interfaces, thus eliminating reader cost and availability as barriers to deployment.

Tokens that act only as storage devices may be used to provide initial, one-way authentication analogous to static passwords. However, because these devices can hold larger, "more random" secret values (that is, an arbitrary collection of bits as opposed to something meaningful or mnemonic to a person), they can provide somewhat better security. Increasingly, tokens of this sort are being used to bootstrap continuous data-origin authentication schemes that are implemented using the processing capabilities of a computer to which the token is (locally) connected. (Recall that the authentication taking place here is authenticating a local computer to a remote computer, not a person to a remote computer.) These schemes are often challenge/response protocols, as described below. Since these protocols are executed in the computer, not the

---

[9]So-called "Web bugs" are another mechanism used to surreptitiously observe an individual's actions online. They are objects, usually one-pixel-square graphic images, embedded within the HTML source on a Web site that cause part of the displayed Web page to be retrieved from another Web site, thereby transmitting information about the requester to a third party. Web bugs are used on a surprisingly large number of sites, primarily for statistical purposes and to gauge the effectiveness of advertising. The information transmitted to the "bugger" includes an IP address and the last site visited and may be linked to cookies to collect individual Web surfing profiles. Web bugs are also embedded in e-mail messages by spammers, who use them to validate live addresses.

[10]The magnetic stripe can abrade, and the data records on it may be degraded by exposure to magnetic fields.

token, they also can make use of secrets stored in the computer rather than on separate hardware storage tokens. The term "software token" has been coined to refer to the use of secrets stored on a computer and employed in conjunction with an authentication protocol. Software tokens are not as secure as hardware storage tokens, since the secrets used by the software are held in files in a computer on a long-term basis. At best, these secrets typically are protected by a password. Thus, any attack against the computer that compromises these files allows an attacker to retrieve the stored secrets through password-guessing attacks. In contrast, a well-designed authentication technology that uses a hardware storage token would read the secret(s) stored on the token, use them, then erase them from the computer memory as quickly as possible. These actions present a smaller window of opportunity for the compromise of the secret(s), making the use of hardware storage tokens potentially more secure. The main attraction of software tokens is the low cost; the software may be free or inexpensive, and there is no need to buy token readers.

Some of the earliest hardware authentication tokens[11] and some of the most popular ones employed today, such as SecurID (see Box 5.3), do not interface directly with an authentication system. Instead, the user is required to act as an interface, relaying information between an information system and the token. Tokens of this sort typically implement a type of authentication known as algorithmic challenge/response, or just challenge/response. Challenge/response schemes operate much like human-enacted authentication scenarios. Most movie goers would recognize the words "Halt! Who goes there?" as the beginning of a challenge/response exchange between a guard and an individual approaching a guarded area. The password in such a scenario would usually change daily, consistent with human limitations for adapting to new passwords. In an online authentication technology, the challenge can change every time, making the corresponding response unique in order to thwart eavesdropping attacks.

Challenge/response schemes are a generic technique to prove knowledge of a secret, sometimes even without disclosing it to the party performing the authentication check.[12] Challenge/response schemes are analogous to Intruder: Friend or foe (IFF) systems originally developed

---

[11]J. Herman, S. Kent, and P. Sevcik. "Personal Authentication System for Access Control to the Defense Data Network." *Proceedings of the 15th Annual IEEE Electronics and Aerospace Systems Conference* (EASCON), September 1982.

[12]Research into a class of algorithms known as "zero knowledge algorithms" is moving work forward in this area. As a starting point for what this work involves, see S. Goldwasser, S. Micali, and C. Rackoff, "The Knowledge Complexity of Interactive Proof-Systems," in *Proceedings of the Seventeenth Annual ACM Symposium on Theory of Computing*,

---

BOX 5.3
SecurID

RSA Security (formerly Security Dynamics) markets a challenge/response card. This card, trademarked SecurID, contains a built-in clock and a liquid crystal display. Rather than requiring the user to obtain a challenge from a host computer, the challenge is implicitly the current time. To gain access, the user merely enters a user ID and then enters the current number displayed on the card. The number displayed changes periodically, usually every 30 seconds to 1 minute depending on the card configuration.

The SecurID has become quite popular in some contexts. It is relatively easy (though not especially convenient) to use, it requires no special hardware, and it is easily integrated with existing, password-style authentication software. Some versions of the card require the user to enter a PIN into the card (where it is combined with the card-resident key), making this into a two-factor authentication system. In this case, even if an adversary acquires a card, the ability to impersonate the affected user depends on guessing the PIN. If the usual practice of monitoring failed log-in attempts is being followed, an adversary guessing PINs for use with a captured card will probably be detected prior to guessing the PIN.

---

by the military for automated authentication of aircraft by ground personnel operating antiaircraft batteries. Although challenge/response systems for information systems were originally implemented using hardware tokens, software tokens now are employed frequently for this purpose and there are manual analogs. Imagine a large sheet of paper with many different numbered passwords. The verifier sends the number; the presenter sends back the corresponding password (which illustrates why these systems are sometimes called one-time password schemes). In practice, the verifier sends some string of characters to the presenter (user); the presenter computes a response value based on that string and on a secret known to the user. This response value is checked by the verifier and serves as the "password" for only one transaction or session. As typically employed in a user-to-system authentication exchange, this is an example of a one-way initial authentication scheme, but

---

New York, ACM Press; O. Goldreich and H. Krawczyk, 1985, "On the Composition of Zero-Knowledge Proof Systems," *Proceedings of 17th International Colloquium on Automata, Languages and Programming* (ICALP), Coventry, U.K, July 16-20, 1990; U. Fiege, A. Fiat, and A. Shamir, "Zero Knowledge Proofs of Identity," *Proceedings of the Nineteenth Annual ACM Conference on Theory of Computing,* New York, ACM Press, 1987; and J. J. Quisquater and L. Guillou, "How to Explain Zero-knowledge Protocols to Your Children," *Advances in Cryptology (Crypto '89),* Springer-Verlag, pp. 628-631, 1990.

it is much more secure, relative to a variety of threats, than are static passwords.

There are many variations on this scheme: Often a shared secret known to both the presenter and the verifier can be used to generate and verify the response. In schemes based on public key cryptosystems, a presenter may employ a private key to generate a response that the verifier checks using the corresponding public key associated with the presenter. These operations can be carried out using software (such as S/Key[13]), or the user may employ a hardware token to perform the calculation. (See Box 5.4, on how such a technology might be used.)

Hardware tokens that contain processors (for example, cryptographic processor smart cards, PC cards, some proximity cards,[14] or USB processor tokens) are qualitatively different from all of the previous token types. They can be much more secure than hardware storage tokens or software tokens, because they can maintain secret values within the card and never export them (i.e., transmit secrets off the card). A smart card typically performs cryptographic operations in the card, using stored secret values to execute parts of an authentication protocol, such as a challenge/response protocol, on behalf of the cardholder. With a token capable of cryptographic operations, the secrets contained in the token are not exposed as a result of inserting the token into a reader, and no secrets are released to the computers to which the readers are attached or transmitted across a communication path. Typically, a user must enter a PIN to enable a smart card token, and the entry of a wrong PIN value multiple times in succession (logically) disables the token. This provides some protection in case the card is lost or stolen. Nonetheless, capable adver-

---

[13]See L. Lamport, "Password Authentication with Insecure Communication," *Communications of the ACM* 24(11)(November 1981):770-772, and Phil Karn's reference implementation of S/Key described in Neil Haller, "The S/Key One-Time Password System," RFC 1760, February 1995; available online at <http://www.faqs.org/rfcs/rfc1760.html>.

[14]A proximity card contains information stored electronically within the card. The information is transmitted via radio over a short distance (typically less than 10 centimeters) after the card is queried. Users like these cards because they require very few steps to perform authentication and therefore are quite fast. These cards are vulnerable to physical attacks that extract data from them. They also may be susceptible to interception of the transmitted data (over a short distance) and to spoofing attacks, in which the attacker transmits the same sort of query as a legitimate verifier and records the response. For disabled users, proximity cards may be attractive alternatives to magnetic-stripe cards since card readers for the former have instructions that are typically visual, they are not always located in positions accessible to those in wheelchairs, and they are hard to insert for those whose manual dexterity is poor. For more, see John Gill and J.N. Slater, "Nightmare on Smart Street," *Tiresias: International Information on Visual Disability*, 2002 (updated), available online at <http://www.tiresias.org/reports/tidecon2.htm>.

BOX 5.4
Token-Based Authentication System: A Scenario

Laura visits BestCare hospital for a chronic illness that requires many laboratory tests and radiological examinations. Dr. Jones, her physician, inquires whether Laura has an Internet-connected computer at her home that she can use to connect to BestCare's Web-based patient information portal. This portal can be used to check results, communicate with various health care providers, request and check clinic scheduling information, view physician-recommended literature, and join health-care-related chat groups. Since Laura has been having a difficult time scheduling her visits by phone and is finding it hard to ask informed questions of her physician during her visits, she eagerly accepts the offer. Dr. Jones then records Laura's acceptance in her computerized record and tells her she will have to click on some health-related pop-up advertisements to receive free access.

BestCare's Web-based patient information center allows patients to check their records and communicate with doctors at their convenience, without having to schedule an appointment. Such a utility saves time for both doctor and patient and helps BestCare honor its commitment to providing continuous care to patients with chronic illnesses. Statistics collected from patients' visits to the site help Dr. Jones with her research in chronic disease management, and BestCare receives additional revenue from healthcare companies in exchange for posting their advertisements on the site.

Because BestCare has decided to require additional security measures protecting patient records from unauthorized access through its Web site, Laura is given a token card in addition to a user ID and a password. At home, Laura asks her son to help; he configures the Web browser, enables the token, and changes the password from the one given to her at the hospital. From now on, Laura will enter her new password in her token card, which then displays a different password that she enters with her user ID to access the portal. She is required to read and accept the privacy notice, which she only skims in her rush to get to the portal. When the portal displays a message that her test results are pending, her son— who is still looking over her shoulder—is curious about the tests. Not wanting to upset her son with information about her unconfirmed diagnosis, Laura decides that she will keep the token in a secure place so that only she can access the portal in the future.

Dr. Jones carries a similar token card to access clinical information about her patients. The system only requires her to use the token when she is not accessing the information from a workstation directly connected to the BestCare network. This reduces the human-effort cost for the care providers but means that the BestCare network must maintain good security with standard firewalls and intrusion detection.

Several parties have been involved in setting up and maintaining the patient information portal. BestCare has outsourced its information technology to Helpful-IT, Inc., and has set up its Internet portal business with its medical records vendor, GoodMedRec Co., which hosts its Web servers and databases with BetterASP, Inc. BestCare has also contracted with several pharmaceutical, nursing home, and

(continues)

BOX 5.4 Continued

other health care companies to advertise their services on its site. It arranged the contracts through an Internet advertising management company named FineClick.

In this scenario, several sets of information are collected. HelpfulIT manages user ID/token/password information in an authentication database. GoodMedRec manages user ID and user demographic information and clinical information in a database. Every time Laura signs on, BetterASP maintains user ID/IP address mappings in its audit systems for performance and billing purposes. On behalf of BestCare, GoodMedRec provides FineClick with an abbreviated set of "clinical codes of interest" in order to conduct customized marketing, and FineClick maintains clinical codes and IP address information for billing.

Authentication/Authorization/Identification

Laura is authorized to view only her own records, not those of other patients. Two-factor authentication, using something she knows (the password) and something she has (the token card), prevents Laura from accessing information that she does not have permission to see. The system records Laura's user ID and date and time of access every time she looks at her records online. Such identification protects BestCare from liability. Laura might also need to identify herself if she wants to ask a doctor a question that pertains to her own medical record. She is not required to identify herself when she searches for general health information, uses the chat groups, or explores advertisements.

Because it is time-consuming for BestCare staff to continually update the Web portal's record of which patient is assigned to which physician, all physicians using the system have been given access to all patient files. Again, it is important for legal reasons to know who has looked at a patient's records, so when Dr. Jones accesses Laura's record using the system, she must be identified and logged as the person who has seen the record.

Two-factor authentication also protects doctor and patient from unauthorized access by outsiders. Even if Laura's token card is stolen, her medical record is safe as long as the thief does not know Laura's password. Unfortunately, Laura has written down her password because she is afraid she might forget it; in doing so, she has made her information more vulnerable.

Dr. Jones is similarly protected from token card theft. However, Dr. Jones has shared her user ID and password with her assistant, who is not otherwise authorized to view confidential patient records. Although Dr. Jones has no reason to doubt her assistant's trustworthiness, such sharing exposes the medical records of all BestCare's patients to unauthorized access and tampering, whether malicious or purely accidental.

There is a downside to using tokens as extra security measures to protect against unauthorized access to medical records; authorized users might be denied access at inconvenient times because of a lost or malfunctioning token. In this scenario, if Dr. Jones is away from the office and her token card is lost or broken, she cannot view Laura's questions as soon as they are asked and Laura's health might be compromised. However, if it becomes common practice for Dr. Jones and her colleagues to circumvent such security measures by calling the office and asking another physician or an administrative assistant to access the record,

Laura's privacy may be compromised. Although BestCare's privacy policies may explicitly address this issue, Laura may not understand its implications.

Breaches

The vice president of HelpfulIT, Inc., is told that patients are having problems accessing its systems from home, and he suspects these problems are associated with FineClick's advertisement-download process. An audit log analysis is initiated, and a staff programmer correlates user IDs, IP addresses, clinical codes, and advertisement clicks from different sources in a spreadsheet. A problem is found in specific codes and advertisements, and it is fixed. The spreadsheet is posted to the help desk as a solution for a possible problem.

Now Laura's clinical data are being used, shared, and cited to resolve an operational problem. The staff member at HelpfulIT, Inc., who resolved the problem does not have medical records access for patients but is now able to combine the user ID, IP address, and types of advertisements (each collected from different interactions) to determine which patient suffers from which illness.

Another major problem relates to the safekeeping of the databases. In light of the increasing number of identified vulnerabilities in systems such as BetterASP's Web servers, the increasing sophistication of attack methods, and the inertia of system administrators when it comes to patching their systems, it is easier than ever to compromise many information systems. Sometimes, inadvertent mistakes lead to the publication of private information over the Internet without adequate authentication and encryption. Misuse and accidental errors by insiders contribute to serious privacy problems.

Although such potential breaches of security and compromises to privacy are sobering to consider, Laura's main concern is that her family remain unaware of her condition until she knows more facts and can share them at the time of her choosing. Back home, Laura's son uses the computer after she is finished exploring BestCare's portal. He clicks the "Back" button on the open browser window and, curious, clicks several more times, eventually reaching a disease management site that Laura had been browsing. His level of concern rising, he checks the browser's history file to identify the last sites visited. On the basis of this indirect and incomplete information, he concludes that his mother is seriously ill and, in a state of great emotion, confronts her. Laura is forced to explain her disease to her son before she is ready to do so.

Privacy Intrusiveness

Token cards are reasonable authentication methods from a security perspective, and this scenario describes how they might be used in a particular context. Potential privacy violations, however, are a result of faults in overall system protection. The scenario demonstrates that the choice of information delivery technology, the decision to allow access by ostensibly uninterested parties for maintenance purposes, and human factors such as password sharing for the sake of convenience, may open up unforeseen vulnerabilities. Many of these same privacy concerns could, however, arise with authentication technologies not based on token cards. How systems are implemented and deployed, and what policies are put in place to govern their usage, all bear on what the privacy implications of authentication systems will be.

saries with access to sophisticated technology (of the sort that might commonly be found in a college physics lab) can extract secret values stored on smart cards.[15] Processor tokens are noticeably more expensive than magnetic-stripe cards or other storage tokens. The cost of readers varies, depending on which token technology is employed.

Often a token of this sort is used only for initial one- or two-way authentication,[16] based on the execution of the cryptographic operations of a challenge/response protocol within the token. This provides a secure foundation for two-way, continuous authentication schemes based on this initial exchange. Responsibility for continuous authentication often is borne by the computer to which the smart card is attached, because smart card interfaces are too slow to deal with all the data transmitted or received on a connection. However, the continuous authentication bootstrapped from a smart card offers the opportunity for better security overall.

Hardware tokens have the desirable security property of not being able to be readily replicated by users, although the difficulty of unauthorized replication varies widely, as noted above. In principle, if one user chooses to share his or her token with another, the first user relinquishes the ability to authenticate himself or herself as long as the hardware token is loaned. This guarantee is diminished with some forms of hardware storage tokens and with software tokens, since one can copy the files that personalize them. The extent to which tokens preclude sharing represents a significant improvement over static passwords. A necessary corollary to this observation is that the loss of any token results in a replacement cost, and the replacement process is more difficult than for a password. A help desk cannot remotely replace a token in the way that it can reset a password. Hardware cryptographic tokens and software tokens entail costs for integration into applications because they execute authentication protocols rather than act just as repositories for secrets.

Something You Are

The final class of technologies—"something you are"— refers to the use of biometrics to authenticate individuals. Biometric authentication, which has received much attention in the media of late, is the automatic

---

[15]See, for example, R. Anderson and M. Kuhn, "Tamper Resistance—A Cautionary Note," *The Second USENIX Workshop on Electronic Commerce Proceedings*, Oakland, Calif., November 18-21, 1996.

[16]Typically, two-way authentication relies on the use of public key cryptography and certificates.

identification or identity verification of human individuals on the basis of behavioral and physiological characteristics.[17]

Biometric authentication is fundamentally different from the other two classes because it does not rely on secrets. Biometrics themselves are not secrets; people commonly leave fingerprints on everything they touch. Our voice, handwriting, and facial image can be captured without our knowledge. Rather, biometric authentication relies on registering and later matching what are believed to be distinguishing physical or behavioral characteristics of individuals. There are many different examples of biometric authentication: it can be based on fingerprints, iris scanning, voice analysis, handwriting dynamics, keystroke dynamics, and so on.

Biometric authentication operates by matching measured physical characteristics of a person against a template or a generating model of these characteristics that was created when the person was registered with an authentication system. The match between a captured biometric and the template is never exact, because of the "noise" associated with the measurement processes, the way the characteristic is presented to the sensor, and changes in the underlying biometric characteristic itself. Thus, these technologies require an administrator to set threshold values and a decision policy that controls how close the match must be and how many attempts to be authenticated the user will be allowed to make.

The scoring aspect of biometrics is a major departure from other classes of individual authentication technologies, which provide a simple, binary determination of whether an authentication attempt was successful. The scoring aspect of biometric authentication technologies means that they exhibit Type I (false negative) and Type II (false positive) errors. Type I errors run the risk of inconveniencing or even alienating individuals whose authentication attempts are erroneously rejected. Type II errors are security and privacy failures, as they represent authentication decisions that might allow unauthorized access. For any specific biometric technology implementation, there is a trade-off between these two types of errors: Changing the scoring to reduce Type I errors increases Type II errors, and vice versa. Some implementations of biometric authentication technologies exhibit relatively poor tradeoffs between these two error types, forcing an administrator to choose between inconveniencing legitimate users while rejecting (appropriately) almost all imposter attempts, or minimizing inconvenience to legitimate users while accepting a higher rate of successful imposters.

---

[17]J.L. Wayman, "Fundamentals of Biometric Authentication Technologies," *International Journal of Imaging and Graphics* 1(1)(2001); B. Miller, "Everything You Need to Know About Biometrics," *PIN Industry Sourcebook*, Warfel and Miller, 1989.

Biometric values that are captured for authentication and transmitted to a remote location for verification must be protected in transit. They are vulnerable to interception and replay, just like (static) passwords, unless suitably protected during transmission across communication networks. It also is important to ensure that the transmitted value represents a legitimate, digitized sample of a user biometric. Otherwise, an attacker might inject a string of bits that purports to be a biometric sample in an effort to subvert the system. Typically (though not always), the range of possible values for a biometric sample is so large that guessing is not a viable means of attack. But since biometric values are not secrets per se, it is conceivable that an attacker has gained access to a user's fingerprint, for example, and has digitized it in an effort to masquerade as the user. Moreover, if unencrypted (or weakly encrypted) biometric templates are stored in centralized authentication servers, an attack against one of these servers could result in the disclosure of the templates for all the users registered with the compromised server. With access to the templates and knowledge of the scoring algorithm, an attacker could engage in off-line analysis to synthesize bit strings that would pass as legitimate biometric samples for specific users.

Today biometric authentication systems are not widely deployed, and there are many implementation variants for the same type of biometric (for example, a plethora of fingerprint systems). However, if biometric authentication were to become widely deployed and if there were significant consolidation and standardization in the industry (resulting in fewer variants), the compromise of an authentication server could have a very significant impact owing to the special characteristics of biometrics: namely, that they are not secret and cannot be easily modified.

As with hardware tokens, the deployment of biometric authentication sensors entails hardware-acquisition costs, although the cost here is typically for each access point of a system rather than for each user of the system. Sensors for biometric authentication have been expensive, and this has been a barrier to adoption. However, the cost of some biometric sensors, especially fingerprint-scanning sensors, has declined, making them affordable for use in individual computers and laptops. Although all biometric measures change over time, an individual cannot forget his or her biometric values, unlike passwords and PINs, nor can they be lost, like hardware tokens. Thus, life-cycle costs can, in principle, be lower for biometric authentication technologies, primarily because of reduced help-desk costs. However, in practice, most biometric authentication systems require the use of a password or PIN to improve security, and this eliminates the cost advantage that would have accrued from fewer help-desk calls. In fact, one can improve the performance of biometric authentication systems in some contexts by offering an alternative authentication mechanism for some individuals who are not compatible with a specific technology. (For example, some percentage of the general population has fingerprints that are not well recognized by fingerprint scanners.)

Finding 5.2: Biometric user-authentication technologies hold the promise of improved user convenience. Vendors of these technologies also promise reduced system management costs, but this has yet to be demonstrated in practice. Moreover, these technologies can pose serious privacy and security concerns if employed in systems that make use of servers to compare biometric samples against stored templates (as is the case in many large-scale systems). Their use in very local contexts (for example, to control access to a laptop or smart card) generally poses fewer security and privacy concerns.

Recommendation 5.2: Biometric technologies should not be used to authenticate users via remote authentication servers because of the potential for large-scale privacy and security compromises in the event of a successful attack (either internal or external) against such servers. The use of biometrics for local authentication—for example, to control access to a private key on a smart card—is a more appropriate type of use for biometrics.

Biometric authentication offers only one-way initial authentication. As noted above, biometric authentication does not provide direct protection for secrets, so it does not provide a basis for bootstrapping from initial to continuous authentication, nor does it support two-way authentication, unlike many of the "something you have" technologies described above. Thus, biometric authentication is not an appropriate replacement for other authentication technologies, specifically for cryptographic technologies used to provide two-way initial authentication and continuous authentication. Box 5.5 provides some commonsense guidelines for the uses of biometric authentication systems.

MULTIFACTOR AUTHENTICATION

It is often asserted that individual authentication can be improved by employing multiple "factors." Generally this translates into using authentication technologies from two of the classes described above. Examples include a PIN plus a hardware token (something you know and something you have) or a PIN and a biometric (something you know and something you are). There is a reasonable basis for this strategy, but it is

---

BOX 5.5
Items to Keep in Mind When Using Biometrics

1. Never design or use a biometric system that allows either remote enrollment or re-enrollment. Such systems have no good way of connecting a user with the enrolled biometric record other than additional authentication, so the advantage of using biometrics is lost.

2. Biometric measures can reveal your identity if they are linked at enrollment or at subsequent usage to your name, Social Security number, or other identifying information.

3. Remember that biometric measures cannot be reissued if stolen or sold. Consequently, your biometric measures will be only as secure as the most insecure site that has them. Do not enroll in a system that does not seek to preserve anonymity unless you have complete trust in the system administration.

4. All biometric access-control systems must have exception-handling mechanisms for those individuals who either cannot enroll or cannot reliably use the system for whatever reason. If you are uncomfortable with enrolling in a biometric system for positive identification, insist on routinely using the exception-handling mechanism instead.

5. The most secure and most privacy-sensitive biometric systems are those in which each user controls his or her own template. However, simply controlling your own biometric template, say by holding it on a token, does not guarantee either privacy or security.

6. Because biometric measures are not perfectly repeatable, are not completely distinctive, and require specialized data collection hardware, biometric systems are not useful for tracking people. Anyone who wants to physically track you will use your credit card purchases, phone records, or cell phone emanations instead. Anyone wanting to track your Internet transactions will do so with cookies, Web logs, or other technologies.

---

not foolproof. The assumption underlying the perceived security benefits of multifactor authentication is that the failure modes for different factors are largely independent. So, for example, a hardware token might be lost or stolen, but the PIN required for use with the token would not be lost or stolen at the same time. This assumption is not always true, however. For example, a PIN attached to a hardware token is compromised at the same time that the token is lost or stolen. If a fingerprint is used to activate a hardware token, is it not likely that copies of the fingerprint will appear on the token itself? As noted earlier, one cannot evaluate the relative security of mechanisms without reference to a threat model, and some threat models undermine the perceived security of multifactor authentication. Nonetheless, multifactor authentication can improve the security of authentication under many circumstances.

CENTRALIZED VERSUS DECENTRALIZED
AUTHENTICATION SYSTEMS

A crucial issue for authentication technologies is whether they are inherently centralized or decentralized. This distinction affects both their deployability and their privacy implications.

Some technologies require little or no infrastructure; any system can make use of such technologies without relying on additional systems for support. This is one of the major drivers of the use of static passwords: They are extremely easy to set up in a highly localized fashion. An application can create and maintain its own password database with about the same effort as that needed for maintaining a database of authorized users. (In fact, doing so properly is rather more complex, but there are numerous poorly implemented password systems.) Some public key authentication technologies have similar decentralized properties. Some challenge/response protocols are designed for local use and require minimal infrastructure. The one-time password[18] and Secure Shell (SSH)[19] protocols are good examples. The latter makes use of public key cryptography but not a public key infrastructure (described later in this section). Both arguably provide a more secure authentication capability than passwords, but they are still intended for use in local contexts, such as a single computer or at most a single organization.

Some types of authentication technologies require some degree of centralization—for example, to help amortize the costs associated with deployment to gain security benefits. Kerberos and public key infrastructure (PKI) are good examples of such systems. In Kerberos, the key distribution center (KDC) is a centralized infrastructure component that stores the passwords of all users, preventing them from having to be shared with each system to which a user connects. The KDC is aware of all sites with which the user interacts, because the KDC is invoked the first time that a user establishes a connection in any given log-in session. The content sent over the connections is not necessarily revealed; nevertheless, the central site operates as the verifier, acting as an intermediary between the user (presenter) and the sites that rely on Kerberos for authentication. The scope of a Kerberos system deployment is typically limited, which in practice mitigates some of the privacy concerns. Although Kerberos systems can be interconnected, most usage of Kerberos is within an individual organization. When cross-realm authentication is employed, only those transactions that involve multiple realms are known

---

[18]See RFC 1760 at <http://www.faqs.org/rfcs/rfc1760.html>.
[19]See <http://www.ietf.org/internet-drafts/draft-ietf-secsh-userauth-16.txt>.

outside a user's home realm.[20]   This limits the adverse privacy aspects of using such a system. However, if a single Kerberos realm was used to authenticate individuals to systems across organizational boundaries, the privacy implications would be much worse. Thus, the same technology can be used in different contexts with vastly different privacy implications. For more information about Kerberos, see Figure 5.1.

The Passport and Liberty systems, though very different in detail, are centralized systems designed expressly to authenticate large user populations to a wide range of disparate systems, with attendant privacy implications. While their designs differ slightly, both offer users the same basic feature: the convenience of single sign-on to a variety of Web services. From a privacy perspective, the obvious drawback to centralized authentication systems is that all Web clients cannot be expected to trust the same authentication service with what could be personally identifying information. Passport and Liberty both address this fundamental obstacle by allowing what they call a federated topology. "Federated," in this context, means that peer authentication services can interoperate with different subsets of service providers. For example, a car rental company could rely on four different airlines' authentication services. Theoretically, a single user could navigate seamlessly between multiply affiliated sites after authenticating only once. Even in their federated form, however, there are two types of privacy risk inherent in these single sign-on systems: exposure of what we call identity data (the set of all information associated with an individual within this identity system) by the authentication service and the aggregation of an entity's (or his or her identifier's) downstream behavior. While the committee did not undertake a detailed analysis of these two systems (one of which is proprietary and one of which has a specification developed and licensed by a private consortium), as with any authentication system the privacy implications will ultimately depend on choices made at the design, implementation, and use stages.[21] Detailed analysis of a particular product is beyond the scope of this report.

Public key infrastructure has often been touted as a universal authentication technology, one that might have national or even global scope.

---

[20]A Kerberos "realm" is a local administrative domain. Typically an organization will have its own realm. Different realms can be configured to interoperate with each other, but this requires explicit action from each organization.

[21]Recently, the FTC stepped in (at the request of privacy advocates) to assure that Microsoft's security and privacy policy is correctly represented to consumers. Many observers commented that this move should be considered a warning that governments internationally will scrutinize how centralized authentication services collect, protect, and use consumer data.

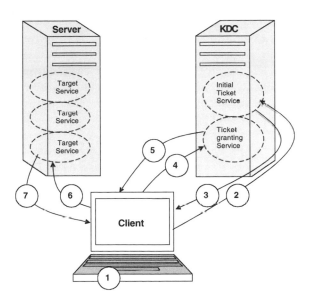

FIGURE 5.1 Kerberos:

1. User provides a principal (user name) and password to the client system.
2. Client queries the Initial Ticket Service of the Kerberos key distribution center (KDC) for a ticket-granting ticket (TGT), which will allow the client to request tickets for specific services later on. The client's request includes a derivative of the user's password, which the Initial Ticket Service verifies.
3. The KDC's Initial Ticket Service provides the client with a dual-encrypted initial TGT containing a log-in session key. The client system converts the user's password into an encryption key and attempts to decrypt the TGT.
4. The client uses the TGT and the log-in session key to request tickets to specific services from the KDC's Ticket-Granting Service.
5. The Ticket-Granting Service decrypts the TGT with its own key, and then decrypts the service request using the TGT's session key. If decryption is successful on both counts, the Ticket-Granting Service accepts the user's authentication and returns a service ticket and a service-session key (encrypted with the log-in session key) for the targeted service. This result can be cached and reused by the client.
6. The client uses the log-in session key provided in step 3 to decrypt the service ticket, gaining access to the service-session key. This key is then used to request access to the target service. This request is accompanied by an encrypted time stamp as an authenticator.
7. Access to the target service is granted. Steps 4 through 7 can be repeated when access to other services is needed; service messages can be encrypted with the service-session key. A time limit is built into the log-in session in steps 3 and 5; the user will need to enter the password again when the log-in session has timed out.

Certainly a very large-scale PKI would have very serious privacy implications, as it might provide a single, uniform identifier that an individual
would employ in transactions with many different organizations. (See
Box 5.6 for a brief description of public key cryptography.) Since each
public key certificate carries a clearly visible identifier for the person
represented by the certificate, it is easy to link different uses of the same
certificate to that person's identity.

The General Services Administration's Access Certificates for Electronic Services (ACES) program, described more fully in Chapter 6 in
this report,[22] has this flavor for citizen interactions with the U.S. government. In Japan, plans call for the creation of a national-level PKI that
would be used not only for individual interactions with the government
but also for a wide range of private sector interactions. VeriSign and
other so-called trusted third party (TTP) certificate authorities (CAs) in
both the United States and Europe promote the notion of using a single
public key certificate as the universal personal authenticator for a wide
range of transactions.

For example, if citizens were issued a single "interact with the government" public key certificate, it might be relatively easy to determine if,
say, the individual who had a reservation to visit Yosemite National Park
was the same person who had sought treatment in a Department of Veter-
ans Affairs (VA) hospital for a sexually transmitted disease. By contrast,
if the VA and the National Park Service each issued their own certificates,
or if they relied on some other decentralized authentication mechanism,
such linkage would be harder to establish. Thus, it is not the use of PKI
per se (except as it is an authentication system with all of the privacy
implications intrinsic to authentication itself—see Chapters 2, 3, and 7 in
this report) but rather the scope of the PKI that influences the privacy of
the authentication system.

PKI technology does not intrinsically require large scale or use across
multiple domains in order to be useful or cost-effective to deploy. This
report has already argued that individuals typically have multiple identities and that most identities are meaningful only in limited contexts, which
suggests that many PKIs could arise, each issuing certificates to individuals in a limited context, with an identifier that is meaningful only in that
context.[23] PKIs of this sort can be privacy-preserving, in contrast to very
large-scale PKIs. Proposals have been made to use PKIs in a highly de-

---

[22]See <http://www.gsa.gov/aces/>.

[23]For another view of PKI, digital certificates, and privacy, see Stefan Brands, *Rethinking
Public Key Infrastructures and Digital Certificates: Building in Privacy*, Cambridge, Mass., MIT
Press, 2000.

BOX 5.6
Public Key Cryptography

Public key cryptosystems were first described in the open literature by Whitfield Diffie and Martin Hellman at Stanford University in 1976.[1] In public key systems, each user has two keys. One is kept private while the other, as the name implies, is usually made public. These keys are mathematically related in such a way that knowledge of the public key does not allow one to determine the corresponding private key. (The reverse may or may not be true, depending on the public key algorithm in question.) This property of public key cryptosystems means that data encrypted with one user's public key can be decrypted using his or her corresponding private key, without sharing the private key with others. Conversely, data that are transformed with a user's private key (digital signing) can be verified with the corresponding public key, again without the need to divulge the key used to generate the signature. This latter relationship is most relevant to user-authentication systems based on public key technology. The use of public key systems significantly transforms the problem of key distribution: Distribution of public keys requires authentication and integrity of the public keys (we have to know whose public keys we are using) but not confidentiality (because the public keys need not be kept secret).

There are two basic ways in which public key systems are used:[2]

- *Encryption.* Public key systems are used to provide confidentiality by having the recipient of a confidential message first provide its public key to the sender. This transaction does not have to be held in secret because the key distribution, the public key, does not have to be kept confidential. The sender then encrypts the communication in the recipient's public key and sends it to the recipient. Only the recipient can decrypt the message using his or her private key.
- *Digital signature.* Public key systems such as the RSA system[3] and the Digital Signature Standard[4] can provide what is often referred to as a "digital signature." Digitally signed data are not encrypted by the process. Instead, they are protected against unauthorized modification, and the identity of the signer of the data can be determined (data origin authentication) if, for example, a PKI has been established (or if the verifier trusts, through some other means, that the public key of the signer is as described). A message or document is digitally signed by transforming the data[5] using the signer's private key.

---

[1]See W. Diffie and M. Hellman, "New Directions in Cryptography," *IEEE Transactions on Information Theory* IT-22(6)(1976):644-654.

[2]A third type of public key cryptosystem, public key agreement algorithms, is not discussed here, since these systems usually are employed for confidentiality but not for authentication.

[3]RSA was developed by Ron Rivest, Adi Shamir, and Leonard Adelman at MIT. See "A Method for Obtaining Digital Signatures and Public-Key Cryptosystems," *Communications of the ACM* 21,2 (February 1978): 120-126.

[4]See *Federal Information Processing Standards Publication 186 on the Digital Signature Standard,* available online at <http://www.itl.nist.gov/fipspubs/fip186.htm>.

[5]In practice, the data to be signed are first compressed in a one-way fashion, using a hash algorithm, and the resulting hash value is digitally signed. This variant on the basic scheme is employed because public key signature operations are relatively slow and signing a large amount of data would be very burdensome.

(continues)

BOX 5.6 Continued

Digital Certificates

Most uses of public key systems require that one know that a given public key belongs to a particular person or organization. One obvious way to obtain the public key securely is to obtain it directly from the sender in a secure out-of-band channel (for example, by way of a personal interaction). This approach, while viable in some circumstances, in general does not scale very well.

However, the very nature of a digital signature lends itself to a solution to this problem. Specifically, if a recipient knows one public key, the issuer of that public key can "vouch" for the association between a different public key and its owner by issuing a digital document of that assertion. With some additional structure, this system becomes the basis for digital certificates, and therefore a PKI. The entity that signs (issues) a certificate usually is referred to as a certificate authority (CA). Note that CAs collect data from many users as part of the certificate issuance (registration) process and assign a single identifier to each user. This practice encourages a user to collapse multiple identities into a single identity for presumed ease of use in interactions with a diverse set of organizations, heightening the risk of linkage.

Because a certificate represents a binding between an identifier (presumably associated with the owner) and a key, it inherently contains some notion of identity. Just how strong this notion is, and the form of identity bound into a certificate, depends on the policies of the CA and on the intended use of the certificate. In some forms, a certificate can contain a name, an e-mail address, or an account number. In others, there may be no meaningful identification, just the public key itself. The basic notion behind the use of a certificate is to establish a certification path between a known public key and the certificate being verified.

---

centralized fashion[24,25] that supports this notion of multiple identities for an individual and thus supports privacy. However, multiple PKIs might impose burdens on users, who would be required to manage the multitude of certificates that would result. In a sense, this is not too different from the common, current situation in which an individual may hold many physical credentials and has to manage their use. If individuals are going to accept and make use of a multitude of PKIs, software needs to provide a user interface that minimizes the burden on users.

---

[24]S. Kent. "How Many Certification Authorities Are Enough?" *Proceedings of MILCOM* (unclassified papers) 97(1)(November 1997):61-68.

[25]S. Kent. "Security Issues in PKI and Certification Authority Design." *Advanced Security Technologies in Networking.* NATO Science Series. Burke, Va., IOS Press, pp. 33-52, 2001.

Finding 5.3: Public certificate authorities and trusted third parties present significant potential privacy and security concerns.

Finding 5.4: Public key infrastructures have a reputation for being difficult to use and hard to deploy. Current products do little to dispel this notion.

Finding 5.5: Many of the problems that appear to be intrinsic to public key infrastructures (as opposed to specific public key infrastructure products) seem to derive from the scope of the public key infrastructures.

Recommendation 5.3: Public key infrastructures should be limited in scope in order to simplify their deployment and to limit adverse privacy effects. Software such as browsers should provide better support for private (versus public) certificate authorities and for the use of private keys and certificates among multiple computers associated with the same user to facilitate the use of private certificate authorities.

This analysis suggests that authentication technologies that imply some degree of centralization can be operated over a range of scales with vastly differing privacy implications. Thus, neither Kerberos nor PKI intrinsically undermines privacy (beyond the fact that they are authentication systems and as such can affect privacy), although each could be used in a way that would do so. In general, decentralized systems tend to be more preserving of privacy: No single party has access to more than its own transaction records. An individual may use the same password for two different Web sites; for a third party to verify this, the party would need at least the cooperation of both sites and (depending on the precise password storage technology being used) perhaps special-purpose monitoring software on both sites. But if users employ the same identifiers at each site, the potential for privacy violations is significantly increased. This same observation applies to any form of decentralized authentication system.

An essential requirement for preserving privacy in authentication systems is allowing an individual to employ a different identifier when he or she asserts a different identity—for example, in different organizational contexts. The use of different identifiers makes it harder to correlate the individual's activities across systems, which helps preserve privacy. This goal can be achieved with technologies ranging from passwords to PKIs. Also, if each system collects less personal information on its users—only what is required to satisfy the requirements of that system—this, too, is privacy-preserving.

> **Finding 5.6: Core authentication technologies are generally more neutral with respect to privacy than is usually believed. How these technologies are designed, developed, and deployed in systems is what most critically determines their privacy implications.**

SECURITY CONSIDERATIONS FOR INDIVIDUAL AUTHENTICATION TECHNOLOGIES

Authentication technologies are often characterized by the security that they offer, specifically in terms of resistance to various types of attack. Many authentication technologies rely on the use of secret values such as passwords, PINs, cryptographic keys, and so on. Secrets may be vulnerable to guessing attacks if they are selected from a set of values that is too small or predictable. Passwords, when selected by individuals and not subject to screening, often exhibit this vulnerability.[26] Secrets also may be compromised by computational attacks, even when the secrets are chosen from large sets of values. For example, a large, randomly chosen cryptographic key would generally be immune to guessing attacks. But this key could be used in an authentication protocol in a manner that permits an attacker to perform computations that reveal the value of the key.

If secrets are transmitted across a communication network, from presenter to verifier, as part of an authentication process, they are vulnerable to interception unless otherwise protected (e.g., by encryption). An encrypted communication path is often necessary, but it is not sufficient to protect secrets against being transmitted. An attacker might masquerade as a system that a user wants to access and thus trick the user into revealing an authentication secret, even though the secret was encrypted en route.[27] A secret need not be transmitted across a network to be subject to attacks of this sort. Several years ago, thieves installed a fake ATM in a

---

[26]In this context, the user (presenter) also is acting as the issuer, and as an issuer is doing a poor job.

[27]This is an example of why two-way authentication is important. A form of this attack sometimes takes place when a user employs Secure Sockets Layer to encrypt communication between a browser and a Web server. The user may reveal credit card account information (account number, expiration date, shipping address, and so on) to a sham merchant, who then can use this information to carry out unauthorized transactions.

shopping mall.[28] Unsuspecting individuals inserted ATM cards and entered PINs, which were collected by the thieves and used to make unauthorized withdrawals from the users' accounts. Thus, even physical proximity and an ability to see a verifier does not ensure that it is the device it appears to be and one to which authentication information should be presented!

Secret values that are too big for individuals to remember must be stored. The way in which the secrets are stored may make them vulnerable. For example, passwords written on a note stuck on a monitor in the workplace may be observed by other employees, custodial staff, or even visitors. Secret values stored in a file on a computer can be compromised by a wide variety of attacks against the computer, ranging from physical theft to network intrusions. Even secret values stored in hardware dedicated to authentication can be extracted illicitly, with varying degrees of difficulty, depending on the technology used to store the secrets.

Often there is a requirement to prevent individuals from sharing authentication data in support of individual accountability. If authentication data are known to individuals or are easily extracted from storage, then individuals may voluntarily make copies and thus circumvent this system goal (see Chapter 4). Even when secrets are stored in physical tokens, the tokens may be loaned to others, in violation of procedural aspects of a security policy.

Sometimes authentication is based not on the possession of a secret value but on the possession of a physical item that is presumed to be resistant to tampering and forgery. An authentication system may be attacked successfully if the assumptions about its tamper- or forgery-resistance prove to be false. In many cases, the security of the credential is derived from the integrity of the data associated with the credential, rather than on the physical characteristics of the credential. For example, a physical credential might contain digitally signed data attesting to a name and employee ID number. Verification of the credential, and thus authentication of the individual possessing the credential, would be based on successful validation of the digital signature associated with the data. Careful use of public key cryptography can make the digital signature highly secure, protecting against modification of the signed data or creation of new, fake signed data. However, it may be quite feasible to copy the data to additional physical credentials. These duplicate credentials represent a form of forgery. Unless the signed data are linked directly to

---

[28]In 1993 in Connecticut, a fraudulent ATM was installed in a shopping center. See the *RISKS* digest for more details; available online at <http://catless.ncl.ac.uk/Risks/14.60.html#subj3>.

the holder of the credential (for example, by means of biometrics), this sort of forgery by duplication is a security concern.

Biometric authentication also relies on the possession of a physical item that is presumed to be resistant to tampering and forgery, namely some measurable part of an individual's body or behavior. Examples include fingerprints, voiceprints, hand geometry, iris patterns, and so on. Biometric values are not secrets; we leave fingerprints on many items that we touch, our voices and facial images may be recorded, and so on.[29] Thus, the security of biometric authentication systems relies extensively on the integrity of the process used to capture the biometric values and on the initial, accurate binding of those values to an identifier. It is critical that later instances of the biometric capture process ensure that it is a real person whose biometric features are being captured—this may mean requiring biometric sensors to be continuously monitored by humans. Biometric authentication systems may be fooled by fake body parts or photographs created to mimic the body parts of real individuals.[30] They also may be attacked by capturing the digitized representation of a biometric feature for an individual and injecting it into the system, claiming that the data are a real scan of some biometric feature.

The preceding analysis of the security vulnerabilities of classes of authentication technologies, while accurate, does not determine whether any of these technologies is suitable for use in any specific context. Instead, a candidate technology must be evaluated relative to a perceived threat in order to determine whether the technology is adequately secure. Nonetheless, it is important to understand these vulnerabilities

---

[29]"The physical characteristics of a person's voice, its tone and manner, as opposed to the content of a specific conversation, are constantly exposed to the public. Like a man's facial characteristics, or handwriting, his voice is repeatedly produced for others to hear. No person can have a reasonable expectation that others will not know the sound of his voice, any more than he can reasonably expect that his face will be a mystery to the world." —Justice Potter Stewart for the majority in *U.S.* v. *Dionisio*, 410 U.S. 1, 1973.

[30]See T. Matsumoto, H. Matsumoto, K. Yamada, and S. Hoshino, "Impact of Artificial Gummy Fingers on Fingerprint Systems," *Proceedings of the International Society for Optical Engineering (SPIE)* 4677 (January 2002), available online at <http://research.nii.ac.jp/kaken-johogaku/reports/H13_overview/A04-00-1.pdf>; L. Thalheim, J. Krissler, and P. Ziegler, "Biometric Access Protection Devices and Their Programs Put to the Test," *c't Magazine* 11 (May 21, 2002):114, available online at <http://www.heise.de/ct/english/02/11/114>; T. van der Putte and J. Keuning, "Biometrical Fingerprint Recognition: Don't Get Your Fingers Burned," *Proceedings of the IFIP TC8/WG8.8 Fourth Working Conference on Smart Card Research and Advanced Applications*, Kluwer Academic Publishers, Dordrecht, The Netherlands, 2000, pp. 289-303, available online at <http://www.keuning.com/biometry/Biometrical_Fingerprint_Recognition.pdf>; and D. Blackburn, M. Bone, P. Grother, and J. Phillips, *Facial Recognition Vendor Test 2000: Evaluation Report*, U.S. Department of Defense, January 2001, available online at <www.frvt.org>.

when evaluating the security characteristics of individual authentication technologies.

COST CONSIDERATIONS FOR INDIVIDUAL AUTHENTICATION TECHNOLOGIES

Costs are an important factor in the selection of authentication technologies. These costs take many forms. Capital costs are associated with the acquisition of any hardware or software needed for an authentication technology. The hardware and software costs may be a function of the number of individuals being authenticated, or of the number of points at which authentication takes place, or both. For example, an authentication system that makes use of hardware tokens has a per user cost, since each user must have his or her own token, and each device that will authenticate the user (for example, each desktop or laptop computer) must be equipped with a reader for the token. A biometric authentication system might typically require readers at each point where individuals are authenticated, and there would be a per-device, not a per-person cost. A software-based authentication system may impose costs only for each computer, not each individual, although licensing terms directed by a vendor might translate into per-user costs as well.

Many authentication systems also make use of some common infrastructure, which also has associated hardware and software acquisition costs. The infrastructure may be offline and infrequently used, or it may be online and require constant availability. In the online case, it may be necessary to acquire replicated components of the infrastructure, to geographically disperse these components, and to arrange for uninterruptible power supplies, in order to ensure high availability. The key distribution center component of a Kerberos system (see Box 5.7) and the ACE/Server used by the SecurID system are examples of the latter sort of infrastructure. A certificate authority in a PKI is an example of the online type of infrastructure component.

Operation of an authentication system involves labor costs of various types. Help desks must be manned to respond to users' questions and problems. If the system relies on secret values that users are required to remember, the help desk will have to interact with users to reset forgotten secret values. If the system makes use of hardware tokens, provisions will have to be made to replace lost or stolen tokens. Users and system administrators must be trained to work with an authentication technology and with that technology's interaction with varying operating systems and applications. Application developers must learn how to make use of an authentication technology and to integrate it into their applications.

Box 5.7
Kerberos

The Kerberos authentication system was developed at the Massachusetts Institute of Technology (MIT) in about 1985 as part of MIT's Project Athena.[1] A Kerberos system consists of three parties: (1) a client, which attempts to authenticate itself to (2) a server and (3) a key distribution center (KDC), also known as a Kerberos server, which acts as an intermediary for the authentication.

Every Kerberos "principal" (either client or server) has a secret key known both by the principal and the KDC. Most Kerberos systems emulate a traditional password-based authentication system inasmuch as the human end user knows a secret password. However, unlike a traditional password-based authentication system, this password is never transmitted over a network and is therefore not easily stolen by eavesdropping. When used, this password is hashed into a secret key that is used to complete the Kerberos protocol.

When a client wishes to make use of a server, it queries the KDC for a "ticket" for the server. The ticket contains the identity of the client along with a time stamp and validity period. This ticket is encrypted by the KDC so that only the server can decrypt it. Among the information encrypted into the ticket is a randomly generated "session" key. The ticket and the session key are then provided to the client by way of a Ticket-Granting Ticket service.

The Ticket-Granting Ticket service is a Kerberos service in which the KDC is also the server. In general, a ticket for the Ticket-Granting Ticket service is obtained at log-in time. Additional tickets are then obtained for other services from the KDC as needed. These additional tickets, encrypted in the session key of the Ticket-Granting Ticket instead of the client's password, are sent by the KDC to the client. This permits the Kerberos system to obtain as many tickets as are necessary without the client's secret key (password) needing to be kept in memory on the client's workstation (computer).

---

[1]For more information on Project Athena, see <http://Web.mit.edu/olh/Welcome/intro.html>.

This brief discussion illustrates how complex it can be to evaluate the cost of an individual authentication system. Initial capital outlays are greater for some types of systems; ongoing costs of other types of systems may eventually outweigh these capital outlays. Different contexts merit different levels of security and will tolerate different costs for authentication technology. Thus, there can be no single right answer to the question of how much authentication technology should cost.

CONCLUDING REMARKS

The preceding chapters describe three different conceptual types of authentication (identity, attribute, and individual), and this chapter fo-

A client's secret key, as mentioned earlier, is typically known to the client as a password, which is hashed into the key when needed. Servers store their secret key (needed to decrypt incoming tickets to obtain the stored session key) somewhere on the server, typically in a file.

Kerberos provides for clients to authenticate themselves to servers and for servers to be authenticated to clients. At the end of a successful authentication transaction, the session key created by the KDC and stored in the ticket is known to both the client and the server. This key can then be used to provide integrity protection for information sent between client and server and for the encryption (confidentiality) of information transfer as well.

Kerberos is an online system. The KDC is required to be involved in most transactions.[2] A ticket is typically issued with a lifetime measured in hours.[3] Short ticket lifetime simplifies the revocation problem. If an entity's key is compromised, all that needs to be done is to change that key in the KDC (and on the server if a server key is compromised). The use of symmetric algorithms means that Kerberos computations are much faster than the equivalent public key operations.

Kerberos still relies on the limited human storage capacity for passwords. It also relies on the user's computer for computational ability, which means that it must be trusted by the user.

Recent work on the Kerberos protocol introduces the use of public key encryption into the initial Ticket Granting Ticket (log-in) transaction. This means that only clients' public keys need to be stored by the KDC, reducing the amount of secret information that needs to be protected by the KDC.

---

[2]But this is not true for all transactions. Once a ticket is obtained by a client for a particular service, that ticket can be reused for multiple transactions without further involvement of the KDC.

[3]In version 4 Kerberos, the maximum ticket lifetime was 21 hours. Version 5 lifts this restriction, but it is still a good idea to limit ticket lifetime.

cuses on the technologies that go into building an authentication system and some of the technology-related decisions that must be made. Some of these decisions will bear on the privacy implications of the overall system. In general, decentralized systems tend to be more preserving of privacy, but the core authentication technologies that make up authentication systems tend to be privacy-neutral. What matters most in terms of privacy are design, implementation, and policy choices, as described elsewhere in this report.

6

Authentication, Privacy, and the Roles of Government

Government institutions play multiple roles in the area where authentication technologies intersect with privacy concerns. Not only do all levels of government (state, federal, and local) use authentication systems, but the technologies are employed within and across government institutions at each level as well. Furthermore, government plays multiple roles in the authentication process. As a relying party, government uses authentication technologies for electronic government applications and for physical and systems security applications. Given the size of its workforce and its user base, government is a significant user of these technologies. The government's role in the authentication process (as regulator, issuer, and relying party) is important, since so many forms of authentication or identification rely on some form of government-issued identity or identifier.

It is not surprising, therefore, that government organizations have conflicting and supporting roles in authentication. As an example, the Social Security Administration (SSA) fills all three roles simultaneously. The Social Security number (SSN) was designed by SSA for its own use in recording earnings. For its intended purpose, in conjunction with other SSA business processes and controls, the SSN's security level meets the SSA's requirements. In this case, the SSA is both the issuing and the relying party, so the incentives for risk mitigation are properly aligned.

When the parties that issue and rely on an identifier are different, the incentives for risk mitigation are not necessarily aligned. For instance, secondary uses of the SSN have proliferated, beginning with their use by the Internal Revenue Service (IRS) and state taxation agencies, and now extending to many private sector organizations such as credit reporting agencies. There is an inherent conflict between the higher confidence levels desired by the relying party and the extra cost imposed on the issuer to meet this confidence level. For example, it is probably neither reasonable nor cost-effective for the SSA to change its SSN issuance and maintenance processes in order to help the private sector manage business risk around creditworthiness just because most credit bureaus use SSNs as unique identifiers for credit history. An examination of the various roles that government fills in authentication processes and privacy protection, anchored by specific examples, helps to explain this complexity.

The issuance of IDs illustrates how different levels of government interact with the public through specific programs for sometimes unique reasons. The principle of federalism—the division (and in some cases overlap) of government responsibilities among federal, state, and local government,[1] designed into the U.S. constitutional form of government— helps to explain why it is important not to view the government role in any area as monolithic.

By design, as protected by public law and policy, government activities are assumed to be fair, impartial, and immune from commercial manipulation.[2] This legal and policy context for the government management of information and related technology makes government use of these technologies a special case and certainly different from their use by the private sector. Individuals who are citizens of or permanent residents in the United States also have a unique relationship with government agencies. Sometimes by choice, and in many instances by compulsion, citizens and residents are both participants in governance and users of government goods and services. For instance, citizens may choose to comment on proposed changes in information-reporting requirements

---

[1]One insightful definition of federalism and its complexity comes from Woodrow Wilson: "To make town, city, county, state, and federal government live with a like strength and an equally assured healthfulness, keeping each unquestionably its own master and yet making all interdependent and cooperative, combining independence and mutual helpfulness." See Woodrow Wilson, "The Study of Administration," *Political Science Quarterly* 2(June 1887):197-222, quoted in Dell S. Wright, "A Century of Intergovernmental Administrative State: Wilson's Federalism, New Deal Intergovernmental Relations, and Contemporary Intergovernmental Management," *A Centennial History of the American Administrative State*, Ralph Clark Chandler, ed. New York, N.Y., The Free Press, 1987, p. 220.

[2]Charles Goodsell. *The Case for Bureaucracy*, 3rd ed. New York, N.Y., Seven Bridges Press, 1994.

such as the questions on census forms. Alternatively, some relationships with government are straightforward and contractual, just as with a business. For example, when it is time to repay student loans, beneficiaries have a legal obligation to return the money that they borrowed from the government with interest.

Unlike private sector organizations, though, public agencies cannot choose their customers. Public law and regulation instead of business plans dictate whether an individual is a beneficiary or a regulated entity. While private sector organizations may only want an individual's business under certain conditions (for example, one can only get a mortgage or a credit card upon meeting certain eligibility criteria), most citizens interact with government organizations from cradle to grave. From the recording of birth to the issuance of death certificates—and annually in between for some government programs—citizens' interaction with government is virtually inescapable.

> **Finding 6.1: Many agencies at different levels of government have multiple, and sometimes conflicting, roles in electronic authentication. They can be regulators of private sector behavior, issuers of identity documents or identifiers, and also relying parties for service delivery.**

REGULATOR OF PRIVATE SECTOR AND PUBLIC AGENCY BEHAVIORS AND PROCESSES

The government acts as a regulator of multiple sectors, including health and medical services, financial services, and education. For this analysis, these regulatory activities are put in three groups: (1) government-wide law and policy that are focused internally on the activities of federal agencies in a particular domain (for example, privacy, electronic government, or computer security); (2) program- or agency-specific law and policy that apply to specific types of transactions but may cut across a number of government agency and private sector organization boundaries for transactions such as federally funded health care or higher education; and (3) public law or policy intended to regulate the information management activities of the private sector broadly or more specifically in certain areas such as financial services. This section summarizes some of this public law and government policy and concludes by identifying some pending legislation that is relevant to privacy and authentication.

Government-wide Law and Policy

Privacy Act and Computer Matching Act

A recent Government Accounting Office (GAO) report[3] refers to the Privacy Act of 1974 (5 U.S.C. Sec. 552a)[4] as the "primary [U.S.] law regulating the federal government's collection and maintenance of personal information." Generally speaking, the Privacy Act aimed at balancing the federal government's need to maintain information about individuals with the rights of individuals to be protected against unwanted invasions of their privacy. The act attempts to regulate the collection, maintenance, use, and dissemination of personal information by federal government agencies. As one source summarizes, the act provides privacy protection in three ways:

1. It sustains some traditional major privacy principles. For example, an agency shall maintain no record describing how any individual exercises rights guaranteed by the First Amendment unless expressly authorized by statute or by the individual about whom the record is maintained or unless pertinent to and within the scope of an authorized law enforcement activity.

2. It provides an individual who is a citizen of the United States, or an alien lawfully admitted for permanent residence, with access and emendation arrangements for records maintained on him or her by most, but not all, federal agencies. General exemptions in this regard are provided for systems of records maintained by the Central Intelligence Agency and federal criminal law enforcement agencies.

3. The act embodies a number of principles of fair information practice. For example, it sets certain conditions concerning the disclosure of personally identifiable information; prescribes requirements for the accounting of certain disclosures of such information; requires agencies to "collect information to the greatest extent practicable directly from the subject individual when the information may result in adverse determinations about an individual's rights, benefits, and privileges under Federal programs"; requires agencies to specify their authority and purposes for collecting personally identifiable information from an individual; requires agencies to "maintain all records which are used by the agency in

---

[3]Government Accounting Office (GAO). *Internet Privacy: Agencies' Efforts to Implement OMB's Privacy Policy* [GGD-00-191]. Washington, D.C., GAO, September 2000. Available online at <http://www.gao.gov/archive/2000/gg00191.pdf>.

[4]The full text of the act itself is available online at <http://www.usdoj.gov/04foia/privstat.htm>.

making any determination about any individual with such accuracy, relevance, timeliness, and completeness as is reasonably necessary to assure fairness to the individual in the determination"; and provides civil and criminal enforcement arrangements.[5]

However, passed in great haste during the final week of the 93rd Congress, the "Act's imprecise language, limited legislative history, and somewhat outdated regulatory guidelines have rendered it a difficult statute to decipher and apply."[6]

One major complicating factor in the implementation and regulation of Privacy Act provisions has been the "lack of specific mechanisms for oversight."[7] Indeed, some have cited the absence of a central agency for the oversight and coordination of the nation's privacy matters as a major reason for the ineffectiveness of American privacy laws in general.[8] In comparison, several other nations have dedicated whole departments and appointed high-level officials to oversee their privacy matters.

The Computer Matching and Privacy Protection Act of 1988 (PL 100-503) amended the Privacy Act of 1974 by adding new provisions regulating the federal government's use of computer matching—the computerized comparison of information about individuals, usually for the purpose of determining the eligibility of those individuals for benefits. The main provisions of the act include the following:

• Give individuals an opportunity to receive notice of computer matching and to contest information before having a benefit denied or terminated;
• Require that federal agencies engaged in matching activities establish data protection boards to oversee matching activities;
• Require federal agencies to verify the findings of computer match-

---

[5]Text for these three items is adapted from Harold C. Relyea, *The Privacy Act: Emerging Issues and Related Legislation,* Congressional Research Service (CRS) Report RL30824, Washington, D.C., CRS, Library of Congress, September 2000.

[6]Department of Justice. "Overview of the Privacy Act of 1974" (Introduction), 2000. Available online at <http://www.usdoj.gov/04foia/1974intro.htm>.

[7]Charles R. Booz. "Electronic Records and the Right to Privacy: At the Core." *Information Management Journal* 35 (3): 18.

[8]See David H. Flaherty, "The Need for an American Privacy Protection Commission," *Government Information Quarterly* 1(3)(1984):235-258. In later work, he also observes that design of the system and policy choices are crucial to privacy protection. See, for example, "Privacy Impact Assessments: An Essential Tool For Data Protection," presentation to a plenary session "New Technologies, Security and Freedom" at the 22nd Annual Meeting of Privacy and Data Protection Officials held in Venice, Italy, September 27-30, 2000. Available online at <http://www.anu.edu.au/people/Roger.Clarke/DV/PIAsFlaherty.html>.

ing programs before suspending, denying, or otherwise "adversely" affecting an individual's benefits; and

• Require agencies to negotiate written agreements with other agencies participating in the matching programs.

An amendment to the act that was passed in 1990 somewhat altered the original act's due process provisions. Specifically, the amendment changed some of the details regarding subject notification of adverse findings and gave data protection boards the ability to waive independent verification of information under certain circumstances.

In December 2000, the Office of Management and Budget (OMB) issued a memorandum reminding federal agencies of the act's requirements.[9,10] According to the memorandum, as "government increasingly moves to electronic collection and dissemination of data, under the Government Paperwork Elimination Act and other programs, opportunities to share data across agencies will likely increase." Therefore, "agencies must pay close attention to handling responsibly their own data and the data they share with or receive from other agencies."

Computer Security Act and Recent Amendments

The Computer Security Act of 1987 (PL 100-235) addressed the importance of ensuring and improving the security and privacy of sensitive information in federal computer systems. The act required that the National Institute of Standards and Technology (formerly the National Bureau of Standards) develop standards and guidelines for computer systems to control loss and unauthorized modification or disclosure of sensitive information and to prevent computer-related fraud and misuse. The act also required that operators of federal computer systems, including both federal agencies and their contractors, establish security plans.[11] Additionally, the law stipulated that agency plans for protecting sensitive information and systems be cost-effective, and most important, it established a standard for risk mitigation. Specifically, the law says that federal agencies must "establish a plan for the security and privacy of each Federal computer system identified by that agency pursuant to subsection (a) that is commensurate with the risk and magnitude or the harm

---

[9]Office of Management and Budget (OMB). "Guidance on Inter-Agency Sharing of Personal Data—Protecting Personal Privacy," M-01-05, December 20. Available online at <http://www.whitehouse.gov/omb/memoranda/m01-05.html>.

[10]This and related activities at OMB were part of the context that led to this study.

[11]For the full text of the act, see <http://www.epic.org/crypto/csa/csa.html>.

resulting from the loss, misuse, or unauthorized access to or modification of the information contained in such system."

Government Paperwork Elimination Act

Part of the impetus for federal agencies to move quickly toward electronic government (and therefore authentication, to an extent) is public law. Enacted in 1998, the Government Paperwork Elimination Act (GPEA)[12] both requires federal agencies to move from paper-based to electronic transactions with the public and provides some of the enablers necessary to make such a transition. It also amplifies federal privacy protections regarding sensitive data collected during the electronic authentication process.

Following on the tradition of the Paperwork Reduction Act (PRA)[13] of 1995, one of the goals of GPEA is to minimize the burden imposed on the public by federal paperwork requirements. More specifically, though, the goal of both the PRA and GPEA is for federal agencies to minimize the information-collection burden on the public, regardless of whether the collection instrument is a paper form, an electronic transaction, or a phone survey.[14] GPEA recognizes the benefits to both federal agencies and the public of moving from paper-based to electronic transactions, including reduced error rates, lower processing costs, and improved customer satisfaction. As a result, GPEA required agencies by the end of Fiscal Year 2003 to provide for the electronic maintenance, submission, or transaction of information as a substitute for paper where practicable. Additionally, the law stipulates that agencies use and accept electronic signatures in this process.

GPEA goes so far as to define the term "electronic signature" and to legitimate the legal force of such signatures in the scope of public interactions with federal agencies.[15] In doing so, federal law and policy help to clear up what has historically been the subject of some debate among federal agencies about what is legally sufficient to "sign" a transaction with a member of the public. Section 1709(1) of GPEA reads:

> The term "electronic signature" means a method of signing an electronic message that—(A) identifies and authenticates a particular person as the

---

[12]Government Paperwork Elimination Act of 1998 (PL 105-277, Div. C, tit XVII).

[13]Paperwork Reduction Act of 1995 (44 U.S.C. Chapter 35).

[14]For background on the goals of GPEA, see Senate Report 105-355, and for background on the PRA and GPEA, see OMB, "Procedures and Guidance; Implementation of the GPEA," *Federal Register*, May 2, 2000.

[15]For more on electronic signatures, see the discussion of the Electronic Signatures in Global and National Commerce Act (E-SIGN) of 2000 later in this chapter.

source of the electronic message; and (B) indicates such person's approval of the information contained in the electronic message.

It is important to note as well what the definition does not do, which is to specify the technologies or policies that an agency might use to comply with this definition. The OMB implementation guidance to federal agencies cites examples of appropriate technologies—shared secrets such as PINs and passwords, digitized signatures or biometrics such as fingerprints, and cryptographic digital signatures such as those used in PKIs.[16] The OMB guidance does, though, suggest an analytical framework for an agency to use to help determine the risk inherent in the transaction it hopes to automate and which authentication technology might most appropriately mitigate that risk.

GPEA also cleared up what might otherwise have been a contentious debate among federal agency general counsel offices throughout Washington, D.C., by addressing directly the enforceability of electronic signatures. For transactions involving electronic records submitted or maintained consistent with the policy enabled by GPEA and using electronic signatures in accordance with the same policy, neither the electronic record nor the signature is to be denied legal effect just because it is electronic instead of paper. Both Congress and the OMB state that the intent is to prevent agencies or the public from reverting to paper instead of electronic transactions and signatures because of concerns that any subsequent prosecution—in a benefits fraud case, for instance—might be thrown out of court.

One other provision of the law pertinent to the topic of this study relates to the protection of information collected in the course of providing electronic signatures services. Consistent with the fair information practices (described in Chapter 3 of this report) and the Privacy Act, GPEA requires that information gathered from the public to facilitate electronic signatures services be disclosed only for that purpose.

Agency- or Program-Specific Law and Policies

Family Educational Rights and Privacy Act

The Family Educational Rights and Privacy Act (FERPA) of 1974 (20 U.S.C. § 1232g; 34 CFR Part 99) is a federal law designed to protect the privacy of a student's education records. The law applies to all schools that receive funds under an applicable program of the U.S. Department of

---

[16]See the Web site <http://www.whitehouse.gov/omb/fedreg/gpea2.html>.

Education. FERPA gives parents certain rights with respect to their children's education records (for example, the right to inspect and review all of the student's education records maintained by the school and the right to request that a school correct records believed to be inaccurate or misleading). These rights transfer to the student, or former student, who has reached the age of 18 or is attending any school beyond the high school level.

Under the law, schools must also have written permission from the parent or eligible student before releasing any information from a student's record. Schools may disclose, with notification, directory-type information, such as a student's name, address, telephone number, date and place of birth, and so on.[17] As schools move toward authentication technologies such as PKI, issues arise as to how FERPA applies.[18]

Health Insurance Portability and Accountability Act

The Health Insurance Portability and Accountability Act (HIPAA),[19] or PL 104-191, was passed by Congress and became law in 1996. Its purpose was, among other things, to improve the continuity of health insurance coverage and the efficiency in health care delivery by mandating standards for electronic data interchanges and to protect the confidentiality and security of health information. Title I of HIPAA deals with health insurance access, portability, and renewability (for example, when a worker loses or changes his or her job), while Title II of the act contains what are referred to as the act's administrative simplification provisions. These provisions fall roughly into three categories: transactions and code set standards,[20] privacy standard,[21] and security standard.[22] The privacy standard, along with the security standard, provides rules for legal controls over patients' medical records.

---

[17]The full text of the act is available online at <http://www.epic.org/privacy/education/ferpa.html>.

[18]EDUCAUSE, an organization that promotes information technology in higher education, has looked at this and related issues in its initiative PKI for Networked Higher Education. See the Web site <http://www.educause.edu/netatedu/groups/pki/> for more information.

[19]The full text of the act is available online at <http://aspe.os.dhhs.gov/admnsimp/pl104191.htm>.

[20]Health Insurance Reform: Standards for Electronic Transactions. 45 CFR Parts 160 and 162. Federal Register: August 17, 2000 (Volume 65, Number 160), pp. 50312-50372.

[21]Standards for Privacy of Individually Identifiable Health Information. 45 CFR Parts 160 through 164. Federal Register: December 28, 2000 (Volume 65, Number 250), pp. 82461-82510.

[22]Security and Electronic Signature Standards: Proposed Rule. 45 CFR Part 142. Federal Register: August 12, 1998 (Volume 63, Number 155), pp. 43241-43280.

The process for creating these standards, or rules, has been fairly complicated. Indeed, according to the Department of Health and Human Services (HHS), the process is a "deliberate [one] designed to achieve consensus within HHS and across other Federal departments."[23] However, in general, once a proposed rule has made its way through several federal groups (such as the HHS Data Council's Committee on Health Data Standards, advisers to the secretary of HHS, and the OMB), the proposal is published and comments from the public are solicited. These comments, which are also open to public view, are then "analyzed and considered in the development of the final rules."[24]

HIPAA is aimed at all organizations that store, process, or transmit electronic health care information through which an individual might be identified. Accordingly, the act applies to virtually all health care organizations, including—among others—health plans (insurers), health care clearinghouses, health care providers (including health maintenance organizations, hospitals, clinics, physician group practices, and single-physician offices), billing agencies, and universities.

HIPAA also provides for serious civil and criminal penalties for failure to comply with the rules. For example, the penalties include fines of up to $25,000 for multiple violations of the same rule in one year, as well as fines of up to $250,000 and up to 10 years' imprisonment for knowingly misusing individually identifiable health information.

The privacy rule formally defines "protected health information," which includes individual patient information such as name, Social Security number, address, and so on; and clinical information such as disease, treatment, drugs, test results, and so on. It permits disclosure of this information for necessary treatment, payment, and operations (TPO) functions. For all other uses, especially for fund-raising and marketing functions, explicit authorization from the patient is required. (There are exceptions, such as for military patients and for clinical research, which is largely governed by the informed consent rule.) If information is provided to an organization not covered by HIPAA for TPO functions (such as a bill collection agency), the rule requires explicit business associate (and possibly chain of trust) agreements that make the recipients responsible for HIPAA-specified privacy and security rules.

The original privacy rule issued in December 2000 required collecting and tracking of a consent form signed by all patients that explained the privacy practices of the institution providing care. Subsequently, a techni-

---

[23]From the Web site <http://aspe.os.dhhs.gov/admnsimp/8steps.htm>.
[24]Ibid.

cal correction proposed in January 2001[25] removed the consent form requirement and replaced it with a privacy notice that does not require a patient's signature. Several basic rights for patients are provided in the privacy rule: the right to access their records, the right to emend those records, and the right to see what disclosures of their information have been made. Institutions are required to employ a privacy officer, who provides services related to the privacy rights of patients.

Fundamental to the privacy rule are the "minimum necessary" and "need to know" principles. Based on these principles, the rule requires institutions to develop and implement policies and procedures to define formal role-based or user-based access authorization rules, and the security rule requires assurance that these policies and procedures are being followed. Additionally, a common and uniform sanctions policy is required for addressing privacy and security policy violations. Patient privacy has always been important in care institutions; the HIPAA privacy rule formalizes the concept in a legal framework with significant penalties for noncompliance.

There are several complexities in meeting HIPAA regulations. If information-access rules are incorrectly defined, the care process could be adversely affected, an obviously unacceptable trade-off. The roles of care providers in an organization are fluid: nurses working in shifts or filling in, on-call consultants rotating on a weekly basis, medical students on monthly rotations, multiple physicians in consulting or specialty roles, and so on. Practically, it is very difficult to assign roles to a fine access granularity and to implement such a system in mostly vendor-supported and heterogeneous clinical application environments without raising the risks to proper health care.

Managing authorizations and tracking privacy notices are operational changes for institutions, but centrally tracking all disclosures for review by the patient if requested is a difficult and costly problem in large institutions. In the context of an academic medical center, for example, HIPAA remains vague in addressing the matter of information collected for and by clinical trial and other kinds of research. Open questions about educational rounds and HIPAA were addressed in the latest rule making, and there are other questions that may be clarified, but only later. The privacy rule was required to be adopted by April 14, 2003, but it is likely that there will be a gradual culture change in care environments toward better privacy protection.

---

[25]Standards for Privacy of Individually Identifiable Health Information; Proposed Rule. 45 CFR Parts 160 through 164. Federal Register: March 27, 2002 (Volume 67, Number 59), pp. 14775-14815.

Regulation of Private Sector Information Management Activity

Electronic Signatures in Global and National Commerce Act

Aimed at eliminating "legal barriers to the use of electronic technology to form and sign contracts, collect and store documents, and send and receive notices and disclosures,"[26] the Electronic Signatures in Global and National Commerce (E-SIGN) Act (PL 106-229) became law in June 2000. The act cleared the way for electronic signatures and contracts to carry the same legal significance as that of traditional paper contracts and handwritten signatures.[27] Indeed, President Clinton signed the act into law with a smart card.

The E-SIGN Act includes consumer consent provisions that "require information to be made available electronically only after the recipient affirmatively consents to receive the information [in that manner]."[28] In fact, recipients must give this consent electronically as well, to ensure that they possess the necessary technological capability (usually Internet access and/or an e-mail account). The act does not specify the use of any particular technological solution; rather, it "leav[es] those choices [up] to the marketplace."[29] However, some critics view this aspect of the act as being a very real disadvantage, fearing a "mishmash of incompatible solutions"[30] and a "standards battle that could take years to resolve."[31]

In 2001, the Federal Trade Commission and the Department of Commerce completed a congressionally mandated study[32] on the impact of the consumer consent provisions of the E-SIGN Act. According to the

---

[26]OMB. "Guidance on Implementing the Electronic Signatures in Global and National Commerce Act" (M-00-15), September 25, 2000. Available online at <http://www.whitehouse.gov/omb/memoranda/m00-15.html>.

[27]Electronic signatures, in this context, are not the same as the digital signatures that were described in Chapter 5. One of the critiques of this law is that electronic signatures do not embody the same security methods and principles as digital signatures.

[28]News Bytes News Networks. "E-SIGN Law Appears to Work Fine So Far—Gov't Study." June 27, 2001.

[29]John Schwartz. "E-Signatures Become Valid for Business." *New York Times*. October 2, 2000, p. C1.

[30]Abby Ellin. "E-Sign on the Dotted Line." *Business 2.0*, November, 2000. Available online at <http://www.business2.com/articles/mag/0,1640,8542,FF.html>.

[31]Jesse Berst. "Sign of Trouble: The Problem with E-Signatures." *ZDNet*, July 17, 2000. Available online at <http://www.zdnet.com/anchordesk/stories/story/0,10738,2604099,00.html>.

[32]Federal Trade Commission (FTC) and Department of Commerce (DOC). *Electronic Signatures in Global and National Commerce Act: The Consumer Consent Provision in Section 101(c)(1)(C)(ii)*. Washington, D.C., FTC, DOC, June 2001. Available online at <http://www.ftc.gov/os/2001/06/esign7.htm>.

report, the act's consumer consent provisions seem to be "working satis-factorily." The report also suggests that "implementation issues [such as signature and authentication standards] should be worked out in the marketplace and through state and federal regulations" rather than by congressional action to "amend the statute."

Financial Services Modernization Act

The Financial Services Modernization Act of 1999 (commonly referred to as the Gramm-Leach-Bliley Act) repealed long-standing legislation that prohibited banks, securities firms, and insurance companies from ventur-ing into business with each other. Under Gramm-Leach-Bliley, these types of companies may now join to form what the act calls financial holdings companies (FHCs). What this means with respect to personal privacy is that, for instance, a consumer's bank can now develop a relationship and share information with that same consumer's insurance company, bro-kerage firm, credit union, or other financial institution, creating new op-portunities to cross-market services.[33]   However, Gramm-Leach-Bliley also contains provisions for protecting consumers' personal information: (1) consumers must be given notice of a company's intent to share their information with a third party and (2) they must be given the option to decline such information sharing.

Nevertheless, Gramm-Leach-Bliley is viewed by many privacy advo-cates as being rife with loopholes—to the point of rendering any privacy protections that it spells out moot. For instance, Dan Gillmor, a technol-ogy columnist, describes what he views as two major problems with the act:

- Consumers must opt out of information sharing—"that is, [con-sumers must] explicitly notify the institutions that they [do not] want their data shared—rather than 'opt in,' which is to allow data sharing only after a consumer gives his or her permission."
- "Affiliated companies (such as those under the same corporate umbrella or in joint marketing deals), so broadly defined as to be almost meaningless, are exempt in every respect."[34]

---

[33]Cecelia Kempler and Robert Wood. 2000, "Living with the Gramm-Leach-Bliley Act." Washington, D.C., LeBoeuf, Lamb, Greene & MacRae L.L.P. Available online at <http://www.insurelegal.com/livingwith031500.html#1>.

[34]Dan Gillmor. "Gramm-Leach's Privacy Problem." *Computerworld* 35 (30)(2001): 34. Available online at <http://www.computerworld.com/cwi/story/0,1199,NAV47-74_STO62385,00.html>.

Business, on the other hand, takes a different view of Gramm-Leach-Bliley. Indeed, most financial holdings companies, while taking into account the additional resources and time they must allocate to meeting the act's privacy provisions, see the act as beneficial to their business. As Federal Reserve Vice Chairman Roger Ferguson put it in a recent speech, Gramm-Leach-Bliley offers "opportunities for banking organizations to expand their lines of business and their range of customer services."[35]

Nevertheless, there has been recent activity within state legislatures to strengthen or "enhance the protections of Gramm-Leach-Bliley, including requiring actual consent—or opt-in—before information sharing,"[36] breeding significant concern among financial firms at the prospect of having to account for up to 50 different state privacy laws along with Gramm-Leach-Bliley.[37]

Another challenge has been the requirement for banks and financial institutions to notify customers, in readable and understandable fashion, about their privacy policies. Privacy advocates have noted that many of the policy notifications were written in hard-to-understand legal language and/or distributed in a way that did not draw attention to what was being disclosed.

Policy Activity in the Early 2000s

The last couple of years have seen a flurry of activity relating to both authentication and privacy issues. Some of this legislation predated the terrorist attacks of September 11, 2001, but a great deal of the new legislation is a direct result of the perceived inadequacies of government information management practices leading up to the attacks. This and the following section include recently enacted legislation whose implementation continues to be planned.

---

[35]Roger W. Ferguson, "Umbrella Supervision: Emerging Approaches," speech before the National Association of Urban Bankers, Urban Financial Services Coalition, San Francisco, Calif., May 26, 2001. Available online at <http://www.federalreserve.gov/boarddocs/speeches/2000/20000526.htm>.

[36]M. Maureen Murphy. *Privacy Protection for Customer Financial Information*, Congressional Research Service (CRS) Report for Congress RS20185. Washington, D.C., CRS, Library of Congress, August 2001.

[37]Indeed, in June 2002, voters in North Dakota approved a referendum that would bar the sale of personal data collected by banks, credit unions, and other financial services firms to third parties. See P. Thibodeau, "N.D. Voters Side Overwhelmingly with Privacy," *ComputerWorld*, June 12, 2002.

USA PATRIOT Act

PL 107-56, Uniting and Strengthening America by Providing Appropriate Tools Required to Intercept and Obstruct Terrorism Act of 2001—the USA PATRIOT Act—gives federal officials broader authority to monitor communications and share information.[38] Enacted in response to the terrorist attacks of September 11, 2001, the act's intent is to combat terrorism, and it encompasses among other things criminal and foreign intelligence investigations, money laundering, and alien terrorists. The most salient effects on individual privacy result from the increased surveillance-related empowerment of government agencies.

In general, there are four surveillance mechanisms provided by U.S. law: interception orders, search warrants, pen registers and trap and trace orders, and subpoenas. Interception orders have given authorities a clearly delineated process for eavesdropping electronically on telephone and face-to-face conversations and electronic communications in serious criminal cases. Search warrants allow the search of premises and the seizure of tangible things, including records. Pen registers and trap-and-trace orders surreptitiously identify the source and destination of calls to and from a particular telephone. Subpoenas compel the production of evidence, including physical items and testimony. There are also differing standards of proof for each of these mechanisms, based on whether domestic law enforcement or foreign intelligence agencies are conducting the surveillance.

The USA PATRIOT Act has changed laws governing all four of the mechanisms described above. It permits pen registers and trap and trace orders for electronic communications, as well as for phone conversations, and authorizes nationwide execution of some surveillance-related court orders. Voice mail is treated like stored e-mail, which gives it less protection than telephone conversations. The act allows interception of communications relevant to the investigation of a suspected computer trespasser and permits sneak-and-peek search warrants and delayed (possibly forever) notification of the subject of the search. It also empowers the attorney general to acquire education records relevant to the investigation of terrorist offenses and to collect DNA samples from prisoners convicted of certain terrorism-related offenses.

The act reduces restrictions on foreign intelligence gathering (that is, on U.S. agencies gathering intelligence about other countries and their citizens) within the United States and facilitates information sharing between foreign intelligence and domestic law enforcement agencies. The

---

[38]See Charles Doyle, *The USA PATRIOT Act: A Sketch*, Congressional Research Service Report RL21203, and Charles Doyle, *The USA PATRIOT Act: A Legal Analysis*, Congressional Research Service Report RL31377.

act eased some of the restrictions on foreign intelligence gathering introduced during the 1970s—it now permits roving surveillance, expands the allowable circumstances for a search or surveillance under the Foreign Intelligence Surveillance Act of 1978 (FISA) (PL 95- 511, 92 Stat. 1783),[39] and sanctions court-ordered access to any tangible item held by lodging, car rental, and storage businesses. Roving surveillance means that warrants need not include specific information about the instrument or location of a search. Unlike domestic law enforcement, FISA searches do not require probable cause of criminality; rather, they require only that the target be suspected of being an agent of a foreign government. Information obtained from these searches may be shared with the FBI. Likewise, domestic law enforcement agencies may also share certain information (e.g., criminal wiretap results) with foreign intelligence agencies.

The USA PATRIOT Act also addresses the financial aspects of terrorism, particularly money laundering. It requires financial services professionals to file suspicious activity reports (SARs) in certain circumstances and also increases "special measures" and "due diligence requirements" related to foreign money laundering. As a result of the act, standards for customer identification and record keeping have become more stringent, and financial institutions are being encouraged to share information with law enforcement agencies.

E-Government Act

The E-Government Act of 2002 (PL 107-347) provides further impetus for the Government Paperwork Elimination Act of 1998 to enable electronic government at the federal level. The act also authorizes increased funding for e-government projects, creates an administrator for a new e-government office within the OMB, extends provisions of the Government Information Security Reform Act of 2000 (PL 106-398, Subtitle G, §1061-1065),[40] provides uniform safeguards to protect the confidentiality

---

[39]For more information on FISA, see <http://www.eff.org/Censorship/Terrorism_militias/fisa_faq.html> and the law itself at <http://www4.law.cornell.edu/uscode/50/ch36.html>.

[40]The Government Information Security Reform Act (GISRA) of 2000 required agencies to report annually to OMB on the security of their information systems and to make information system security part of their regular process of doing business (e.g., in budget requests). Under a sunset provision, GISRA was originally intended to expire in November 2002; however, the Federal Information Security Management Act (H.R. 3844), which was later incorporated into the E-Government Act, made the GISRA provisions mentioned above permanent. See Judi Hasson, "Egov Agenda Takes Shape," *Federal Computer Week*, December 2, 2002. Available online at <http://www.fcw.com/fcw/articles/2002/1202/news-egov-12-02-02.asp>.

of information collected from the public for statistical purposes, and requires the issuance of government-wide policies for standards for federal Web site usability and for records management for federal Web sites. Especially relevant for this report, the law includes provisions on electronic signature technologies and privacy impact analyses.

The provision concerning electronic signature technologies is intended to promote the compatibility of agency solutions. Executive agencies must ensure that their use and acceptance of electronic signatures to secure electronic transactions with the federal government are compatible with the pertinent policies issued by the OMB. The law further designates the General Services Administration (GSA) as the lead federal agency to create a framework for the interoperability of electronic signatures solutions, which is to include digital signatures.[41]

The privacy provisions of the act recognize that more citizen-centered e-government requires an exchange of personally identifiable information between users and federal agencies. In response, the act requires that agencies conduct privacy impact statements when developing or procuring a new information system. While the act leaves the details of the content of privacy impact statements to the OMB to develop, it is reasonable to assume that the OMB will use the best practice of the Chief Information Officers (CIO) Council as a starting point for this policy.[42]

As of this writing, there are still many implementation details to be worked out, but this new law clearly provides more tools for agencies that seek to implement authentication technologies and to consider the privacy implications of those decisions.

Homeland Security Act of 2002

The Homeland Security Act of 2002 (PL 107-296) establishes a cabinet-level Department of Homeland Security, bringing together a myriad of federal agencies currently spread among a number of federal-level cabinet agencies and executive branch organizations. As a consumer of intelligence data from the FBI and CIA as well as a coordinator of the dissemination of such data throughout the federal government and to state and local governments, the new Department of Homeland Security will have significant information management responsibilities that have both authentication and privacy implications. Much of this information management would appear to fall under the purview of the undersecretary

---

[41] GSA's Federal Bridge Certification Authority is a move in this direction; for more information, see <http://www.cio.gov/fbca/>.

[42] See the CIO Council's Web site for information on the IRS's implementation of the privacy impact statement as a best practice. Available online at <http://www.cio.gov/documents/pia_for_it_irs_model.pdf>.

for information analysis and infrastructure protection; the delegation of such responsibilities requires more scrutiny.

Summary

In recent years, the desire for highly integrated electronic government is driving government organizations toward interagency and intergovernmental authentication technology and policy solutions.[43] The Access Certificates for Electronic Services (ACES) system, described later in this chapter, is an example of such a proposed solution. However, complications arise when this type of solution is undertaken in the public sector. For example, public sector authentication solutions often involve significant roles for private sector trusted third parties, complicating roles and responsibilities and therefore accountability. In addition, single-sign-on approaches allow interaction with multiple government agencies, but might lead to many of the privacy concerns cited in this report. It is not clear that the current privacy policy framework is sufficiently robust or flexible to provide the privacy protections needed to accommodate these approaches (see Chapter 3 in this report for more on the current state of privacy law and policy in the United States). While there may be a desire for a simple, secure, privacy-preserving means by which citizens can interact with multiple government agencies, it is difficult to satisfy all of these criteria simultaneously. Indeed, as is clear from the discussion in this chapter, privacy law and policy in the United States tend to be without overarching or apparent unifying principles. The lack of cohesiveness in the legal and policy framework could lead to gaps, inconsistencies, and overlaps, making compliance difficult and potentially more expensive.

GOVERNMENT AS ISSUER OF IDENTITY DOCUMENTS

The preceding sections addressed the first role of government, as regulator, and this section discusses its second role with respect to authentication—as an issuer of identity documents, often in conjunction with the private sector. Anyone who has traveled on a commercial airline since September 11, 2001, has a sense of the unique role that government fills in issuing identification documents. The airlines, enforcing regulations issued by the federal government, are quite clear in their instruc-

---

[43]See Computer Science and Telecommunications Board, National Research Council, *Information Technology Research, Innovation, and E-Government*, Washington, D.C., National Academy Press, 2002, for a broad look at e-government innovation and approaches that can help accelerate innovation in government.

tions; passengers must present a "government-issued photo ID."[44]   A photo ID issued by a traveler's employer is not sufficient.   It must be government-issued.   The government is able to compel individuals to hold certain IDs and follow specified processes in order to help ensure the integrity of the ID issuing process.   As a result, government-issued IDs are presumed to be of higher quality than those issued by private organizations (although fraudulent government IDs are demonstrably not hard to come by). (See Box 6.1 for a general discussion of credentials presented by those wishing to be authenticated.)

The integrity of any authentication system that relies on a government-issued identifier depends on the integrity of a small number of foundation ID documents issued by government organizations.   What is somewhat surprising, though, is how circular the process of either obtaining, getting a duplicate, or even retiring a government-issued ID is and how involved in the process the private sector is.   As discussed below, hospital staff play an integral role in recording birth information that is used for the issuance of birth certificates and then Social Security numbers.   It is also possible to get printed copies of birth certificates from private sector companies working on behalf of local governments.[45]   At the other end of the continuum of life, private funeral directors often issue death records for sharing with a variety of government organizations.

The first identity document issued for most native-born U.S. citizens is a birth certificate.   Birth and death records are maintained by municipal governments.   Many births (all of those outside public hospitals) occur without the presence of any government employee.   Many a new parent has faced the admonition from hospital staff not to leave the hospital without naming the new child, making it possible for the city or county office of vital records to record the birth and issue a birth certificate.   In the case of a small local government, a town clerk may serve this function. It is interesting to note, however, that the hospital staff play a role in documenting the birth for purposes of establishing the identity of the child and his or her relationship to its parents.   A delivery room nurse and the physician who delivered the child are likely to sign the paperwork necessary to obtain the birth certificate.   The presence of a nonmedical government employee during childbirth would, in fact, probably be considered to constitute a significant invasion of privacy.

---

[44]See the Web site <http://www.tsa.gov/workingwithtsa/travel.shtm> for federal rules on government-issued IDs for flying commercially. John Gilmore is presently challenging these regulations in federal court. See <http://cryptome.org/freetotravel.htm> for a chronology of that suit.

[45]See, for example, the Web site <http://www.vitalchek.com/provider_overview.asp> for information on obtaining birth certificates and other vital records.

BOX 6.1
On the Nature of Credentials

Understanding the nature of credentials is an important component of understanding authentication technologies, processes, and systems, since the "verifier" in an authentication transaction verifies credentials presented by the "presenter." Credentials may be bound in some way to the individual to whom they were issued, or they may be bearer credentials. The former are necessary for identification, while the latter may be acceptable for some forms of authorization. A driver's license or a passport is an example of the former, while an admission ticket for an entertainment event or a discount coupon is an example of the latter. Cash is a true bearer credential with very good anticounterfeit protection. A credential intended to be bound to a specific individual should effect the binding in some way that can be checked by a verifier; otherwise it risks becoming a bearer credential. Most driver's licenses, employee ID cards, and all passports include a photo to allow a human verifier to determine if the individual presenting the credential is the one to whom the credential was issued. Machine-verifiable credentials may be bound to bearers through use of personal identification numbers or biometrics.

Most credit cards do not include a photo, even though they are credentials intended for use by a specific individual. Instead, most credit cards contain a signature strip, and verifiers (merchants) are supposed to compare the purchaser's signature with that on the card for what are referred to as "card present" transactions. This signature-verification approach to user authentication is generally poorer than the photo ID approach, and it is not always used by merchants, especially in the United States. A growing number of credit card transactions are conducted as mail order or telephone order (MOTO) transactions or Internet transactions, and in these cases neither a photo nor a signature is available to the verifier to be checked. To help address this deficiency, credit card verification generally entails an online check. This is necessary in part because the credit card, as an authorization credential, is tied to data that cannot easily be maintained on the credit card, for example, the outstanding purchase total relative to the cardholder's credit limit.

This example points to another aspect of credential systems: off-line versus online verification. Thanks in part to ubiquitous networking, credit cards have effectively become online verification systems, which they were not when they were first used. Online verification may be effected simply by querying a database using an identifier (for example, a credit card number), or it may involve a complex interaction between the credential and its issuer (for example, as many smart cards operate). Online verification also is attractive in that it supports rapid revocation of credentials. Many credentials are issued with an explicit period of validity. They must be periodically renewed. The issuer can revoke a credential by refusing to renew it, but this is not a very responsive way to revoke a credential. If failure to renew is the only way to revoke a credential, the issuer must trade off the costs of more frequent renewal against accepting the costs imposed by delaying revocation until the next renewal period. If the issuer can physically recall a credential, an intermediate form of revocation is possible; but in a world where an increasing number of transactions are not conducted in person, physical revocation is often not a viable option. (If one tried to use an invalid credit card in a store, it might be

(continues)

BOX 6.1   Continued

retained or destroyed by the merchant, but card confiscation is not possible when the transaction is conducted via the phone, mail, or Internet.)

For any physical credential, there is always a concern about how easily the credential can be forged or altered. If one can readily modify a credential or create a bogus credential and have a verifier accept the credential as valid, then the credential system has failed. For credit cards, knowledge of a legitimate credit card number (plus expiration date and billing address) is sufficient to effect most MOTO transactions. Credit card account numbers (and expiration dates and addresses) cannot be well-protected secrets, because they must be transmitted to merchants to effect transactions. This points out a fundamental deficiency of credit cards as credentials in the MOTO environment: the information needed to pose as the legitimate cardholder is not a well-protected secret. Ancillary measures are adopted by merchants to counter credit card fraud—for example, reliance on automatic number identification (ANI) for phone orders placed to toll free numbers, and shipping only to the billing address associated with an account.

An obvious security concern for physical credentials is the ability of a verifier to detect forgeries. Many driver's licenses and current U.S. passports include antitamper and anticounterfeiting measures—for example, holograms that are designed to make it easy for a human verifier to determine if the credential is legitimate. Many credit cards also make use of holograms, to raise the bar against generation of fake physical credit cards. If legitimate credentials come in many forms, the verifier is less likely to be able to spot fakes. Birth certificates exhibit this problem (among others), since there are more than 17,000 jurisdictions that may issue these documents, and the formats vary widely. Machine-verifiable credentials ameliorate this problem, but they are typically more expensive to create, and the cost of deploying verification technology also creates barriers to deployment.

Against this backdrop, one can examine various forms of credentials to see how they rate. For example, a driver's license is an identity credential for a named

It is also important to note that not all births occur in hospitals. Besides the proverbial delivery in a taxicab, one must consider home births and so on. The U.S. Constitution defines anyone born in the United States as a citizen, whether or not he or she is born in a hospital (at the time the Constitution was written, far fewer children were born in hospitals), so that (hypothetical) controls on birth certificates based on hospital licensing would miss some number of children. In effect, the issuance of a birth certificate approximates the issuance of an identity certificate at birth.

In the past, human witnesses could serve to authenticate someone's identity in the way that the birth certificate is meant to do now. Children tended to be born at home, in the presence of witnesses from the local community. They grew up among family and neighbors, many of whom remained available for later testimony as to the identity of the eventual individual. It carries a photo of the individual to whom it was issued and is designed for off-line verification by a human. It can be physically revoked by a law enforcement officer or officer of the court. Because of wide variability in formats and anticounterfeiting measures, forged licenses may be hard to detect, especially when the license does not purport to be from the state in which it is being verified. A license typically contains data—for example, home address—which are not well maintained on the credential and which are not generally essential to the primary function for which the license was issued.

A combination of a user ID and a password constitutes a bearer credential in practice, even when the intention is otherwise. Authentication takes place over a network, and any binding to an individual is based on the assumption that the user did not share the password and that the pair was not guessed by an attacker.

Most credit cards are essentially bearer credentials, although that is not the intention. Cards that bear a photo of the cardholder offer added protection in card-present transactions but do not improve the security of MOTO transactions. Counterfeit cards, even ones that make use of holograms, have been produced by thieves, demonstrating the limits of current, anticounterfeiting measures.

A smart card with a photo ID is a hybrid form of individual credential designed for both human verification and machine-based, typically online, verification. The human verification aspect of such cards is vulnerable to tampering attacks, except to the extent that anticounterfeiting measures are applied. The machine verification aspect of these cards can be of very high quality: That is, creating a fake public key certificate that would be accepted by the verifier can be made infeasible from a mathematical perspective. However, it may be possible to covertly acquire the private key and certificate of a legitimate individual from his or her card and insert them into a smart card with another individual's photo, thus allowing the second individual to pose as the first for both human and machine verification purposes. This illustrates the difficulty of developing very high assurance credential technology, although technology of this sort does pose significant barriers to counterfeiting.

adult. In other words, family and neighbors could testify to continuity of identity despite biometric changes in the identified person. The current birth certificate is meant to serve as a substitute, but it has several flaws of its own.[46]

---

[46]There are many contexts in which human witnesses serve as verifiers of identity of either people or objects. For example, chains of custody in court cases require human witnesses to testify to the provenance of something admitted into evidence. Human witnesses can, of course, authenticate other individuals; this requires establishing the authority and veracity of the witness. This report does not investigate the pros and cons of human witness testimony, as the committee's charge was to examine authentication *technologies*, but certainly there are situations in which human witness testimony may be the best (or only) method available for verifying identity.

There is, of course, a human element in the issuance procedure, so there are errors both of commission (for example, not accounting properly for stillborn children or creating fraudulent documentation of a "birth" that never occurred) and omission (childbirths that go unrecorded).[47] As in all automated systems, there must be a manual process for handling these errors, and the impact of the errors must be considered. In addition, in order to ensure that the document refers to the correct individual when it is issued, it is important to issue the initial identity document as close to birth as possible. This begs the question of whether biometrics of some sort are needed, which raises some interesting problems with respect to the many biometrics (including footprints, which are standard in some locales) that might be used as part of an identity document for a small child. Photographs of newborn infant faces are difficult to use for anything other than determining the race of the child, if that. Eye color changes over the first year of life, and newborns have not yet acquired their permanent hair color. While fingerprints are set at birth, there are some important technical limitations: the ridges are so close together that a standard 500-dots-per-inch scanner does not have enough resolution to scan them accurately, and today's algorithms do not handle finger growth, which causes the ridges to spread farther apart.

The Social Security Administration (SSA) has some nearly unique technical requirements for its system of authenticating people. Parents are given a strong incentive to get an SSN for their child before filing the first federal income tax return after the child's birth: They must do so to claim the child as a dependent (this is a relatively recent change). Hence, the SSN is likely to be issued near the time of birth. While some children have large enough unearned incomes to require paying taxes, many children will have no use for their SSN until they are teenagers getting their first summer jobs. The first technical requirement, therefore, is that although the binding between a person and his or her SSN will sit dormant for approximately 15 years, it must routinely be verifiable at that later time. Very few commercial systems have this property: If they have not

---

[47]There are other randomization processes at work in addition to errors in documentation. It is known, for instance, that on rare occasions parents have taken the wrong child home from a hospital nursery. As discussed already, family mobility is a randomizer for the early childhood years. A child whose parents move frequently while the child is maturing can lose all witnesses to his or her identity continuity except for his or her parents, and if those parents should die or otherwise not be acceptable as witnesses, that child would have no witnesses to identity. As individuals urbanize and become more mobile, if the only method of establishing identity is through human witnesses to identity continuity, it may not be possible to establish identity with close to 100 percent confidence. Put another way, it may be becoming easier for someone to infiltrate an urbanized nation under an assumed identity.

interacted with a customer for 15 years, very few, if any, businesses are required (or want, for that matter) to keep that customer record. Until recently, most people had little or no contact with the SSA during their working years. Now, people receive annual account statements (previously called Personal Earnings and Benefits Estimate) from the SSA. If the statement is correct, there is no need for follow-up, so individuals may still go three to four decades between their first contributions and their next interaction with the SSA, when they claim benefits after retirement. Hence the second technical requirement: The authentication technology needs to work with absolutely minimal interaction over spans of 50 or more years.[48] This requirement suggests that authentication systems that must persist for long periods of time will have to support renewal, as systems (presumably) change over time.[49]

A third technical requirement for the SSA system of authenticating people is that the system must work for the entire population, not just a significant percentage. As interaction with the SSA, the IRS, and other government agencies is legally mandatory, not being able to authenticate to them is not an option. Either the authentication system must work for everyone (for example, ruling out biometrics that have significant failure rates for reasons beyond people's control), or there must be a non-onerous exception mechanism. Declaring that certain sets of people are not worth serving (or going to great lengths to serve) is an option in most commercial contexts, but not for the government. If the choice is to include an exception mechanism, it will need to be designed in from the beginning, and the security implications of the exception mechanism will need thorough analysis, since experience indicates that security problems are often found in little-used parts of systems.

> **Finding 6.2: Electronic authentication is qualitatively different for the public sector and the private sector because of a government's unique relationship with its citizens:**
>
> **a. Many of the transactions are mandatory.**
> **b. Government agencies cannot choose to serve only selected market segments. Thus, the user population with which they must deal is very heterogeneous and possibly difficult to serve electronically.**

---

[48]It should be noted that no cryptographic system other than the one-time pad has remained secure for 50 years in modern history.

[49]Note that this may mean more than just changing key sizes, as is done for some authentication algorithms; other cryptographic parts of the system, such as hash functions, may need replacing.

  c. **Relationships between governments and citizens are sometimes cradle to grave but characterized by intermittent contacts, which creates challenges for technical authentication solutions.**
  d. **Individuals may have higher expectations for government agencies than for other organizations when it comes to protecting the security and privacy of personal data.**

This finding echoes the analysis in CSTB's 2002 report *Information Technology Research, Innovation, and E-Government*,[50] which described special considerations in e-government. Ubiquity (access for everyone, anywhere, anytime) and trustworthiness (citizens will not tolerate unauthorized or accidental disclosure of personal information) were described as areas in which government leads in demand for technologies.

The Tangled Web of Government-Issued Identity Documents

It is overly simplistic to view government as monolithic. It may turn out that each agency picks its own authentication technology and deploys it among the user base that the agency serves. Some agencies may voluntarily agree to use another agency's authenticators. In fact, most models of e-government presume a degree of integration among government agencies and between levels of government.[51,52] Making such electronic interactions work seamlessly for users will require a degree of interoperability for both policy and technology. To this end, as noted in the discussion of the E-Government Act, the federal government is sponsoring the deployment of a PKI that will authenticate transactions across the federal government and (potentially) with state governments as well. In many cases, the government will both issue and rely on the authenticator. As discussed below, once an individual has one of the widely recognized government-issued IDs, he or she can obtain other government-issued IDs. In essence, government acts as a certificate authority (CA) of sorts in the issuance of these documents. (Figure 6.1 illustrates the interdependencies of foundational identity documents.)

---

[50]Computer Science and Telecommunications Board, National Research Council. *Information Technology Research, Innovation, and E-Government*. Washington, D.C., National Academy Press, 2002.

[51]For example, see K. Layne and J. Lee, "Developing Fully Functional E-Government: A Four Stage Model," *Government Information Quarterly* 18: 122-136, and Janine S. Hiller and France Bélanger, "Privacy Strategies for Electronic Government," *E-Government 2001*, Mark A. Abramson and Grady E. Means, eds. New York, Rowman and Littlefield, 2001.

[52]See also the white paper "Federal Electronic Government Infrastructure: The E-Authentication Gateway—Connecting People to Services," available online at <http://www.cio.gov/eauthentication/presentations/authentication_gateway_whitepaper.pdf>.

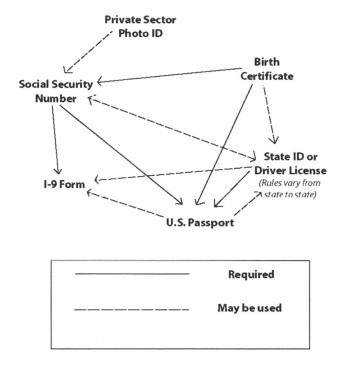

FIGURE 6.1 Interdependencies of foundational identity documents issued by both governments and the private sector.

Issuance of an SSN requires proof of age and of citizenship or appropriate noncitizen status and a current proof of identity. For adults, the proof of identity is generally another government-issued photo identification, although it need not be: nonphotographic government records such as marriage and divorce records and adoption records are also accepted. Additionally, some private sector identification cards are accepted: for example, employer and school ID cards (usually with photographs), along with insurance policies and ID cards (usually without photographs). For a child, proof of identity is based on a parent's vouching for the child's name, possibly indirectly through the hospital's registrar and/or county/state officials.

A California state ID card (for identification purposes, equivalent to a driver's license), for example, is issued upon presentation of a birth certificate, passport, or expiring ID card and proof of SSN. As noted earlier, it is difficult to link the birth certificate to the person applying for the ID card. In the United States, state ID cards are the dominant form of photo identification. Most private organizations rely on state ID cards for everyday transactions—for example, paying by check, setting up a video rental account, and so on.

Acquiring a U.S. passport requires a birth certificate, a prior passport or other proof of citizenship, and current proof of identity—that is, a local, state, or federal government-issued photo identification, including state ID cards and U.S. passports. An SSN must be stated on the passport application. The passport is sufficient to request any of the three other forms of identification. In addition, a passport is sufficient proof of identity and authorization to satisfy the U.S. Department of Justice I-9 form.[53] Alternatively, the I-9 is most commonly satisfied with a state ID card and a Social Security card. Other possibilities (for example, other military or government ID cards) also exist but are used relatively rarely. Most large employers will issue their own photo identification, which is occasionally used outside the place of employment—for example, for verifying eligibility for various corporate discounts.

The forms of identification described above have several noteworthy features. Birth certificates are generally issued by municipal jurisdictions, state ID cards by states, and Social Security cards and passports by different agencies within the federal government. Weaknesses in various documents, particularly the difficulty of binding a birth certificate to a specific person, are addressed by the business practices of the various agencies. In general, a birth certificate alone is insufficient evidence for the generation of other identity documents. In the United States, each agency has its own policy for what it accepts, while in Australia this concept has been formalized in the "100 points of proof" model.[54] The formalization occurs through the assignment of points to different identifying documents. For instance, a current Australian passport is worth 70 points, a bank statement is worth 40 points, and employment records are worth 10 points. Different services require different point totals. The decentralized nature of this arrangement means that no single entity has a completely authoritative database. The evidence required for the initial government-issued identity document, the birth certificate, is often attested to by private sector employees. It should also be noted that the United States is a nation of immigrants—documents prepared overseas may introduce even more uncertainty into the system.[55] All of these factors contribute to the difficulty that the relying party may have in verifying the documents.

---

[53]The I-9 form is required to be completed by all new employees so that their employer can verify their employment eligibility.

[54]See the Web sites <http://www.centrelink.gov.au/internet/internet.nsf/multifilestores/poi0110t/$File/poi0110en.pdf> and <http://www.whittlesea.vic.gov.au/enquiries/eserv_user.asp>.

[55]Note the case of Danny Alimonte, born in the Dominican Republic. His eligibility to play Little League baseball came into dispute during the 2001 Little League World Series. It

As the authentication environment changes over time, with fewer people to attest to the provenance of a person and more and more authentication happening electronically, it will be necessary to revisit the security of foundational identity documents. Today's systems have worked reasonably well, but it will become increasingly easy for correlated information about an identity to be acquired by someone with malicious intent. For many purposes, birth identity becomes largely irrelevant later in life. Birth certificates, which are bearer credentials, suffer from the problems inherent in all bearer credentials. However, stronger alternatives, such as DNA, are very expensive, may be unpopular with large segments of society, and raise new privacy and technical challenges.

Recommendation 6.1: Birth certificates should not be relied upon as the sole base identity document. Supplemented with supporting evidence, birth certificates can be used when proof of citizenship is a requirement.

Threats to Foundational Documents

As noted previously, government-issued identity documents are the foundational documents relied upon by many authentication systems in both the public and private sectors. Any analysis of such systems must therefore take into account the threat model faced in the issuance and use of those documents.[56] Only after the threats against the relied-upon documents are understood can the threat faced by the system under analysis be considered. As discussed in Chapter 4, in order to evaluate the security of any authentication system, one first needs to define the threat faced by the system.[57]

---

was unclear whether Danny was 12 or 14 years old. Dominican Republic birth records from the mid-1980s yielded inconsistent answers. He was eventually declared ineligible.

[56]This discussion applies as well to the generation of identity documents that does not take place under governmental purview. However, given that in practice many authentication systems do ultimately rely on a government-issued identification document, the discussion is in that context.

[57]It is worth remembering that authentication is often the first step in authorization. The many authorization policies that different government and private sector parties may have are outside the scope of this report. However, from a privacy perspective, it is often better to handle authorization directly, rather than as a function of identity (verified through authentication). For example, one can anonymously watch a movie: one goes to the ticket window, purchases a ticket with cash, gives the ticket to the ticket collector, and enters the theater. No record is ever made of the identity of the moviegoer. On the other hand, many moviegoers voluntarily give up some amount of privacy to purchase tickets with a credit card, possibly beforehand, over the telephone or the Internet.

The attacks against generation systems for traditional foundational document fall into these general categories:

- Obtaining a fraudulent identity document,
- Passing off someone else's valid identity document as one's own,
- Modifying the contents of a valid identity document,
- Compromising private information stored in a back-end system, and
- Unauthorized modification of information stored in a back-end system.

Motivations for these attacks can vary, of course, ranging from the desire to purchase alcohol when under age to the desire to move easily through security checkpoints in order to perpetrate a terrorist act. Attacks could be aimed at individuals (as in the case of identity theft) or at undermining public and private institutions. The disparity of possible motivations highlights another way (see Chapter 4) in which secondary use is dangerous: Namely, it makes it difficult to determine the danger posed by a security breach or attack. Given the myriad uses of driver's licenses, for example, it is incredibly difficult to ascertain the danger from a successful attack against a motor vehicles department database. Each of these attacks is discussed in more detail below.

- *Fraudulent identity documents.* These are a major problem in today's systems. The problem includes both external threats (for example, someone getting a driver's license with someone else's birth certificate and SSN) and internal threats (for example, a corrupt clerk at the DMV issuing driver's licenses without checking supporting documentation). It is worth noting that this kind of fraud happens only on a small scale (in terms of the percentage of identity documents issued), but it is a relatively easy way for a determined person to circumvent the system.
- *Imposters.* One can attempt to pass off someone else's identity document as one's own. Regardless of how the identity document is acquired (for example, a driver's license stolen in transit or a lost wallet found on the beach), the technical problem is the binding of the document to its holder. Photo identification represents a primitive biometric aimed at solving this problem. It has the advantages of being self-contained and requiring no infrastructure to support verification. The problem is that faces can change dramatically over time, and some identity documents have long lives (for example, with automatic renewal, the picture on a driver's license can easily be 8 or more years old).
- *Document modification.* Identity documents may be fraudulently altered (for example, the substitution of photographs on a passport or

driver's license). Preventing this sort of attack requires technical measures in the identity document (for example, holograms on driver's licenses or embossed seals on passport photos). Document modification is an attack on the integrity of the document itself; in the digital world, cryptographic integrity techniques such as message authentication codes (MACs) and digital signatures, when properly used, provide strong protection against such attacks.

• *Compromising confidential information.* Many information systems store confidential personal information that is not physically present on the identity document. For example, California and New Jersey driver's licenses show only the mailing address of their holder, not the street address, if two different addresses are on file. However, an attacker compromising the relevant database could learn the street address of any license holder.

• *Modifying computerized records.* Given that most identity authentication systems have computerized data records and that additional information may be stored in those systems, one also must be concerned about modification of that information. For example, driver's license suspensions in some states are handled by electronically marking the appropriate record as having suspended driving privileges, while the license holder is permitted to retain the physical license (and hence to continue to use it as state-issued photo identification—for example, for cashing checks). If an attacker changed this flag, either someone could drive who should not be driving, or someone innocent could be caught driving with a supposedly suspended license. The back-end database, not the physical document, is the arbiter of license status.

Moving to digital credentials will not change these basic categories of fraud. Depending on the technology chosen for authentication, the distribution of fraud among these categories may change. For example, the use of cryptographic integrity techniques for digital credentials would make document modification extremely difficult, if not impossible, assuming that the technology is properly implemented.

A major change between traditional authentication and digital authentication is the scale of likely fraud. With today's systems, one of the primary weaknesses relates to the validity of a specific instance of an identity document and permeates all of the first three categories above (fraudulent documents, imposters, and document modification). However, controls generally work well enough to prevent the widespread dissemination of fraudulent identity documents. As we move forward into a world of digital identity documents, the issuing process is still extremely important. All the cryptography in the world cannot overcome weakness in this step, because cryptographic notions of trust (and validity) are necessarily relative: They can only be as trustworthy (in the best case) as something else. The hope is that this trust chain is firmly anchored by a statement acknowledged as true in the real world. It is unfortunate that all too many people (including those who should know better) have a tendency to trust as accurate anything that the computer says, even in situations where they would not trust a paper document.

The ability to generate fraudulent identity documents on a small scale tends to have a minor impact on the overall system. However, in a digital world, the compromise of secret information—for example, of a signing key or other methods of accessing the document-issuing system—could open the way to massive issuance or use of fraudulent identity documents. The compromise of back-end systems today is already a problem for the last two categories of threats (compromising information and modifying records). One has to consider the difference in speed of propagation of security breaches. Electronic issuance of identity certificates can go orders of magnitude faster than the issuance of paper-based identity certificates.

> **Finding 6.3: Many of the foundational identification documents used to establish individual user identity are very poor from a security perspective, often as a result of having been generated by a diverse set of issuers that may lack an ongoing interest in ensuring the documents' validity and reliability. Birth certificates are especially poor as base identity documents, because they cannot be readily tied to an individual.**

> **Finding 6.4: Scale is a major factor in the implications of authentication for privacy and identity theft. The bulk compromise of private information (which is more likely to occur when such information is accessible online) or the compromise of a widely relied on document-issuing system can lead to massive issuance or use of fraudulent identity documents. The result would adversely affect individual privacy and private- and public-sector processes.**

> **Recommendation 6.2: Organizations that maintain online-accessible databases containing information used to authenticate large numbers of users should employ high-quality information security measures to protect that information. Wherever possible, authentication servers should employ mechanisms that do not require the storage of secrets.**

GOVERNMENT AS RELYING PARTY FOR
AUTHENTICATION SERVICES

Government, in addition to *issuing* identity documents, is also a *relying* party (that is, it makes payments, allows access to records, and distributes benefits electronically based on claims made by users) for authentication systems to administer public programs at all levels (federal, state, and local). In fact, the government faces some unique challenges as a relying party, owing to its large size and multifaceted nature. It should be noted that government revenues and expenditures are an order of magnitude larger than those of the largest private corporations in the United States. The government's customer base is everything from an individual citizen to neighborhood nonprofit organizations to large, multinational corporations. In some cases, the interactions between government and varied customers are for the same purpose—for example, paying income taxes. In other cases, the interactions are very different—for example, military procurements tend to come from government contractors, not from private citizens.

Additionally, the functions of government are spread among a multitude of federal, state, county, and local agencies. Government units are organized by function (health and welfare, defense, education, public works, and so on), regardless of how people might interact with them. For example, a small businessperson such as a farmer probably has interactions and transactions with several agencies within the federal government—the Department of Agriculture, the Internal Revenue Service, the Department of Labor, and perhaps the Small Business Administration. At the state level, state tax, labor, and agriculture agencies may have their own set of reporting requirements and benefits but may also pass along some programs funded by the federal government.

There is a belief, held mainly by information technology and public administration professionals, that applications of technology through e-government could reorient public organizations, causing them to become more responsive to the needs of users.[58] As discussed earlier, GPEA is driving federal agencies to move information and transactions to the Internet. For many public sector organizations, though, the move to e-government was already under way before the enactment of GPEA gave statutory impetus to federal agency efforts. Through the Office of Man-

---

[58]For some selected visions of e-government, see the National Association of Chief Information Officers, online at <http://www.nascio.org/publications/digital_government_report_2001.pdf>; Council for Excellence in Government, online at <http://www.excelgov.org/usermedia/images/uploads/PDFs/the_next_american_revolution.pdf>; or OMB e-government strategy, online at <http://www.whitehouse.gov/omb/inforeg/egovstrategy.pdf>.

agement and Budget, the federal government has identified 24 e-government projects that might offer a variety of electronic services between government and citizens, government and business, and government and government (that is, between federal, state, and local governments), and several administrative efforts that are for internal use in federal agencies.[59] For the most part, the task force that recommended this list to OMB found that these efforts had been under way for some time and predated GPEA.

Cutting through the organizational complexity, though, requires a degree of consistency in policy, management, and technology that is rarely found in the paper-based world. Many government agencies, most notably some leading federal agencies, are investing heavily in PKI as the means to deploy an electronic authentication system that will work universally for users of government programs.

The next three subsections describe ways in which the government has tried to authenticate citizens in different contexts. The first is a detailed discussion of a program—Access Certificates for Electronic Services (ACES)—that the federal government had endorsed as a way to authenticate users across a variety of program and organizational lines, the second describes the Internal Revenue Service's electronic tax filing programs, and the third describes the Social Security Administration's attempt at remote authentication for access to earnings and benefits statements. Brief concluding remarks follow.

Access Certificates for Electronic Services

ACES is a program instituted by the GSA. The program's primary purpose is to provide a PKI to facilitate secure online citizen transactions with government agencies.[60] Under ACES, a user acquires a public key certificate by interacting with one of a small number of selected, commercial CAs. These CAs commit to certification policies and procedures consistent with a model established by GSA for this purpose. This procedure is intended to ensure uniform quality of user authentication and status checking for federal agencies that act as relying parties—that is, that accept these certificates to identify users.

The user employs a certificate issued by an ACES-approved CA and the corresponding private key when engaging in transactions with participating government agencies. Federal agencies developing PKI-enabled

---

[59]See the Web site <http://www.egov.gov/egovreport-3.htm> for a more detailed description of these 24 initiatives.

[60]The General Services Administration is a federal management agency that sets policy in areas related to federal procurement, real estate, and information resources.

applications are encouraged to take advantage of the Certificate Authentication Module (CAM)—a GSA-supplied and Mitretek-developed software—to verify an ACES certificate prior to use. The CAM is designed to perform the requisite certificate validation checks, relieving application developers of the need to implement this complex PKI software. The CAM always verifies the revocation status of an ACES certificate by contacting an Online Certificate Status Protocol (OCSP) server operated by the CA that issued the certificate. (The rationale for adopting this specific revocation-status-checking mechanism is described later.)

To acquire a certificate, a user provides a CA with some personal information to verify the user's claimed identity. The standards for this verification are established by GSA and thus are uniform for all of the CAs providing the service (within the procedural security limits that these CAs enforce). The form of identity established through this interaction is a name.

The identification provided by this type of interaction generally will not be sufficient to identify the user uniquely to a government agency, since many users may share the same name—for example, John Smith. Thus, ACES certificates generally will be ambiguous relative to the ID requirements for any government agency. An agency may identify a user on the basis of both a name and an SSN or other parameters (for example, home address, age, birth date, and so on.) Thus, when the user contacts an agency for the first time with his or her ACES certificate, the user will need to provide this other information to an agency server to establish the correspondence with the user's record in the agency database. If this is the user's first contact of any form with the agency, the agency will need to verify the supplied information as, for example, the SSA does by consulting with other government records. This procedure needs to be repeated by the user when he or she initially contacts an agency. Each agency must then find a means for binding the ACES certificate to the user identity in that agency's database—for example, on the basis of the CA name and serial number of the certificate or a hash of the public key from the certificate. (The CA name and serial number are unique to the user, but they will change whenever the user renews the certificate, because a new serial number must be assigned to every certificate issued by the CA, even if the user merely renews the certificate. This procedure suggests that users may have to reauthenticate themselves periodically to each agency when the user's certificate expires, using whatever means the agency employed to effect the initial binding between an ACES certificate and its records. If the hash of the public key of the certificate is employed, similar problems arise whenever the user changes his or her key pair.)

Under the terms of the ACES program, neither the user nor the government pays the CA for issuing an ACES certificate. Instead, every time an individual uses a certificate in a transaction with a government agency, the agency pays. The government agency pays the issuing CA for the revocation status check (via OCSP, usually invoked by the CAM), thus providing the financial motivation for CAs to issue these certificates. ACES avoids the need for government agencies to make up-front investments in establishing a PKI to support this sort of e-government service. It also avoids the need for these agencies to act as CAs. Instead, the agencies pay for the PKI on a sort of installment basis, indefinitely. (This arrangement is analogous in many ways to the government allowing a private company to build a toll road and then collect the tolls, forever.)

It has been suggested that ACES is an appropriate way to enable citizen e-government because the technical aspects of CA operation exceed the capabilities of most government agencies. However, since the certificates issued by the CAs are not sufficient to identify individuals uniquely relative to agency database records, each agency ultimately acts as a registration authority (RA) when it establishes the correspondence between the certificate holder and the database records. The RA function, while less technical than that of the CA, is usually the most security-critical procedure of CA operation, so agencies have not avoided the need to participate in PKI management as a result of ACES. Arguably, the agencies have databases that are ideal for identifying their users to the granularity required to ensure authorized access to records and to effect authenticated transactions. Thus, the use of commercial CAs to issue user certificates does not relieve government agencies of the burden of performing this security-critical function. It is true that CA operation does require specialized technical capabilities, and the ACES program avoids the need for agencies to acquire these capabilities. However, it is not clear that an agency with the IT resources needed to create and operate PKI-enabled applications could not also operate a CA for the users that it serves by means of these applications.

The Internal Revenue Service—Electronic Tax Filing

The IRS has been working to increase the volume of the electronic filing of individual tax returns since the program began in the late 1980s. While IRS e-file has been described as a pioneer program in electronic government, it is interesting to note that for many years the IRS required that electronically filed returns be accompanied by paper signature documents. Only since 1999 has the IRS begun to make the e-file program a totally paperless process, including electronic authentication, for some selected taxpayers.

Fortunately for the IRS, there is public law and policy that supports electronic authentication. The basic requirement in the Internal Revenue

Code is that tax returns be signed. However, the law does not specify what constitutes a signing and, in fact, Treasury regulations give the IRS commissioner broad discretion to determine what constitutes a signing. Additionally, the IRS Reform and Restructuring Act of 1998 (PL 105-206) speaks directly to the issue of electronic signatures and provides that they are criminally and civilly equivalent to paper signatures.

There is only one direct channel for the public to e-file with the IRS. Through the Telefile program, the IRS "invites" taxpayers to participate by getting a specially designed tax package. Invitations go to taxpayers on the basis of expected eligibility (as a 1040EZ filer, with income less than $50,000, or as a single filer with no dependents). The package includes instructions for how to file using a Touch-Tone phone and a customer service number (CSN), which is a four-digit PIN. IRS relies on the CSN used by the taxpayer to sign the return, but that does not authenticate the transaction, since the CSN is not a unique identifier. The IRS authenticates the transaction by comparing data elements—the CSN, date of birth, taxpayer identification number (generally an SSN), and a name presented by the taxpayer—to those same data elements maintained in IRS databases.

What makes authentication for IRS e-file somewhat challenging is the role of intermediaries between the IRS and the taxpayer. In addition to the direct provision of service through Telefile, the IRS relies extensively on intermediaries to deliver its electronic filing products to the public. Generally, over half the individual tax returns filed with the IRS are prepared by tax preparers such as commercial services, certified public accountants, and enrolled agents. Tax preparers do an even larger percentage of the returns prepared for e-file, a program that emerged out of a partnership between the IRS and H&R Block. A subset of preparers, authorized e-file providers, are authorized to e-file individual tax returns for their clients. The authorization, in this case, refers to the fact that the IRS regulates the preparers that can e-file in some detail.

Prior to 1999, the only way for a taxpayer to sign a return filed through a preparer was to fill out a paper signature document, called a jurat, which the preparer also had to sign and then send to the IRS within 48 hours of the IRS accepting the return electronically. The requirement for the preparer to file the jurat with the IRS is contained in IRS Revenue Procedures governing the behaviors of authorized e-file providers, which also require them to exercise due diligence in verifying the identity of taxpayers by requesting forms of identification to help validate claimed identity. Similarly, the taxpayer who used personal computer or Web-based tax preparation software prior to 1999 had to complete a jurat and send it to the IRS after the return was acknowledged as accepted. (As a side note, the return can only be transmitted to the IRS through a third-party transmitter authorized by the IRS.)

Beginning in 1999, the IRS built on experience of the Telefile program to issue e-file customer numbers (ECNs) to those individuals who had filed their returns using Web-based or personal computer tax preparation software the previous year. Much as with Telefile, these selected taxpayers got a sealed postcard that explained program eligibility and contained one CSN (two for joint filers).

As part of a parallel pilot in 1999, those taxpayers using an authorized e-file provider could avoid the use of a jurat. In the presence of the preparer, taxpayer(s) would select their own PIN(s), to be used to sign the return. IRS Revenue Procedures required that the taxpayers physically enter their self-selected PINs on the preparer's keyboard. As part of the signing process, the preparer and taxpayers also record the PIN(s) and other data from the return on a worksheet that both the preparer and taxpayer(s) retain.

In both of the 1999 electronic signature efforts, much as with Telefile, the IRS used the PIN-like four-digit number (for example, CSN, ECN, self-selected PIN) to sign the returns. This procedure meets the legal requirement for a return to be signed. Used in combination with other data presented by the taxpayer(s), the IRS is able to authenticate the transaction to ensure that the taxpayer is who he or she claims to be. The need for such authentication results from the use of a four-digit PIN that is not a unique identifier. Additionally, authentication beyond the signing of the return is necessary because of the business risks associated with refund fraud. The IRS refers to the need for "revenue protection."[61] Since the initial offering in 1999 and 2000, the IRS has evolved its electronic authentication efforts for taxpayers filing from home using the Web, tax preparation software and/or the services of a tax preparer. The primary difference now is that the IRS no longer mails out the ECN to home filers and instead allows taxpayers to self-select a PIN for signing purposes. Additionally, the signing is bound to the transaction by the taxpayer(s) providing information from the previous year's tax return like Adjusted Gross Income (AGI) so the IRS can validate claimed identity of the taxpayer beyond name, address, and taxpayer identification number.

---

[61]Given that over 70 percent of individual tax returns result in a refund and that there is a history of individuals trying to defraud the government by seeking refunds they are not entitled to, this is a significant business risk. It is interesting to note that the shift from paper-based to electronic signing altered the IRS's ability to prevent some refund fraud. For instance, the use of the CSN in the case of Telefile and the ECN in the first 2 years of that effort, in conjunction with other identifying data, provides an extra check up-front that is not possible with paper-based signings.

The Social Security Administration and PEBES

One of the more infamous cases of privacy involving authentication colliding with e-government capabilities comes from the SSA's Online PEBES initiative.[62] In 1997, the SSA had to bring down its otherwise-successful Web-based capability allowing individuals to request and ultimately receive a Personal Earnings and Benefits Estimate Statement (PEBES) over the Web. The SSA took this action after a *USA Today* article and subsequent stories in other national news outlets raised concerns about the how the SSA authorized the release of a PEBES to an individual electronically (described below). Although PEBES provided dramatically improved service through reduced cycle times and cost per transaction, SSA yielded to congressional pressure and suspended the service owing to the public outcry resulting from the national media coverage.

Historically, SSA had provided PEBES to those who made a request over the phone or by mail if the requester produced three identifiers (SSN, date of birth, and name), without validating if the requester was really the person related to that record. For instance, it was quite possible that a wife could have provided the requested information and obtained her husband's PEBES using that business rule. Using this process, SSA filled literally millions of requests per year for PEBES by mail and over the phone.

To improve service and reduce the workload of the shrinking SSA staff, the organization launched an effort to fulfill requests for PEBES through a self-service application over the Web. Initially the SSA provided partial electronic service, taking the request electronically but reverting to paper by mailing the report to the address provided in the request. Over time, and after considering the results of pilot testing and some risk analyses, the SSA launched the fully interactive version by which the PEBES was delivered back to the requester electronically. As an acknowledgment that moving this kind of transaction (even just the PEBES request portion) to the Web might entail more risk, the SSA added more data elements to the identifiers used in the knowledge-based authentication that had been used for the previous 25 years. The Web-based self-service application would now require the requester to provide place of birth and mother's maiden name in addition to the three elements listed above.

---

[62]Zachary Tumin. "Social Security on the Web: The Case of the Online PEBES." *Strategic Computing & Telecommunications in the Public Sector*. Boston, John F. Kennedy School of Government, Harvard University, 1998.

The fully interactive PEBES was up for approximately 1 month before the press depicted the offering as "social insecurity." The concern expressed by the press and by several senators who wrote to the commissioner of the SSA soon after the story broke was that the data elements used in the knowledge-based authentication system might well be known to people other than the owner of the data (and of the related PEBES report). More than even disgruntled spouses (or ex-spouses), close friends or other individuals who might be able to assemble the required data elements could gain access to the PEBES that they were not entitled to.[63]

The three examples—ACES, the IRS and electronic tax filing, and the SSA and PEBES—illustrate the complexity of authentication and security requirements and privacy. The IRS and the SSA have different threat models and different security and privacy requirements, demonstrating once again that monolithic solutions, even at the federal level, are unlikely to be satisfactory.

NATIONWIDE IDENTITY SYSTEMS

The federal government is not the only government body that plays a role in authentication and privacy considerations. It is through local governments that most individuals acquire identification documents. State governments also play a key part in individual authentication—for example, in the issuance of driver's licenses by state departments of motor vehicles (DMVs). The committee's first report, *IDs—Not That Easy*,[64] examined the concept of a nationwide identity system, raising numerous policy and technological questions that would need to be answered if such a system were to be put into place. In such a hypothetical system, government would likely fill all three roles: regulator, issuing party, and relying party.

As noted in *IDs—Not That Easy*, state driver's licenses already constitute a large-scale (nationwide and, in some cases, international) system of identification and authentication. Earlier in this report, it was noted that secondary use of state driver's licenses and state IDs raises significant privacy and security concerns. Recognizing the ease with which such documents can be fraudulently reproduced or obtained, there have been proposals to strengthen driver's licenses. The American Association of

---

[63]For SSA's own analysis of PEBES, see "Privacy and Customer Service in the Electronic Age: Report to Our Customers," available online at <http://www.ssa.gov/reports/service/>.

[64]Computer Science and Telecommunications Board, National Research Council. *IDs—Not That Easy: Questions About Nationwide Identity Systems*. Washington, D.C., National Academy Press, 2002.

Motor Vehicle Administrators is in the process of developing and proposing standards to do that.[65] They include provisions for the use of biometrics to tie a driver to his or her license; some states already require fingerprints. As with any system that uses biometrics, however, care must be taken to mitigate threats against the resulting database.

> Finding 6.5: State-issued driver's licenses are a de facto nationwide identity system. They are widely accepted for transactions that require a form of government-issued photo ID.

> Finding 6.6: Nationwide identity systems by definition create a widespread and widely used form of identification, which could easily result in inappropriate linkages among nominally independent databases. While it may be possible to create a nationwide identity system that would address some privacy and security concerns, the challenges of doing so are daunting.

> Recommendation 6.3: If biometrics are used to uniquely identify license holders and to prevent duplicate issuance, care must be taken to prevent exploitation of the resulting centralized database and any samples gathered.

> Recommendation 6.4: New proposals for improved driver's license systems should be subject to the analysis presented in this report by the National Research Council's Committee on Authentication Technologies and Their Privacy Implications and in the earlier (2002) report by the same committee: IDs— Not That Easy: Questions About Nationwide Identity Systems.

CONCLUDING REMARKS

Government organizations, especially federal agencies, must live with a plethora of legal and policy demands and guidelines in the area of authentication and privacy, as well as provide accountability and submit to oversight. While citizens demand ease of use, they also expect security and privacy protection for the information that in many cases they are required to provide to the government. Reconciling this tension is a continuing challenge for any institution, but especially for the government, owing to its unique role and requirements. This report emphasizes the need to avoid authentication or identification when mere authoriza-

---

[65]More information is available online at <http://www.aamva.org/IDSecurity/>.

tion will suffice. In the case of government, respecting the legitimate function of anonymity is even more crucial. Given the often obligatory relationship between citizen and government, allowing anonymity and therefore increased privacy protection when possible not only increases efficiency (by avoiding the need to employ complicated authentication machinery before a transaction) but also enables the many advantages of privacy protection described in Chapter 3. (A simple example in which authentication is not required for interaction with the government is the downloading of tax forms. The identity of the person downloading certain forms does not need to be verified before the forms are made available. The same holds true for many public records.)

> **Finding 6.7: Preserving the ability of citizens to interact anonymously with other citizens, with business, and with the government is important because it avoids the unnecessary accumulation of identification data that could deter free speech and inhibit legitimate access to public records.**

E-government is a driver for authentication and privacy solutions that place greater emphasis on government as a relying party than as an issuer of ID documents. Systems that depend on a common identifier in government are subject to the privacy risks associated with the potential for inappropriate data aggregation and (inadvertent or deliberate) information sharing in ways that the individual providing the information did not expect. Care must be taken to adhere to the principles in the Privacy Act of 1974 and the privacy principles described in Chapter 3 of this report.

> **Finding 6.8: Interagency and intergovernmental authentication solutions that rely on a common identifier create a fundamental tension with the privacy principles enshrined in the Privacy Act of 1974, given the risks associated with data aggregation and sharing.**

Finally, while this chapter emphasizes many of the unique constraints under which government must operate, government is not immune to the challenges faced by the private sector when developing authentication systems, many of which are touched on in the preceding chapters. Threat models must be understood before proceeding, and the goals of any authentication system should be well articulated.

7

A Toolkit for Privacy in the Context of Authentication

The preceding chapters provide an in-depth look at authentication, abstractly and with respect to particular technologies, as well as an overview of privacy and a look at government-specific issues related to authentication and privacy. This concluding chapter provides a toolkit that can aid in designing an authentication system that is sensitive to privacy concerns. It focuses on the three types of authentication identified in Chapter 1:

- *Individual authentication* is the process of establishing an understood level of confidence that an identifier refers to a specific individual.
- *Identity authentication* is the process of establishing an understood level of confidence that an identifier refers to an identity. The authenticated identity may or may not be linkable to an individual.
- *Attribute authentication* is the process of establishing an understood level of confidence that an attribute applies to a specific individual.

Authentication systems using one or more of these techniques are generally deployed to meet one of two goals:

- *Limiting access.* Authentication may be used to limit who enters or accesses a given area/resource and/or to control what they do once granted entrance or access.
- *Monitoring.* Authentication may be used to enable monitoring of system use. This may occur regardless of whether decisions about access

to or use of resources are being made on the basis of authentication. Such authentication is conducted to support real-time and retrospective uses, including audits to assess liability or blame, to mete out rewards and praise, to provide for accountability, or to make behavior-based decisions such as those made by marketers.

Privacy issues arise in all systems that exercise control over access or monitor behavior, regardless of the method of authentication used. As described in Chapter 3, the decision to authenticate, whatever the reason, may affect decisional privacy, bodily integrity privacy, information privacy, and communications privacy. As noted earlier, affecting privacy is not always equivalent to violating privacy. Without delving into the normative decisions surrounding what is an appropriate level of sensitivity to privacy, this chapter describes how choices made at the outset of system design and deployment can have baseline privacy implications that should be taken into account.

The choice of attribute, identity, or individual authentication is a substantial determinant of how large an effect on privacy the authentication system will have. However, for cases in which the resource to be protected is itself private information or something else to which access must be controlled in order to protect privacy, a privacy-invasive authentication system may be necessary and appropriate. Such an authentication system also may be warranted in other contexts for other reasons. Thus, examining the privacy consequences of authentication technology is best done in tandem with evaluating the nature of the resource that the authentication system is deployed to protect.

As mentioned above, access control can be supported by proving that one is allowed to do something or by proving that one is not on a list of those prohibited from doing something. This proof can be provided using attribute, identity, or individual authentication methods. For example, sensitive areas in a workplace are frequently limited to those individuals who can prove that they are on the list of those permitted access. This proof may come in the form of an attribute authentication system (the employee has a property that permits access), an identity authentication system (the identification number given the employee permits access), or an individual authentication system (the individuals on this list are permitted access). In contrast, it is common for bars and nightclubs to have rules about those individuals who may *not* enter. When individuals present themselves for entry, those who possess certain traits (such as being underage or being someone who is not welcome by the owner) may not enter. The under-21 criterion uses an attribute authentication system, and a driver's license or other age-verification documents are used to make age-based decisions about entry. An individual authentication system, albeit usually a low-tech one, is used to prohibit from entering those whom the owner has indicated are not welcome.

An attribute authentication system deployed in either of the contexts described above (employment or bar) need not maintain a database. In each situation, the decision to permit or deny entry is based on an attribute that, as far as the authentication system is concerned, any individual may possess. In contrast, an identity or individual authentication system in these two contexts potentially is implemented quite differently.[1] In the employment context, the identity or individual authentication system must contain a record on everyone who is allowed to enter. In the bar context, the identity or individual authentication system will only contain information on those who cannot enter (such as the list of people the owner has indicated are unwelcome and the fact that those under 21 are not allowed in). An important consequence flows from this limitation. In the employment scenario, the system easily allows for additional controls over the individual once he or she enters the building, and it potentially supports monitoring of those within the system even where such monitoring is unrelated to decisions about access to or use of a resource. In the bar scenario, on the other hand, the system put in place generally will not provide any means for controlling or monitoring those who enter based on the way they authenticated themselves.

An authentication system designed to limit the access of a specific group of individuals has no further privacy consequences for those not on the initial list if the system is designed so as to limit its function to its goal. These examples illustrate that the privacy implications of authentication systems stem from implementation and system design choices and not necessarily from the reasons for which the authentication system is needed or the form of authentication technology employed. In the next section, a detailed toolkit is presented for thinking through how different choices in the design of an authentication system can have an impact on privacy.

PRIVACY-IMPACT TOOLKIT

The choice among an attribute authentication system, an identity authentication system, and an individual authentication system bears sub-

---

[1]In considering the distinction between identity and attribute authentication, note that identity authentication, which assumes the existence of an identity and a unique identifier, allows for the creation of longitudinal records. In attribute authentication, if the attribute chosen is sufficiently distinctive it is functionally equivalent to an identity authentication system, in which case the attribute may be more accurately labeled an identifier, thereby eroding the protections that might otherwise be provided by an attribute authentication system.

stantially on the privacy consequences of the system. Viewed independently of the resource they are designed to protect, attribute authentication systems present the fewest privacy problems and individual authentication systems the most. Nevertheless, in some instances individual authentication systems may be appropriate for privacy, security, or other reasons.

Separate from the type of authentication, the overall scope of the system will have obvious implications for user privacy. To limit effects on the privacy of users, systems should collect information on the fewest individuals possible. Not all access-control decisions contemplate or require auditing. While many access-control systems, particularly those that control access to sensitive or valuable information or resources, explicitly call for auditing, it is possible to design a system that supports access control but not auditing.[2] Where auditing is not contemplated or necessary, the scope of the system should be narrowed. For example, if auditing is not needed, then once a decision to permit access or action is rendered, there may be no reason to store and maintain data about the decision and many privacy reasons to destroy it.

In general, when developing an authentication system, several questions must be answered that go beyond the scope of the system and what type of authentication will be used. Decisions will need to be made about which attributes to use, which identifiers will be needed, which identity will be associated with the identifier, and how the level of confidence needed for authentication will be reached. The answers to each of these questions will have implications for privacy. Below, the four types of privacy described in Chapter 3 (information, decisional, bodily integrity, and communications) are discussed in the context of each of the above questions. The analysis proposed here is technology-independent, for the most part, and can be applied to almost any proposed authentication system.

Attribute Choice

Attribute authentication and, frequently, identity authentication and individual authentication require the collection or creation of attributes that the system uses to determine whether to grant an individual access during the authentication phase. In an attribute authentication system, the attribute alone will be the thing being authenticated. In an identity authentication system, the identifier will correlate to some collection of

---

[2]For example, auditing may not be necessary when controlling access to theaters, amusement parks, or other "one-time pay to enter" locales.

information that the system considers to be an identity. The identity may be nothing more than an e-mail account that bears no obvious relation to the underlying individual and the password that accesses it (in other words not john.mulligan@example.com, but abracadabra@example.com). In an individual authentication system, however, the identity, which potentially includes attributes as well as personal information, is distinctive to a given individual. For example, when a driver's license is initially issued, an effort is made to bind the driver's license number (nothing necessarily individual about it at this point) to an identity that is distinct enough to be linked, in theory, to the individual who requested the license. Part of the identity comprises attributes such as eye and hair color, height, weight, a photographic image of the individual, and so on.

Information Privacy

To analyze how the choice of attribute(s) may implicate information privacy, it is useful to consider the fair information principles detailed in Table 3.1 in Chapter 3.

Several characteristics of an attribute may be related to collecting the minimum amount of information needed for authentication. For example, the more distinctive the attribute is in relation to the individual, the easier it will be to establish the necessary level of confidence that the attribute applies to a specific individual; conversely, this may increase the potential for privacy problems. When a large group of individuals is allowed to access a resource, the selection of a unique attribute may inappropriately create opportunities for revelation of the individual to whom the attribute pertains. The selection of an overly distinctive attribute in such a situation would violate the minimization principle. However, the selection of a unique attribute may be appropriate where attribute authentication is being used to limit access to an individual or a small set of individuals. For example, the use of a highly distinctive attribute to control access to personal information about an individual maintained by a third party may meet the minimization principle and be necessary to protect against inappropriate access to the personal information in question.

Regardless of whether the choice of a highly distinctive attribute is appropriate, the more sensitive or revealing the attribute is, the greater the information privacy problems raised. Thus, greater attention must be paid to protecting against misuse and disclosure. Similarly, the more attributes collected for authentication (regardless of whether they are appropriate), the greater the information privacy problems raised. Clearly there are trade-offs between the privacy implications an attribute poses and that attribute's security value. Ideally, attributes should be selected that minimize the privacy effect and maximize the security potential.

In selecting an attribute, the quality of the data represented should also be examined. The attribute should be relevant to the system. For example, organizational role might be an appropriate attribute in an employment context but not in a retail context; eye color might be appropriate for physical access systems but not online systems. If an attribute is subject to change, then in some circumstances it may not be a good attribute to select because its quality may be compromised. For example, hair color may be a poor choice of attributes if the goal is to limit access to individuals whose hair is naturally a given shade. In other circumstances the changeable nature of the attribute may improve its value as an authentication attribute. For example, the use of last-deposit or last-withdrawal information in a financial context as an attribute may meet the data-quality standard despite its variable nature. The fact that the value of these attributes changes frequently means that ongoing system compromise is less likely if the value is guessed or stolen.

The accuracy of an attribute should also be considered. Different systems may tolerate different levels of accuracy. In general, to enhance privacy protection, a system should select an attribute that is relevant, accurate, and fresh. If the levels of accuracy, relevance, and reliability of an attribute are high, the number of attributes can be minimized.

In selecting an attribute, system designers should also consider how widely it is used in other systems. If an attribute is widely used, it can more easily facilitate secondary uses and record linkages from and to other systems. A less widely used attribute (ideally an attribute unique to the system) is less likely to serve as a link between the records of disparate systems. In addition, if an attribute is unique to a system, and the attribute space is sufficiently large and the attributes are randomly distributed in that space, then the system is less vulnerable to outside attacks based on attribute guessing. To limit the likelihood that its value will be compromised, an attribute used for authentication purposes should not be used for other system purposes. For example, any attribute used as an identifier in a system (perhaps an account number) is likely to be exposed to a wide range of individuals and/or system elements and thus is a poor choice as an authentication attribute.

In order to protect privacy, the security level that the system accords an authentication attribute should be consistent with the value of the attribute, as well as the value of the data that can be accessed on the basis of knowledge of the attribute. If an attribute is sensitive or unique, its value to the individual may go well beyond its value to the system as an authenticator. The data subject's valuation of the attribute and the consequent security that it should be afforded may not be immediately obvious to system developers or users.

To better protect information privacy (and in accordance with fair information principles), once an attribute is selected, individuals should receive clear notice about whether information regarding that attribute will be retained in a separate authentication system of records, what the uses of that system are, who has access to it, and what rights the individual has with respect to accessing the system. The system should also specify how controls on the attribute authentication system will be enforced and to whom the system is accountable.

Decisional Privacy

The choice of attributes may affect decisional privacy. In addition to raising information privacy problems, the choice of a sensitive or revealing attribute(s) may also affect the individual's willingness to participate in the system for which authentication is sought and to engage in activities that might result in the collection or generation of additional sensitive or revealing information. Examples of attributes that are themselves revealing or sensitive are political party, religion, and weight.

Bodily Integrity Privacy

Bodily integrity privacy may also be affected by the choice of attributes. For example, the collection of blood in order to ascertain blood type as an attribute, or of DNA in order to screen for a genetic attribute raises two types of privacy issues that have implications for bodily integrity. First, the collection of the attribute may be physically intrusive or invasive. Second, once collected, the attribute may reveal additional information about an individual's physiological or psychological condition (such as a predisposition to certain diseases), as well as information about an individual's recent activities (such as pregnancy or drug use).

Communications Privacy

If identifiers such as network or communication system addresses (or even phone numbers) are mislabeled and used as authentication attributes, communications privacy can be implicated. These addresses can facilitate collection and analysis of information about the individual that can be correlated with other records.

Summary of Attribute Choice Discussion

This analysis indicates that an attribute selected for an authentication system that minimizes privacy implications should:

- Not be unique to an individual unless tightly controlled access is required,
  - Not be widely used in other systems,
  - Not be sensitive or revealing,
  - Be relevant to the system, accurate, and fresh,
  - Require no physical contact,
  - Entail obvious (as opposed to covert) collection, and
  - Not be related to communication activities.

Identifier Selection

Identity authentication and individual authentication systems both use identifiers to tie individuals to an identity within the system. Both systems require the selection or construction of an identifier, such as a name, a random number, or a tax ID number. The choice of or creation of an identifier raises privacy concerns.

Information Privacy

To analyze how the choice or creation of an identifier may implicate information privacy, consider once again the fair information principles in Table 3.1 in Chapter 3.

The principle of limiting the collection of information is raised by the selection or construction of an identifier. First, the minimization aspect of the collection-limitation principle requires that efforts be made to limit the collection of information to what is necessary to support the transaction. The selection of an identifier that in itself has meaning, is important, or is revealing (if unnecessary to the underlying purpose of the transaction) would violate this principle. An effort should be made to use identifiers that are not themselves personal information. Thus, randomness and system exclusivity are valuable traits in an identifier. As discussed above, these traits are valuable from the perspective of system security as well. An identifier that is created or constructed for the purpose of authentication in that one system will offer more protection for both privacy and security than will an identifier selected from or based upon existing identifiers.

Because the identifier is being selected for its capacity to link to the individual in the context of an individual authentication system, the information privacy concerns are greater than they are in attribute and identity authentication. To best protect privacy, identifiable information should be collected only when critical to the relationship or transaction that is being authenticated. The individual should consent to the collection, and the minimum amount of identifiable information should be collected and retained. The relevance, accuracy, and timeliness of the identifier should be maintained and, when necessary, updated. Restrictions on secondary uses of the identifier are important in order to safeguard the privacy of the individual and to preserve the security of the authentication system. The individual should have clear rights to access information about how data are protected and used by the authentication system and the individual should have the right to challenge, correct, and amend any information related to the identifier or its uses.

The privacy question related to how involved an individual should be in the selection or creation of an identifier is an interesting one. It would appear at first that allowing the individual to select an identifier would maximize the individual's control and involvement and allow that person to establish a desired level of privacy. Yet studies on users indicate that individuals are likely to select an identifier that they can easily remember and, in most cases, an identifier that they use elsewhere or that is related to some personal information (see Chapter 4 for more on usability). A random identifier, created exclusively for use in that system, will provide more protection from an information privacy perspective but will be more cumbersome for the individual to use and remember. However, technical mechanisms can be employed to minimize these inconveniences.[3]

Decisional Privacy

An identifier that is randomly created and used exclusively for a particular authentication system will pose fewer adverse implications for decisional privacy than an identifier that reflects or contains personal information. The selection of an identifier that can be linked to the individual is likely to pose greater risks to decisional privacy than the selection of an attribute or identifier that cannot be linked. Such a system would not provide for anonymous or pseudonymous participation. Instead, it will be possible to associate a particular individual's involvement with the activity. Depending on the activity, it is possible that the selection of an identifier linked to the individual will cause some individuals not to participate.

---

[3]For example, in Web access contexts, a different public key certificate can be created for use with each Web site, and browser software can automatically interact with the site to select the right certificate when the site is visited. This affords a high degree of privacy relative to linkage concerns, and it can provide a very convenient individual authentication interface.

Bodily Integrity Privacy

Identifiers, unlike attributes, generally do not represent a characteristic of an individual and thus are not likely to affect bodily integrity. The selection of an identifier that could be associated with physical characteristics or physical activities of an individual may affect bodily integrity if the collection of the identifier was physically intrusive, invasive, or intimidating.

Communications Privacy

Communications privacy is affected if the identifier is the individual's network or communication system address or number (telephone number, e-mail address, IP address, and so on). If the identifier is related to the communication activities of an individual, its collection raises questions of communication privacy, because it would enable linking between authentication and communication activities. For example, if the identifier could be linked both to the individual and to the communications activities of the individual (phone number or e-mail address), it could significantly compromise communications privacy. This information would be valuable to both the system collecting the information and also to those outside the system, especially for law enforcement and other investigative purposes. To minimize privacy implications and enhance security, it would be best if the identifier used in an authentication system is not related to communications. However, if the system for which access is being authenticated is a communications system, then use of a communications identifier would be appropriate, as it would be information that is germane to the system.

Summary of Identifier Selection Discussion

This analysis indicates that an identifier selected for an authentication system that also minimizes privacy implications should:

- Be unique to the system (possibly random),
- Not be widely used,
- Not be sensitive or revealing,
- Require little or no physical contact,
- Entail obvious (as opposed to covert) collection/assignment, and
- Not be related to communication activities.

Identity Selection

In both identity and individual authentication systems, identifiers are often associated with other data records. Even in an individual authentication system that does not have as a primary goal the creation of an identity record, these data records constitute a de facto identity of the entity pointed to by the identifier. There are, accordingly, three types of individual/identity authentication systems, each with different privacy concerns:

1. *Purely individual authentication systems.* In these systems, the identifier itself is the only information about the entity available to the system; no additional data records are associated with the entity's identifier. In this case, the privacy analysis above regarding the selection of an identifier applies directly.

2. *Self-contained identity authentication systems.* In these systems, an entity's identifier is linked to data records that are held within the system and contain identity information about the entity; this information may include the history of the entity's access to the system. In these systems, an entity's identifier is not linked to information about the entity outside the system. For example, a system-specific number might be assigned to each entity in the system. In this case, no new privacy issues are introduced.

3. *Non-self-contained identity authentication systems.* In these systems, the identifier used by the system to refer to an entity is also linked to data records that are held outside the system and contain identity information about the entity. For example, a system of this type might maintain an entity's credit card number, which is linked by credit agencies' external systems to the entity's transaction history and credit rating. In this case, new privacy issues arise; these issues are explored below.

Information Privacy

If the system identity is associated with a particular individual, all the fair information principles should be honored in order to best protect privacy. An authentication system that is organized in such a way that a particular individual's privacy may be compromised requires the following: the individual's knowledge and consent; collection of the minimum amount of information and publication, including specific examples, of the level of collection required; that the information be relevant, accurate, timely, and complete; that information collected be used only for the specific purpose for which it was collected, unless the individual consents or a valid court order is issued; that the individual have the right to access, challenge, correct, and amend information; and that the system be maintained with the highest level of security. All of the issues related to identifier selection and information privacy remain present in the context of identity selection.

Decisional Privacy

Viewed independently of context, individual authentication systems pose the greatest risk to decisional privacy. The creation of transactional information about authentication events that is closely tied to a given individual has the greatest potential to have a chilling effect on individuals who do not want their identity associated with an activity or organization. Similarly, individually identified transactional records about authentication events are more likely to be reused by third parties (law enforcement, private litigants, hackers, and so on). Individually identified records are more easily repurposed and reused.

Bodily Integrity and Communications Privacy

The discussions in the "Identifier Selection" section above about issues related to bodily integrity and communications privacy also apply here.

The Authentication Phase

This phase determines whether the attribute, identifier, or identity refers to the individual being authenticated at the level of confidence required by the system. This determination is usually accomplished by observation of the individual or by challenging the individual to produce something supporting the claim. (For example, requiring a card and PIN at an ATM, requiring a badge to be swiped as the bearer enters a building, and requiring a password at an e-commerce Web site are all authentication phases within their respective systems.)

Information Privacy

Whether records of the act of authentication are kept, including, for example, time and date logs, implicates information privacy most directly. If such transactional records are kept—for example, to provide an audit trail for security purposes—then the system should minimize the amount of information collected. The individual should also be notified that the information is being kept as part of a system, how long it will be kept, who has access to the system, and what other uses may be made of the information. The individual should be able to access the record and correct or amend it if necessary. The system should limit the retention of records containing information about authentication acts as well as secondary uses of or access to such records.

Decisional Privacy

The intrusiveness and visibility of the authentication phase may also affect decisional privacy. The attribute or identifier itself may not be particularly revealing or sensitive, but the process for verification may be so revealing as to inhibit someone from participating. If the individual is challenged to produce something supporting the attribute or identity claimed, decisional privacy may be affected if the challenge seems to be intimidating or if the supporting evidence is revealing or sensitive. Decisional privacy is directly affected by the creation of transactional records of authentication events to support auditing.

Bodily Integrity

The authentication phase may also affect bodily integrity if the observation of the attribute requires close or direct contact with the individual or observation that appears intrusive. If the authentication phase requires the individual to produce physical evidence of an attribute, the individual's bodily integrity may be compromised. For example, a casual observation that someone is 5 feet 6 inches tall is not likely to affect someone's sense of bodily integrity, while actually measuring someone is likely to affect that sense.

Communications Privacy

If the authentication phase requires the use of a communications system, communications privacy may be implicated. Any authentication that occurs on the Internet, for example, involves communications privacy. The question of who has access to the content of the authentication and to the transactional information generated during the communication should be addressed before the authentication system is implemented. Again, the creation and maintenance of transactional records of authentication events (or the authentication events that are unrelated to the need to control system access) may raise particularly troubling issues of communications privacy. If the monitoring reveals information about whom an individual associates or communicates with, directly or indirectly, the system will infringe on communications privacy. Finally, if the authentication phase entails use of a communications system that can be associated with a particular individual, then communications privacy may be affected because the system will generate content and transactional information linked to the individual.

Summary of Authentication Phase Discussion

This analysis indicates that in order to minimize privacy consequences, the following goals should be kept in mind when designing the authentication phase of an authentication system:

- Choose the minimum level of confidence in the authentication that supports the system needs. These needs could be satisfied in range of ways: from self-reported, to verified by the second party to the transaction, to verified by a third party, to verified by multiple third parties, to polling government sources, and so on.
- Establish processes to achieve this level of confidence and make sure that the individual being authenticated is involved in the authentication.
- Ensure that the system does only what it sets out to do (e.g., access control, monitoring, or some combination of these).
- Limit the maintenance and storage of transactional records to the minimum amount necessary.
- Set destruction policies for those records that need to be kept for limited periods.
- Segregate authentication information from transactional data subsequent to authentication events.
- Create technical and procedural strategies that limit the ability to connect authentication information with specific authentication events.
- Understand and consider the security risks of authentication activity data storage, including risks of unauthorized access, unauthorized use by those with authorized access, and legally compelled access.

CONCLUDING REMARKS

The development, implementation, and broad deployment of authentication systems require thinking carefully about the role of identity and privacy in a free, open, and democratic society. Privacy, including control over the disclosure of one's identity and the ability to remain anonymous, is an essential ingredient of a functioning democracy. It is a precondition for the exercise of constitutionally protected freedoms, such as the freedom of association. It supports the robust exercise of freedom of expression by, for example, creating psychological space for political dissent. It maintains social norms that protect human dignity and autonomy by enabling expressions of respect and intimacy and the establishment of boundaries between oneself and one's community.

Information collected in or generated by authentication systems can be valuable and revealing. It may document where individuals have been, what resources they have sought, what individuals or institutions they have chosen to associate with, and so on. It is likely to be sought by law enforcement, commercial entities, and private parties. If individuals fear unchecked scrutiny, they will be less likely to vigorously participate in the political process and in society in general. If individuals are denied physical and mental privacy—from the government, corporations, and other individuals—they are less able to explore ideas, formulate personal opinions, and express and act on these beliefs. In the context of systems that mediate access to political, cultural or artistic information and/or provide state and private parties with access to personal information, identity and individual authentication mechanisms chill the free flow of information and free association. At the same time, "privacy" is often used as a pretext to hide illegal activities, and society has, at times, a legitimate interest in requiring authentication or identification. This requirement may stem from the need to validate claims to rights and privileges or the need to hold individuals responsible for their activities.

The decision about where to deploy identity authentication systems— be it only where today confirmation of identity is already required, or in a greater range of circumstances—will shape society in both obvious and subtle ways. Because many privacy breaches are easy to conceal and/or are unreported, failing to protect privacy may cost less in the short run than the initial outlay required to establish sound procedural and technical privacy protections. In addition, establishing practices and technical measures that protect privacy costs money at the outset. If individuals whose information was compromised and agencies responsible for enforcing privacy laws were informed of privacy breaches, there would be greater incentive to proactively implement technologies and policies that protect privacy. Even if the choice is made to institute authentication systems only where people today attempt to discern identity, the creation of reliable, inexpensive systems will inevitably invite function creep and unplanned-for secondary uses unless action is taken to avoid these problems. The role of attribute authentication in protecting privacy is underexplored and may be a way to mitigate some of these concerns.

It is critical that there be analysis of the intended context and usage models and thoughtful decision making about what system requirements are. To best protect privacy, the privacy consequences of both the intended design and deployment and the potential secondary uses of authentication systems must be taken into consideration by vendors, users, policy makers, and the general public.

APPENDIXES

Appendix A

Biographies of Committee Members and Staff

COMMITTEE MEMBERS

STEPHEN T. KENT, *Chair*, is chief scientist in information security at BBN Technologies, a part of Verizon Communications. During the past two decades, Dr. Kent's research and development activities have included the design and development of user authentication and access control systems, network layer encryption and access control systems, secure transport layer protocols, secure e-mail technology, multilevel secure (X.500) directory systems, and public key certification authority systems. His most recent work focuses on security for Internet routing, very high speed Internet Protocol (IP) encryption, and high-assurance cryptographic modules. Dr. Kent served as a member of the Internet Architecture Board (1983-1994), and he chaired the Privacy and Security Research Group of the Internet Research Task Force (1985-1998). He chaired the Privacy Enhanced Mail working group of the Internet Engineering Task Force from 1990 to 1995 and has co-chaired the Public Key Infrastructure Working Group since 1995. He is the primary author of the core IPsec standards: RFCs 2401, 2402, and 2406. He is a member of the editorial board of the *Journal of Computer Security* (1995 to the present), serves on the board of the Security Research Alliance, and served on the board of directors of the International Association for Cryptologic Research (1982-1989). Dr. Kent was a member of the National Research Council's (NRC's) Information Systems Trustworthiness Committee (1996-1998), which produced *Trust in Cyberspace*. His other NRC service includes membership

197

on the Committee on Rights and Responsibilities of Participants in Networked Communities (1993-1994), the Technical Assessment Panel for the NIST Computer Systems Laboratory (1990-1992), and the Secure Systems Study Committee (1988-1990). The U.S. Secretary of Commerce appointed Dr. Kent as chair of the Federal Advisory Committee to Develop a Federal Information Processing Standard for Federal Key Management Infrastructure (1996-1998). The author of two book chapters and numerous technical papers on network security, Dr. Kent has served as a referee, panelist, and session chair for a number of conferences. Since 1977 he has lectured on network security on behalf of government agencies, universities, and private companies throughout the United States, Europe, Australia, and the Far East. Dr. Kent received the B.S. degree in mathematics, summa cum laude, from Loyola University of New Orleans and the S.M., E.E., and Ph.D. degrees in computer science from the Massachusetts Institute of Technology. He is a fellow of the Association for Computing Machinery and a member of the Internet Society and Sigma Xi.

MICHAEL ANGELO is currently a staff fellow at Compaq Computer Corporation and runs a laboratory at Compaq that assesses biometrics and other security-enhancing technologies, such as smart cards. He is considered a subject-matter expert for security and its associated technologies. His job is to provide technical guidance and input into strategic planning and development of secure solutions. In addition, he is responsible for providing technical assistance to the corporate security team. Dr. Angelo possesses expertise in both biometric and token access authentication technology, including technical threat model and implementation analysis, as well as risk reduction enhancement methodology, applied computer system security, computer forensics, advanced data-protection methodologies, and practical encryption techniques. His experience comprises 15 years in designing, implementing, managing, and supporting secure intra- and internets, including gateways, firewalls, and sentinels, and 20 years working at the kernel level of numerous operating systems, including a wide variety of hardware platforms (from personal computers to supercomputers) and software platforms (including UNIX [several flavors], MS-DOS/Windows/NT, and VMS). He holds several patents. Dr. Angelo has been active in a number of trade standards organizations: the Trusted Computing Platform Association, Americans for Computer Privacy, the Bureau of Export Administration Technical Advisory Committee, the Information Security Exploratory Committee, the Key Recovery Alliance, the Computer Systems Policy Project, the Cross-Industry Working Team Security Working Group, and the National Institute of Standards and Technology's Industry Key Escrow Working Group.

STEVEN BELLOVIN is a fellow at AT&T Research. He received a B.A. degree from Columbia University and M.S. and Ph.D. degrees in computer science from the University of North Carolina at Chapel Hill. While a graduate student, he helped create Netnews; for this, he and the other collaborators were awarded the 1995 USENIX Lifetime Achievement Award. At AT&T Laboratories, Dr. Bellovin does research in networks and security and why the two do not get along. He has embraced a number of public interest causes and weighed in (e.g., through his writings) on initiatives (e.g., in the areas of cryptography and law enforcement) that appear to threaten privacy. He is currently focusing on cryptographic protocols and network management. Dr. Bellovin is the coauthor of the book *Firewalls and Internet Security: Repelling the Wily Hacker,* and he is one of the Security Area directors for the Internet Engineering Task Force. He was a member of the CSTB committee that produced *Trust in Cyberspace* (1999) and served on the Information Technology subcommittee of the group that produced the NRC report *Making the Nation Safer.* He has been a member of the National Academy of Engineering since 2001.

BOB BLAKLEY is chief scientist for security and privacy at IBM Tivoli Software. He is general chair of the 2003 Institute for Electrical and Electronics Engineers Security and Privacy Conference and has served as general chair of the Association for Computing Machinery's (ACM's) New Security Paradigms Workshop. He was named Distinguished Security Practitioner by the 2002 ACM Computer Security and Applications Conference and serves on the editorial board for the *International Journal of Information Security.* Dr. Blakley was the editor of the Object Management Group's Common Object Request Broker Architecture (CORBA) security specification and is the author of *CORBA Security: An Introduction to Safe Computing with Objects,* published by Addison-Wesley. Dr. Blakley was also the editor of the Open Group's Authorization Application Programming Interface specification and the OASIS Security Services Technical Committee's Security Assertion Markup Language specification effort. He has been involved in cryptography and data security design work since 1979 and has authored or coauthored seven papers on cryptography, secret-sharing schemes, access control, and other aspects of computer security. He holds nine patents on security-related technologies. Dr. Blakley received an A.B. in classics from Princeton University and a master's degree and a Ph.D. in computer and communications sciences from the University of Michigan.

DREW DEAN is a computer scientist at SRI International. He joined SRI in July 2001; prior to that he was a member of the research staff at Xerox PARC. He pioneered the systematic study of Java security and more recently has worked across a wide range of security issues, including denial of service, the theory of access control, and IP traceback. Among his publications, he has received a Best Student Paper award from the ACM Computer and Communications Security conference (1997), an Outstanding Paper award from the ACM Symposium on Operating System Principles (1997), and a Best Paper Award from the Internet Society's Network and Distributed Systems Security Symposium (2001). Dr. Dean is a member of the editorial board of Springer-Verlag's *International Journal of Information Security*. Dr. Dean holds M.A. and Ph.D. degrees from Princeton University and a B.S. degree from Carnegie Mellon University, all in computer science.

BARBARA FOX is a senior software architect in cryptography and digital rights management at Microsoft Corporation and is currently a senior fellow at the Kennedy School of Government at Harvard University. She serves on the technical advisory board of The Creative Commons and the board of directors of the International Financial Cryptography Association. Ms. Fox joined Microsoft in 1993 as director of advanced product development and led the company's electronic commerce technology development group. She has coauthored Internet standards in the areas of Public Key Infrastructure and XML security. Her research at Harvard focuses on digital copyright law, public policy, and privacy.

STEPHEN H. HOLDEN is an assistant professor in the Department of Information Systems at the University of Maryland, Baltimore County. Dr. Holden's research, publications, and teachings leverage his substantial federal government experience in government-wide policy in information technology management and electronic government. He left the Internal Revenue Service (IRS) in 2000 after a 16-year career in the federal career service. While at the IRS, he served as the program executive for electronic tax administration (ETA) modernization, reporting to the assistant commissioner (ETA). He also served on the Federal Public Key Infrastructure Steering Committee during his time at the IRS. Prior to going to the IRS, Dr. Holden worked for 10 years at the Office of Management and Budget, doing a variety of policy, management, and budget analysis work. His federal civil servant career began in 1983 when he was a Presidential management intern at the Naval Sea Systems Command. He holds a Ph.D. in public administration and public affairs from Virginia Polytechnic and State University, a Master of Public Administration, and a B.A. in public management from the University of Maine.

DEIRDRE MULLIGAN was recently appointed director of the new Samuelson Law, Technology and Public Policy Clinic at the University of

California, Berkeley, School of Law (Boalt Hall). While attending Georgetown University Law Center, Ms. Mulligan worked at the American Civil Liberties Union's Privacy and Technology project, where she honed her interest in preserving and enhancing civil liberties and democratic values. After law school, she became a founding member of the Center for Democracy and Technology, a high-tech public interest organization for civil liberties based in Washington, D.C. For the past 6 years, Mulligan has been staff counsel at the center. She has worked with federal lawmakers, government agencies, the judicial system, public interest organizations, and the high-tech business community, with the goal of enhancing individual privacy on the Internet, thwarting threats to free speech on the Internet, and limiting governmental access to private data. She has testified in several settings and has contributed to technical standards development. Ms. Mulligan received her J.D., cum laude, from Georgetown University Law Center in 1994 and a B.A. in architecture and art history from Smith College in 1988.

JUDITH S. OLSON is the Richard W. Pew Chair in Human Computer Interaction at the University of Michigan. She is also a professor in the School of Information, Computer and Information Systems, the Business School, and the Department of Psychology. Her research interests include computer-supported cooperative work, human-computer interaction, the design of business information systems for organizational effectiveness, and cognitive psychology. Dr. Olson's recent research focuses on the nature of group work and the design and evaluation of technology to support it. This field combines cognitive and social psychology with the design of information systems. She began her career at the University of Michigan in the Department of Psychology, served as a technical supervisor for human factors in systems engineering at Bell Laboratories in New Jersey, and returned to the University of Michigan, first to the Business School and then the new School of Information. She has more than 60 publications in journals and books and has served on a number of national committees, including the National Research Council's Committee on Human Factors and the council of the Association for Computing Machinery (ACM). She has recently been appointed to the CHI Academy of the ACM's Special Interest Group for Human-Computer Interaction. Dr. Olson earned a B.A. in mathematics and psychology from Northwestern University in 1965 and her Ph.D. 4 years later in the same disciplines from the University of Michigan.

JOE PATO is the principal scientist for the HP Labs Trust, Security and Privacy research program. He has also served as chief technology officer for Hewlett-Packard's Internet Security Solutions Division. Mr. Pato's current research focus is the security needs of collaborative enterprises on the Internet, addressing both interenterprise models and the needs of lightweight instruments and peripherals directly attached to the Internet. Specifically, he is looking at critical infrastructure protection and the confluence of trust, e-services, and mobility. These interests have led him to look at the preservation of Internet communication in the event of cyberterrorism, trust frameworks for mobile environments, and how to apply privacy considerations in complex systems. His work in cybercrime and homeland security recently led him to become one of the founders and board members of the IT Sector Information Sharing and Analysis Center. His past work included the design of delegation protocols for secure distributed computation, key exchange protocols, interdomain trust structures, the development of public- and secret-key-based infrastructures, and the more general development of distributed enterprise environments. Mr. Pato has participated on several standards or advisory committees for the Institute for Electrical and Electronics Engineers, American National Standards Institute, National Institute of Standards and Technology, Department of Commerce, Worldwide Web Consortium, Financial Services Technology Consortium, and Common Open System Environment. He is currently the co-chair of the OASIS Security Services Technical Committee, which is developing Security Assertions Markup Language.

RADIA PERLMAN is a Distinguished Engineer at Sun Microsystems Laboratories. She is the architect for a group that does research in network security issues, recently most focused on public key infrastructure deployment. Some of the group's implementation will be distributed as part of a reference implementation for Java. Dr. Perlman is the author of many papers in the field of network security, as well as coauthor of a textbook on network security (and author of a textbook on lower-layer networking protocols). She is well known for her work on sabotage-proof routing protocols. Her work on lower-layer protocols, also well known, forms the basis of modern bridging, switching, and routing protocols. This expertise is crucial to understanding the technology behind such things as providing Internet anonymity. Dr. Perlman has about 50 issued patents, a Ph.D. in computer science from the Massachusetts Institute of Technology, and S.B. and S.M. degrees in mathematics from MIT. She was recently awarded an honorary doctorate from the Royal Institute of Technology, Sweden.

PRISCILLA M. REGAN is an associate professor in the Department of Public and International Affairs at George Mason University. Prior to joining that faculty in 1989, she was a senior analyst in the congressional

Office of Technology Assessment (1984-1989) and an assistant professor of politics and government at the University of Puget Sound (1979-1984). Since the mid-1970s, Dr. Regan's primary research interest has been analysis of the social, policy, and legal implications of the organizational use of new information and communications technologies. She has published more than 20 articles or book chapters, as well as *Legislating Privacy: Technology, Social Values, and Public Policy* (University of North Carolina Press, 1995). As a recognized researcher in this area, Dr. Regan has testified before Congress and participated in meetings held by the Department of Commerce, the Federal Trade Commission, the Social Security Administration, and the Census Bureau. She received her Ph.D. in government from Cornell University in 1981 and her B.A. from Mount Holyoke College in 1972.

JEFFREY SCHILLER received his S.B. in electrical engineering (1979) from the Massachusetts Institute of Technology (MIT). As MIT network manager, he has managed the MIT Campus Computer Network since its inception in 1984. Before that, he maintained MIT's Multiplexed Information and Computing Service (Multics) time-sharing system during the time of the ARPANET TCP/IP conversion. He is an author of MIT's Kerberos authentication system. Mr. Schiller is the Internet Engineering Steering Group's area director for security. He is responsible for overseeing security-related working groups of the Internet Engineering Task Force. He was responsible for releasing a U.S. legal freeware version of the popular PGP (Pretty Good Privacy) encryption program. Mr. Schiller is also responsible for the development and deployment of an X.509-based public key infrastructure at MIT. He is also the technical lead for the new Higher Education Certifying Authority being operated by the Corporation for Research and Educational Networking. Mr. Schiller is also a founding member of the Steering Group of the New England Academic and Research Network (NEARnet). NEARnet, now part of Genuity, Inc., is a major nationwide Internet service provider.

SOUMITRA SENGUPTA is assistant professor in the Department of Medical Informatics at Columbia University. Dr. Sengupta has focused his work on the challenges of security and privacy in health care, complementing his academic work by service as security officer for the New York Presbyterian Healthcare System. His research interests are in the areas of distributed systems, their monitoring, management, and security aspects, and their application in a health care environment. He is interested in the architectural design and engineering concerns of building large, functioning systems over heterogeneous platforms and protocols. Dr. Sengupta holds a B.E. from Birla Institute of Technology and Science (electrical and electronics engineering), Pilani, India, and M.S. and Ph.D. degrees from the State University of New York at Stony Brook, New York, in computer science. He was a member of the Association for Computing Machinery (1984-1994), the Institute for Electrical and Electronics Engineers (IEEE) Computer Society (1984-1992) and is currently a member of the American Medical Informatics Association.

JAMES L. WAYMAN has been the director of the Biometrics Test Center at San Jose State University in California since 1995. The Test Center is funded by the U.S. government and other national governments to develop standards and scientific test and analysis methods and to advise on the use or nonuse of biometric identification technologies. The test center served as the U.S. National Biometrics Test Center from 1997 to 2000. Dr. Wayman received the Ph.D. degree in engineering from the University of California at Santa Barbara in 1980 and joined the faculty of the Department of Mathematics at the U.S. Naval Postgraduate School in 1981. In 1986, he became a full-time researcher for the Department of Defense in the areas of technical security and biometrics. Dr. Wayman holds three patents in speech processing and is the author of dozens of articles in books, technical journals, and conference proceedings on biometrics, speech compression, acoustics, and network control. He serves on the editorial boards of two journals and on several national and international biometrics standards committees. He is a senior member of the Institute for Electrical and Electronic Engineers.

DANIEL J. WEITZNER is the director of the World Wide Web Consortium's (W3C's) Technology and Society activities. As such, he is responsible for the development of technology standards that enable the Web to address social, legal, and public policy concerns such as privacy, free speech, protection of minors, authentication, intellectual property, and identification. He is also the W3C's chief liaison to public policy communities around the world and a member of the Internet Corporation for Assigned Names and Numbers Protocol Supporting Organization Protocol Council. Mr. Weitzner holds a research appointment at the Massachusetts Institute of Technology's (MIT's) Laboratory for Computer Science and teaches Internet public policy at MIT. Before joining the W3C, he was cofounder and deputy director of the Center for Democracy and Technology, an Internet civil liberties organization in Washington, D.C. He was also deputy policy director of the Electronic Frontier Foundation. As one of the leading figures in the Internet public policy community, he was the first to advocate user control technologies such as content filtering and rating to protect children and avoid government censorship of the Internet. These arguments played a critical role in the 1997 U.S. Supreme Court case, *Reno* v. *ACLU*, awarding the highest free speech protections to the Internet. He successfully advocated the adoption of amendments to the Electronic Communications Privacy Act creating new privacy protections for online transactional information such as Web site access logs. Mr. Weitzner has a degree in law from Buffalo Law School and a B.A. in Philosophy from Swarthmore College. His publications on communications policy have appeared in the *Yale Law Review*, *Global Networks*, *Computerworld*, *Wired Magazine*, *Social Research, Electronic Networking: Research, Applications and Policy*, and *The Whole Earth Review*. He is also a commentator for National Public Radio's Marketplace Radio.

STAFF

LYNETTE I. MILLETT is a study director and program officer with the Computer Science and Telecommunications Board (CSTB) of the National Research Council. She is currently involved in several CSTB projects, including a study examining certification and dependable systems, a comprehensive exploration of privacy in the information age, and a look at the fundamentals of computer science as a research discipline. She is also exploring possible study options for CSTB with respect to the issues of biometrics and open source software development. She recently completed a CSTB study that produced *Embedded, Everywhere: A Research Agenda for Networked Systems of Embedded Computers*. Before joining CSTB, Ms. Millett was involved in research on static analysis techniques for concurrent programming languages as well as research on value-sensitive design and informed consent online. She has an M.Sc., is "ABD" in computer science from Cornell University, and has a B.A. in mathematics and computer science from Colby College. Her graduate work was supported by both a National Science Foundation graduate fellowship and an Intel graduate fellowship.

JENNIFER M. BISHOP has been a senior project assistant with the Computer Science and Telecommunications Board (CSTB) since October 2001. She is currently supporting several projects, including Digital Archiving and the National Archives and Records Administration; Computing Frontiers: Prospects from Biology; and Telecommunications Research and Development. She also maintains CSTB's contact database, handles updates to the CSTB Web site, and has designed book covers for several reports. Prior to her move to Washington, D.C., Ms. Bishop worked for the City of Ithaca, New York, coordinating the police department's transition to a new SQL-based time accrual and scheduling application. Her other work

experience includes designing customized hospitality-industry performance reports for RealTime Hotel Reports, maintaining the police records
database for the City of Ithaca, and hand-painting furniture for
Mackenzie-Childs, Ltd., of Aurora, New York. She is an artist working in
oil and mixed media. Ms. Bishop holds a B.F.A (2001) in studio art from
Cornell University.

Appendix B

Briefers to the Study Committee

Although the briefers listed below provided many useful inputs to the committee, they were not asked to endorse the conclusions or recommendations, nor did they see the final draft of the report before its release.

MARCH 13-14, 2001
WASHINGTON, D.C.

Roger Baker, Department of Commerce and CIO Council
Daniel Chenok, Office of Information and Regulatory Affairs, Office of Management and Budget
Sara Hamer, Social Security Administration
John Woodward, RAND

MAY 30-31, 2001
WASHINGTON, D.C.

Lt. Col. Robert Bollig, Executive Officer, Department of Defense, Biometrics Management Office
Mike Green, Director, Department of Defense, PKI Program Management Office
Cathy Hotka, Vice President, Information Technology for the National Retail Federation
Mark MacCarthy, Senior Vice President for Public Policy, VISA USA

David Temoshok, Office of Governmentwide Policy, General Services
    Administration
Richard Varn, Chief Information Officer, State of Iowa

WORKSHOP
OCTOBER 3-4, 2001
HERNDON, VIRGINIA

Michael Aisenberg, VeriSign
Kim Alexander, California Voter Foundation
Brian Arbogast, Microsoft Corporation
Paul Barrett, Real User Corporation
Stefan Brands, McGill University
Roger Clarke, Xamax Consultancy Pty Ltd and the Australian National
    University
John Daugman, University of Cambridge
Mark Forman, Office of Management and Budget
Chris Hoofnagle, Electronic Privacy Information Center
Paul Van Oorschot, Entrust, Inc.
Margot Saunders, National Consumer Law Center
Judith Spencer, General Services Administration
Peter Swire, George Washington University Law School
Paul Syverson, Naval Research Laboratory
Brian Tretick, Privacy Assurance and Advisory Services, Ernst & Young

JANUARY 9, 2002
PALO ALTO, CALIFORNIA

Christopher Kuner, Morrison and Foerster LLP

MARCH 13-14, 2002
WASHINGTON, D.C.

Patti Gavin, Social Security Administration
Fred Graf, Social Security Administration
Jay Maxwell, American Association of Motor Vehicles Administrators
Joe Sanders, New York State Department of Motor Vehicles

Appendix C

Some Key Concepts

Attribute. An attribute describes a property associated with an individual.

Attribute Authentication. Attribute authentication is the process of establishing an understood level of confidence that an attribute applies to a specific individual.

Authentication. Authentication is the process of establishing confidence in the truth of some claim.

Authenticator. An authenticator is evidence that is presented to support the authentication of a claim. It increases confidence in the truth of the claim.

Authorization. Authorization is the process of deciding what an individual ought to be allowed to do.

Biometrics. Biometrics is the automatic identification or identity verification of individuals on the basis of behavioral or physiological characteristics.

Bodily Integrity. Bodily integrity in the context of privacy refers to those issues involving intrusive or invasive searches and seizures.

Certification Authority. A certification authority is the entity that issues a digital certificate in a public key cryptosystem.

Communications Privacy. Communications privacy is a subset of information privacy that protects the confidentiality of individuals' communications.

Credential. Credentials are objects that are verified when presented to the verifier in an authentication transaction. Credentials may be bound in some way to the individual to whom they were issued, or they may be bearer credentials. The former are necessary for identification, while the latter may be acceptable for some forms of authorization.

Decisional Privacy. Decisional privacy protects the individual from interference with decisions about self and family.

Identification. Identification is the process of using claimed or observed attributes of an individual to infer who the individual is.

Identifier. An identifier points to an individual. An identifier can be a name, a serial number, or some other pointer to the entity being identified.

Identity. The identity of X is the set of information about individual X that is associated with that individual in a particular identity system Y. However, Y is not always named explicitly.

Identity Authentication. Identity authentication is the process of establishing an understood level of confidence that an identifier refers to an identity. It may or may not be possible to link the authenticated identity to an individual.

Individual Authentication. Individual authentication is the process of establishing an understood level of confidence that an identifier refers to a specific individual.

Information Privacy. Information privacy protects the individual's interest in controlling the flow of information about the self to others.

Password. A sequence of characters, presumed to be secret, that is divulged in order to gain access to a system or resource.

Privacy. Privacy is a multifaceted term, with many contextually dependent meanings. One aspect of the right to privacy is the right of an individual to decide for himself or herself when and on what terms his or her attributes should be revealed.

Private Key. In public key cryptography systems, a private key is a value (key), presumed to be secret, and typically known only to one party. The party uses the private key to digitally sign data or to decrypt data (or keys) encrypted for that party using the party's public key.

Public Key. In public key cryptography systems, a public key is a value used to verify a digital signature generated using a corresponding private key, or used to encrypt data that can be decrypted using the corresponding private key.

Public Key Certificate. Sometimes called a digital certificate, a public key certificate contains attributes, typically including an identifier, that are bound to a public key via the use of a digital signature.

Public Key Infrastructure. A public key infrastructure (PKI) consists of a set of technical and procedural measures used to manage public keys embedded in digital certificates. The keys in such certificates may be used to enable secure communication and data exchange over potentially insecure networks.

Registration Authority. A registration authority is the entity in a PKI that establishes a correspondence between an identifier that will appear in a certificate and an individual.

Security. Security refers to a collection of safeguards that ensure the confidentiality of information, protect the integrity of information, ensure the availability of information, account for use of the system, and protect the system(s) and/or network(s) used to process the information.

Threat. A threat is a motivated, capable adversary. The adversary is motivated to violate the security of a target (system) and has the capability to mount attacks that will exploit vulnerabilities of the target.

What Is CSTB?

As a part of the National Research Council, the Computer Science and Telecommunications Board (CSTB) was established in 1986 to provide independent advice to the federal government on technical and public policy issues relating to computing and communications. Composed of leaders from industry and academia, CSTB conducts studies of critical national issues and makes recommendations to government, industry, and academic researchers. CSTB also provides a neutral meeting ground for consideration of complex issues where resolution and action may be premature. It convenes invitational discussions that bring together principals from the public and private sectors, assuring consideration of all perspectives. The majority of CSTB's work is requested by federal agencies and Congress, consistent with its National Academies context.

A pioneer in framing and analyzing Internet policy issues, CSTB is unique in its comprehensive scope and effective, interdisciplinary appraisal of technical, economic, social, and policy issues. Beginning with early work in computer and communications security, cyber-assurance and information systems trustworthiness have been a cross-cutting theme in CSTB's work. CSTB has produced several reports known as classics in the field, and it continues to address these topics as they grow in importance.

To do its work, CSTB draws on some of the best minds in the country, inviting experts to participate in its projects as a public service. Studies are conducted by balanced committees without direct financial interests in the topics they are addressing. Those committees meet, confer electronically, and build analyses through their deliberations. Additional expertise from around the country is tapped in a rigorous process of review and critique, further enhancing the quality of CSTB reports. By engaging groups of principals, CSTB obtains the facts and insights critical to assessing key issues.

The mission of CSTB is to

- *Respond to requests* from the government, nonprofit organizations, and private industry for advice on computer and telecommunications issues and from the government for advice on computer and telecommunications systems planning, utilization, and modernization;
- *Monitor and promote the health of the fields* of computer science and telecommunications, with attention to issues of human resources, information infrastructure, and societal impacts;
- *Initiate and conduct studies* involving computer science, computer technology, and telecommunications as critical resources; and
- *Foster interaction* among the disciplines underlying computing and telecommunications technologies and other fields, at large and within the National Academies.

As of 2003, CSTB activities with security and privacy components address privacy in the information age, critical information infrastructure protection, authentication technologies and their privacy implications, information technology for countering terrorism, and geospatial information systems. Additional studies examine broadband, digital government, the fundamentals of computer science, limiting children's access to pornography on the Internet, digital archiving and preservation, and Internet navigation and the domain name system. Explorations touching on security and privacy are under way in the areas of the insider threat, cybersecurity research, cybersecurity principles and practices, dependable/safe software systems, biometrics, wireless communications and spectrum management, open source software, digital democracy, the "digital divide," manageable systems, information technology and journalism, supercomputing, and information technology and education.

More information about CSTB can be obtained online at <http://www.cstb.org>.